R12

# A Time Before New Hampshire

# A Time Before
# New Hampshire

## THE STORY OF A LAND
## AND NATIVE PEOPLES

### MICHAEL J. CADUTO

ILLUSTRATED BY
ADELAIDE TYROL

UNIVERSITY OF NEW HAMPSHIRE

PUBLISHED BY UNIVERSITY PRESS OF NEW ENGLAND

HANOVER AND LONDON

University of New Hampshire
Published by University Press of New England
37 Lafayette St., Lebanon, NH 03766
© 2003 by Michael J. Caduto

Printed in the United States of America
5 4 3 2 1

Library of Congress Cataloging-in-Publication Data

Caduto, Michael J.
 A time before New Hampshire : the story of a land and Native peoples /
by Michael J. Caduto ; illustrated by Adelaide Tyrol.
    p.   cm.
Includes bibliographical references and index.
 ISBN 1–58465–185–7
 1. Indians of North America—New Hampshire.  2. Historical
geology—New Hampshire.  I. Title.
 E78.N54 C33 2003
 974.2'01—dc21                                    2002012160

*Permission to include the following is gratefully acknowledged:*

The photographs by Michael J. Caduto that appear throughout this book are reprinted with his permission, © 2003 by Michael J. Caduto.

The illustrations by Adelaide Tyrol that appear throughout this book and on cover are reprinted with her permission, © 2003 by Adelaide Tyrol.

The photographs that appear on pages 13, 16, 69, and 124 are used with permission, © 2001 by the New Hampshire Historical Society.

The photographs that appear on pages 17, 20, and 26, from negatives GEO80872c, GEO85829c, and GEO80821c, respectively, are included with permission from the Field Museum, Chicago, Illinois.

The illustration that appears on page 19 is redrawn from an illustration found in Chet Raymo and Maureen Raymo, *Written in Stone: A Geologic History of the Northeastern United States* (2001) and is used with permission from the author and Black Dome Press, Hensonville, New York.

The photograph that appears on page 24 is used with permission (© 2002) from Mark S. Twickler, Associate Director, Climate Change Research Center, Institute for the Study of Earth, Oceans and Space (EOS), University of New Hampshire, Durham, New Hampshire.

The illustrations that appear on pages 34, 35, and 54 are redrawn here with permission from © Bradford B. Van Diver. *Roadside Geology of Vermont and New Hampshire*. 1987 Missoula, Montana: Mountain Press Publishing Co.

The illustrations that appear on pages 58 and 59 are from Michael J. Caduto's *Pond and Brook: A Guide to Nature in Freshwater Environments,* published by University Press of New England, Hanover, New Hampshire (© 1990), and are used here with permission from the artist, Joan Thomson.

The photograph that appears on page 68 of this book, which was taken by Hugh Raup, is reproduced with permission of the Harvard Forest Archives, Petersham, Massachusetts.

The illustration that appears on page 105 of this book is based on an illustration found in William A. Haviland and Marjory W. Power's *The Original Vermonters: Native Inhabitants, Past and Present* (1994) and is included with permission from the University Press of New England, Hanover, New Hampshire.

The maps that appear on pages 160 and 219 are used with permission, ©2003 by Michael J. Caduto.

The photograph that appears on page 176 is used with permission from the Hood Museum of Art, Dartmouth College, Hanover, New Hampshire; gift of Miss Helen Toussaint. Photograph by Jeffrey Nintzel.

*(continues on page 266)*

*For the Alnôbak*

*With gratitude*
*for your respectful ways,*
*and for the legacy of Wôbanaki,*
*Dawnland.*
*Oliwni.*

# CONTENTS

# PREFACE

As an ecologist and student of Native peoples, I have asked myself many times whether a book ought to be written that is largely defined by political boundaries. The first piece of the 9,300-square-mile parcel of land that we now call New Hampshire was delineated by the English in 1629; a date so recent that the state's entire political history spans an infinitesimal moment of the 650 million years of geologic time recorded in the rocks. New Hampshire's brief coastline shares much of the same marine and estuarine character as the coast of neighboring Maine and Massachusetts. As for geology, soils, and the nature of biological communities, New Hampshire's northern, eastern, and southern boundaries are meaningless lines drawn arbitrarily across an ecological continuum. The red-tailed hawk stoops on a meadow vole regardless of where its impending meal is eligible to vote.

Serendipitously, however, the southern half of New Hampshire's western boundary along the far shore of the Connecticut River is distinguished by much more than the result of a capricious historical political decision. By sensing and following a relatively weak zone in Earth's crust, the river has eroded a fairly straight course where it runs from about Woodsville to the Massachusetts border. This part of the Connecticut River traces a major tectonic boundary where deposits from the floor of an ancient sea and remnants of an arc of volcanic islands collided with the margin of the ancestral North American plate about 445 million years ago.

Developing from distinct geologic foundations, the genesis of soils as well as the evolution of their associated plant and animal communities varies across the river lineament. One might argue that these differences have given rise in recent centuries to the divergent social, political, and economic entities that we now know as New Hampshire and Vermont. This boundary—the eastern edge of the ancestral North American tectonic plate and the western edge of New Hampshire's roots in a crescent of ancient volcanic islands—is worthy of being a point of departure for defining this book.

The eastern border of New Hampshire weaves along a diffuse cultural boundary between the western and eastern peoples of the "Dawnland,"

*Wôbanaki.* With customs and languages that are similar, yet distinct, their ancestors have coexisted for thousands of years along a shared continuum of culture and geography. Their story cuts a broad swath through history, a time that begins with the hunting of the large mammals and witnesses their passing, a time that sees long periods of heating and cooling and responsive shifts in the wild and human communities of the region. The Native peoples are deeply rooted through a connection to this land whose antiquity dwarfs the mere centuries that have unfolded since strangers sailed to these shores.

The original peoples of New Hampshire are brethren, in both blood and cultural traditions, to their relatives in Vermont, southern Quebec, western Maine, and northwestern Massachusetts. They are part of a larger group known as the Western *Abenaki,* "Dawn Land People." The word "Abenaki" is based on a given name used by the Montagnais who live north of the St. Lawrence River, a name that was altered by use among the Francophone settlers of Quebec in the late 1620s. The Abenaki's traditional name for themselves is *Alnôbak,* "The People."

In addition to New Hampshire's distinctive location, the real value of defining and telling the story of the land and the peoples within her boundaries, of the particular relationship that has unfolded between the natural world and the Native peoples of this region, is to connect with that most powerful point of reference for human beings: our sense of place. For residents of the Granite State, this is a book about the history of your home. For immediate neighbors and visitors from greater distances, this book helps you to understand the story of New Hampshire and, through association, recounts the broader epic of the Northeast and beyond.

# ACKNOWLEDGMENTS

More than any other book I have written, *A Time Before New Hampshire* demanded that I journey into the most recent findings in disparate academic fields, ranging from geology and glaciology to archaeology and paleonology. The help I received from the generous reviewers in the following list, all experts in their respective fields, was essential for completing this book. Since many of these fields of study rely on interpretations of physical and biological signs of what happened thousands of years ago, the meanings of some findings are both uncertain and hotly debated. Each of these reviewers corrected the factual inaccuracies that they found in the manuscript and offered their perspectives on subjects of controversy. They may not necessarily agree with how I present the past in those cases where we base our conclusions on evolving interpretations of a sometimes incomplete knowledge.

I am deeply grateful to each of the following reviewers for the many hours spent pouring over the manuscript and for assisting over the telephone when urgent questions arose: Thomas R. Armstrong, Ph.D., Research Geologist, United States Geological Survey; Eugene L. Boudette, Ph.D., United States Geological Survey (ret.) and New Hampshire State Geologist (ret.); Jeanne A. Brink, Native American educator and consultant; Victoria Bunker, Ph.D.; Colin Calloway, Ph.D., Chair, Native American Studies Center at Dartmouth College; Jere Daniell, Ph.D., Professor of History, Dartmouth College; James di Properzio, science editor; Gary W. Hume, Ph.D., New Hampshire State Archaeologist (ret.); Charles W. Johnson, Vermont State Naturalist (ret.); Carl Koteff, Ph.D., United States Geological Survey; Donna Roberts Moody, Repatriation and Site Protection Coordinator for the Abenaki Nation; Dr. James B. Petersen, Associate Professor and Chair of the Department of Anthropology, University of Vermont; Mark Suomala, Naturalist and Nature Tours Coordinator, Audubon Society of New Hampshire; Peter A. Thomas, Ph.D., former Director, Consulting Archaeology Program, University of Vermont; Charlie True, a member of the Council of the Abenaki Nation of New Hampshire.

Professor Wallace A. Bothner, Ph.D., and Linda Wrightsman of the Department of Earth Sciences at the University of New Hampshire provided numerous leads, afforded access to Dr. Donald Chapman's slides, and shared the Department's collection of minerals. Dr. P. Thompson Davis of the Department of Natural Sciences at Bentley College in Waltham, Massachusetts, generously shared his expertise on the glaciology of the White Mountains. I followed many solid leads provided by Dr. David Wunsch, New Hampshire's State Geologist. Jane S. Potter offered her assistance with the search for sources to interpret post-glacial environments. A great help both in providing photographs and tracking down other sources was Dr. Mark S. Twickler, Associate Director of the Climate Change Research Center, Institute for the Study of Earth, Oceans and Space (EOS) at the University of New Hampshire.

During the course of the past twenty years since I moved to Gedakina, I have learned much from the Abenaki peoples and their friends. In particular I would like to acknowledge Jeff Benay, Doris Minckler, Joseph Bruchac, John Moody, Donna Roberts Moody, Michael Delaney, Kenny Maskell, Chief Charlie True, and other respected leaders who have passed away: Chief Homer St. Francis, Chief Blackie Lampman, and Chief Stephen Laurent.

Adelaide Tyrol's magnificent illustrations bring these words and images to life in a way that helps us to better see and feel that these peoples and places of the past were once alive. Stacy Miller LaBare showed a steadfast hand as she drafted the maps of the Ancient Trails of *Wôbiwajoak* (the White Mountains) and of Native New Hampshire: The Alnôbak circa 1600.

No one could have possibly shown more patience with the many delays as this book wended its way from my imagination to the page. A heartfelt thanks to the staff at the University Press of New England who worked so hard to weave the piles of photos and illustrations into the text in such a pleasing way.

My gratitude goes out to the families of the Lanzas and the Yorks, who provided some quiet writing space in the old carriage house and schoolhouse.

A special "thank you" to my wife, Marie, and to all family and friends who accepted my absences when this project demanded every ounce of the time, energy, and attention I could muster. And thanks to Squirrel, whose gentle presence was always there to sooth during my moments of creative angst.

# A Time Before New Hampshire

# Introduction
## Waves In Time

*A* wave curls and glistens in the late-day sun until the breaker froths and engulfs your bare feet, folding you in an effervescent mist. Tugging as it recedes, it draws you toward Ocean's bosom, to where time forever turns back on itself; where present and past are brief moments on the eternal circle. Water and sand cave beneath your feet, pull you down, and invite you to meld with the grains of sand, to return home once again.

New Hampshire's seacoast is a brief, varied stretch of sandy beaches, rocky shores, marshes, and other estuarine riches. Her inland is dotted with wetlands and dappled with expansive lakes. These are our mentors: they remind us that history is a succession of waves and tides washing, ebbing, and flowing on the shores of this land in a dance between life and the elements.

For nearly 650 million years, encompassing four major geologic events, waves of rock sheets driven by convective forces deep within Earth's molten mantle have displaced this land. Mountains have risen, then eroded to their roots. Seas have opened and closed. Continental glaciers have advanced and melted back; seas of ice moving at a millennial pace, driven by global cycles of cooling and warming. Successive waves of plant and animal communities have come and gone in response to these changes like kelp swaying in the longshore current of time.

The lives of the primal world and the ancient peoples who walked upon its shifting rocks of time are not wholly encompassed in the evidence of life in the ancient seas, in bands and sheets of folded crystalline rock, in the archaic fragments of stone and bone that lie buried in the soil. Science tells us that New Hampshire's Native people have lived here for some 11,000 years; a mere blink of an eye compared to the venerable past as told in their Creation stories. In the ever-changing land of long ago, they breathed the breath of aged trees, hunted beasts of immense proportions, ate quiet meals together, shared stories around the cooking fire, and stared up at starry skies that magnified the fastness of a magnificent, unforgiving wilderness. Nature was, and is, seen as an expression of a Creator: a boundless generative force whose essence of unknowable mystery dwells in all that is encompassed in Earth and Sky, in this world and beyond.

After the last continental glacier retreated about 14,000 years ago, and in the warm habitable interstices that punctuated the periods in between earlier ice sheets, waves of indigenous peoples have ebbed and flowed. In recent centuries, waves of migrants from distant realms set foot upon these shores, bearing alien plants and animals. These invaders swept through this land—a cultural and biological hurricane that forever altered the native communities.

History is an egalitarian arbiter of the past in this recounting of the epochs. The artifice of "prehistory" draws a temporal line between the eons that passed before the coming of Europeans and the centuries that followed. Did the tree that fell in the pre-European forest make a sound when it crashed to the ground? Perhaps we should ask the squirrel who was crushed beneath its trunk where it was gnawing on the shell of an acorn, the family of sapsuckers who were trapped inside their arboreal nest when the trunk landed full on its doorway, or the ancient people who later gathered the dead, dried branches and threw them upon the fire to cook a meal of caribou flanks. In this account, every event is historic— whether preserved in signs etched in the rocks themselves, in the pollen record of bog peat, in the tales of wonder retold in ancient oral tradition, or in the pages of a book.

Our humanity enables us to connect easily with the aspects of *A Time Before New Hampshire* that tell the story of the indigenous peoples of this region, but our imaginations stretch to enfold the complexities and vast expanses of time encountered during the periods of geologic and glacial history. Although this entire book is based on the knowledge that we now possess, there is a particular sense of certainty in chapters 1 through 3, in which the story of Earth's past is related. In comparison, the living human history of chapters 4 to 11 unfolds as a relatively fluid, interpretive experience. This is reflected in the transition of tone and voice when moving from these earlier chapters to the latter. The conventional names used by anthropologists and archaeologists when referring to the chronological *periods* of cultural history in the Northeast correlate with the chapters in Part II and Part III of this book: *Paleoindian* (chapter 4), *Archaic* (chapter 5), *Woodland* (chapters 6–10), and *Contact* (chapter 11).

Throughout *A Time Before New Hampshire,* I have based this story on exhaustive research in numerous disciplines. The facts that form the foundation for this book have been drawn from such fields as geology, glaciology, climatology, archaeology, anthropology, ecology, forestry, wildlife management, paleobotany, and cultural history. In places, where there are gaps in our knowledge due to scant evidence and the lack of clarity that comes from glimpsing people, places, and environments from vast temporal distances, I have added a touch of breath to re-animate the natural history and events in the lives of ancient peoples, to re-create experiences that, while archaic to us, were once lived in the present as the heart of daily life. Skeletons of hard facts grow flesh and come to life in these pages as I draw on more than twenty five years of work in the sciences. I also plumb the depths of what I have learned through extensive research and by what I have experienced during two decades of personal and professional relationships with the Native peoples of North America, particularly those of New Hampshire and Vermont.

While creating these vignettes of lives past, I draw on details that are accurate to the best of our knowledge, such as clothing, tools, crafts, foods, environments, dates, places, and ecological settings. In a few of the sketches in chapters 4 and 5, I use my imagination to flesh out the details of how the lives and spiritual practices of ancient peoples unfolded. The opening story from 11,000 years ago that depicts a family in Jefferson, New Hampshire, builds upon our specific knowledge of that site and is also based on our awareness that ancient peoples of the Northeast sought help from the powers embodied in projectile points made from quartz crystal, powers that could help them find the game animals they needed to live.

Throughout this narrative, I have placed you, the reader, into the midst of archaic environments and the lives of ancient peoples. No matter where you now live, or in what place you may find yourself as you enter the world herein, it is my hope that this story, which spans 4.6 billion years, will transport you into the present of the past. May this journey help you to see and understand that the places we call home have evolved in the vastness of time; that we live in a here and now that was forged in the crucible of Earth's fires, sculpted by the forces of nature, and ceaselessly altered by the capricious hands of humankind.

PART I

# The Foundation

# 1. The Primordium

The age of the world is great enough for our imaginations,
even according to the Mosaic account, without borrowing
any years from the geologist.
—Henry David Thoreau,
*A Week on the Concord and Merrimack Rivers,* 1849

*L*ong before Thoreau paddled and portaged through the heart of southern New Hampshire, a Scottish farmer experienced a geologic epiphany while walking along the cliffs of Arthur's Seat in Edinburgh. James Hutton's vision transformed our awareness of Earth history from biblical revelation to the realm of science. Hutton eventually published *Theory of the Earth* sixty-four years before Thoreau's account of his journey up the Concord and Merrimack rivers came into print. In his book, Hutton described for the first time the concept that Earth's rock is part of a cycle that turns once every few hundred million years: a process of emergence, erosion, deposition, alteration by heat and pressure and, finally, re-emergence.[1]

Earth's immense age humbles even this nearly imperceptible turn of the geologic screw. Science tells us that some 4.6 billion years ago, a universal explosion created a vast nebula. Our solar system coalesced from this cloud of interstellar gas and dust. Gradually, over the first 500 million years, radioactivity warmed the center of Earth's gaseous sphere, causing heavy elements to melt, sink, and form a *core* of nickel and iron. Lighter elements rose to the surface. The pressure of gravity in this ever-denser core generated more heat, which melted Earth's entire sphere.

Hundreds of millions of years passed. Earth cooled as its heat dissipated into space. The inner core solidified while the outer core remained molten. A *mantle* of rock-forming elements now surrounded the core and the entire

These cliffs in Edinburgh, Scotland, inspired James
Hutton's vision of a dynamic geology. Located in
Holyrood Park, the rocks of Arthur's Seat are the
remnants of an ancient volcano. *Photo by Michael
J. Caduto.*

sphere was covered by a hard, stony shell or *crust*. Picture the pit, flesh, and
skin of an avocado and you have a good image of the three major components of Earth's structure—the core, mantle, and crust (figure 1-1).

On the surface, the roiling waters of Earth's primordial seas were
whipped by violent storms as lightning cracked the air charged by the
highly ionized atmosphere that was forming. Earth was a billion years old
before conditions in her primordial sea could support life. The booms of
lightning and unbroken periods of relentless rain must have been punctuated by periods when the clouds parted and her surface was illuminated
by magnificent sunrises and sunsets whose reddish-orange hues painted a
lifeless, elemental world. When life arrived, it was not heralded by the
flash of a bat's wing or the cry of a gull. At some generative point in time,
a single living cell arose, nurtured in this warm pelagic bosom. A human

FIGURE 1-1. Earth's avocado-like structure. The metallic inner *core* is surrounded by the *mantle* of rock-forming elements. Both are enclosed within a stony *crust.*

witness to this event would have seen and heard nothing as the first primitive ancestor of today's Cyanobacteria or "blue-green algae" appeared. As these photosynthetic algae used the sun's energy for growth and metabolism, they emitted the first oxygen into Earth's atmosphere. The oldest known rocks on Earth, which were discovered on the continent of Australia, date back to this time of more than 3.5 billion years ago.

In New England, there is no evidence of what occurred during the vast space of the next 2.6 billion years. The oldest known rocks in the chain of Appalachian mountains are 1.5 billion years old and are now visible at an outcrop just west of New Hampshire in Felchville (Reading), Vermont.[2] And up on the slopes of the Adirondack Mountains, a portion of Earth's skin now lies exposed that formed near the end of this long expanse of time more than 1 billion years ago.

The feeling of solidity and permanence beneath a hiker's feet as she slabs up the side of a mountain is born of humankind's temporal awareness. We perceive each step along the trail as motion, but when we stop walking the rocks appear to be a dormant bulk of minerals beneath our feet. We are caught in a moment too brief to notice Earth's movements. In Earth history, that one step, and even the sum of our steps—the duration of a human life—spans an infinitesimal amount of time. If the building of a mountain chain occurred in the blink of a geologic eye, the span of a human life would be imperceptible—a rocky eyelid frozen in mid-blink.

What animates the ground we walk on? Heat and convection within Earth's core and mantle are the engines that drive the changes on her surface. Intense pressures have created a partially molten mass of minerals in the outer mantle. As the malleable rock in this region heats up, it becomes less dense and rises toward the surface, where it eventually cools, sinks, re-heats, and rises. This slow, constant movement of about 1 inch each year causes this plastic rock to rise and fall in circular currents. When the partially molten rock rises to the surface, it is pushed aside by still more rock moving up beneath it. This creates horizontal currents that move the hard crust above.

Riding on this geologic sea of partially molten rock are the thirteen plates that make up Earth's surface. When the convective currents below the crust converge and push two plates together, one plate rides over the other and pushes it down into the mantle. The upper plate rises up to form a mountain range. For this reason, they are called *tectonic plates,* from the Greek *tekton* for "builder." A trench, called a *subduction zone,* forms along the edge of the plate being pushed down, where part of Earth's crust is being consumed. Stand on the Vermont side of the Connecticut River in Brattleboro or Bellows Falls and look east toward the dramatic cliffs that form the edge of southwestern New Hampshire and you will see one of the most interesting and complex geologic features in the world. You are in the subduction zone on the eastern edge of the ancient North American tectonic plate, viewing outcroppings of rock along the western face of an escarpment on which are exposed the layers of three distinct terranes, including the remnants of an ancient chain of equatorial volcanos beneath an upper layer that was originally part of the African continent.[3] This boundary marks a zone where entirely different geologic realms crushed together 400 million years ago.

Land mass shrinks where tectonic plates meet, so it must generate somewhere else. In *rift zones*—places where tectonic plates are pulling apart, such as along the deep-sea Atlantic ridge in between the continents of North America and Europe—Earth's crust becomes so thin that molten rock called *magma* pushes up and forms new crust of dense basalt on the ocean floor. Rising magma helps to drive this process by pushing the plates apart. Deep canyons form in many of these rift zones. Volcanos also rise up in some of these regions as the magma erupts, cools, and hardens (figure 1-2). Eruptions occur along ocean ridges as well as in zones where plates are colliding, where the crust is pushed into the magma and melted. In the midst of this cycle, the less-dense rocks of the continents rise up and form the regions of dry land that "float" on the denser basalt below.

Cooling rock contracts and often forms cracks or *joints.* When magma pushes up into a joint and hardens it forms a *dike.* The Flume, which is found about 4 miles south of Franconia Notch at the base of Mount Liberty, is a classic dike. Flume Brook eroded the softer basalt dike that had intruded into a joint in the harder, surrounding Conway granite. The resulting chasm is 700 feet long, up to 70 feet high, and from 12 to 20 feet wide. Walk along the trail that runs through the Flume dike and you occupy a space that once was solid rock, eroded away by the patient, powerful hand of water and all that it carries. Sabbaday Falls, found along the

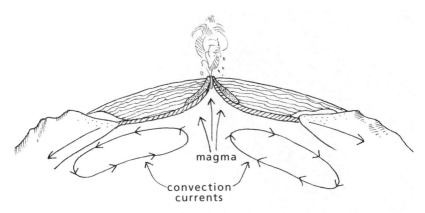

FIGURE 1-2. A *rift zone* where new crust is generated. Convection currents within the mantle, as well as the rising magma, push apart the two tectonic plates above. New crust is generated on the ocean floor and volcanos form as molten magma erupts, cools, and solidifies. Deep trenches form along many oceanic rift zones.

Kancamagus Highway, is another beautiful landform cut when Sabbaday Brook eroded a basalt dike running through Concord granite. Many basalt dikes are found amid the rugged outcrops in the northern parts of the New Hampshire coast south of the wide harbor at the mouth of the Piscataqua River, which consist largely of older volcanic rock and sediments that have been metamorphosed into schist and gneiss. These persistent rocks have formed coves that shelter a number of small, intimate beaches.

Over time, sediments are washed away by rushing water, abraded by the wind, and rendered by heating and cooling and the relentless forces of expanding ice. During the colonial period, local rock was quarried in winter by drilling a row of holes near the edge of an exposed outcrop, then filling each hole with water. The combined expansive forces of the columns of ice in the holes split off rock slabs of even width. Jeremy Belknap describes the sculpting power of the elements in *The History of New Hampshire:*

> In the year 1746, a party who were ranging the woods, in the neighbourhood of the White Mountains, on a warm day, in the month of March, were alarmed with a repeated noise, which they supposed to be the firing of guns. On further search, they found it to be caused by rocks, falling from the south side of a steep mountain.[4]

Rocks are the mineral pages of an ancient book that records the dynamic expression of Earth's ever-changing nature. As rock erodes from the uplands, the sediments are carried down to the ocean by streams and

*Left:* A basaltic dike atop Mount Chocorua. As the granite that formed this bedrock was cooling, it contracted and cracked, and basalt welled up into the joint. *Photo by Michael J. Caduto.*

*Opposite:* The Flume in Franconia Notch was created as Flume Brook eroded a massive basalt dike that had intruded into a joint in the surrounding granite. *Photo courtesy New Hampshire Historical Society.*

rivers and deposited into layers. This process, along with the actions of glaciers and waves over time, is how the sandy beaches along the coast of southern New Hampshire were formed, where the slate bedrock is more easily eroded than the metamorphic rocks to the north. Over time, sediments of sand, silt, and clay that are compressed by the layers above them are cemented, solidified, and hardened to form *sedimentary rocks* such as sandstone. Clay is the parent material of shale, but limestone, which has a high calcium content, is a sedimentary rock that forms from the shell remnants of a multitude of sea creatures. Mountains are usually built of igneous and metamorphic rock because sedimentary rocks erode as mountains rise.

Any rock that is once again subject to heat, pressure, or chemical action, but that does not melt, is transformed as it recrystallizes into a *metamorphic rock*. Sandstone metamorphoses into quartzite, limestone becomes marble, and shale changes into slate and schist. Metamorphic rocks, which compose nearly one-half of New Hampshire's bedrock, are crystalline and often appear as wavy bands and stripes.[5] The major

mountain ranges and some well-known peaks in this region consist of metamorphic rock, including New Hampshire's Presidential range, Vermont's Green Mountains, and the Taconics, as well as Mount Moosilauke and Mount Monadnock.

When the sedimentary and metamorphic rocks of Earth's crust lie within the portion of a tectonic plate that is being pushed down into the mantle, those rocks are once again compacted, heated, and consumed into the partially molten mass. Wherever this molten material cools and solidifies, it forms *igneous* rocks such as granite and quartz. Igneous rocks are hard because they consist of interlocking crystals that form as the molten magma slowly cools. Mica, quartz, and feldspar, and their respective colors of black, white, and pink, are the basic components of granite, which comprises about one-half of New Hampshire's exposed bedrock.[6] Because this rock cooled over a long period of time while still miles beneath Earth's surface, it is called *plutonic* rock.

Mountains and volcanos arise as rocks on the overriding plate are pushed up and folded. In places, magma erupts from volcanos and forms pumice, a kind of igneous rock that cools too quickly to align into crystals. Once again, from these lofty slopes, the process of erosion begins anew. During the entire circuit of the *rock cycle,* it may take a few hundred million years for a portion of Earth to make the journey from crust to mantle to crust.

The hands of time and geologic forces never rest. New Hampshire's backbone—which begins with Mount Monadnock in the south, continues north through the New Hampshire highlands, and stretches to the White Mountains—was born of a massive tectonic collision some 380 million years ago that pushed her jagged summits to frigid heights of over 25,000 feet. The peaks that we see today are the erosion-resistant roots of those ancient Acadian mountains. A multitude of forces have worked and reworked this foundation: erosion, metamorphism, folding, faulting, and a gradual uplifting over time. Earth is a tireless sculptor.

The north face of Mount Monadnock. *Photo by Michael J. Caduto.*

# 2. The Crucible and the Cauldron

Almost every thing in nature, which can be supposed
capable of inspiring ideas of the sublime and beautiful, is
here realized. Aged mountains, stupendous elevations,
rolling clouds, impending rocks, verdant woods, chrystal
streams, the gentle rill, and the roaring torrent, all conspire
to amaze, to soothe and to enrapture.

—Jeremy Belknap, A.M.,
*The History of New Hampshire,* 1792

Earth's early history occurred in an expanse of time unimaginable from a human frame of reference. Even her "recent" history is hard to fathom for beings whose immediate points of reference are
each sunrise and sunset. Geologists measure the age of rocks by dating
nuclear isotopes and by studying the signs of ancient biology recorded in
fossils. When a new deposit of rock forms, the radioactive isotopes that
are naturally found in that rock begin to decay at a constant rate. The age
of rocks is discerned by measuring the amount of radioactive decay that
has occurred in particular minerals within that rock. Rocks that are of
similar age can be discovered by studying the fossils they contain.
Wherever the age of the ancient plants and animals preserved in layers of
rock is alike, then so is the relative age of those rocks.

A geologist's signposts along the geologic time line, moving from
larger to smaller spans of time, consist of the *era, period* and *epoch.*
While useful to those who are students of the generic nomenclature, these
names can be cumbersome when trying to envision the web of geologic
and biologic developments that occurred over hundreds of millions of
years. A geologic time line correlates these dates and years with the
marker names used by geologists.

To untangle the web of geologic time, we are going to set a twenty-
four-hour clock that covers a period starting 650 million years ago, the
age of the most ancient rocks in New Hampshire. As the clock ticks down

to the present, each second will mark the passing of 7,523 years. On this time scale, the 14,000 years that have passed since the most recent *Wisconsinan* ice sheet melted from New Hampshire amounts to 1.9 seconds. A mere .13 seconds measures the last millennium.

▧ ➡ ➡ 12:00 A.M. (650 million years ago)   Our geologic clock starts to tick. Rocks are now forming that will one day be found along the Atlantic coastal plain and in the nearby *piedmont,* the "foothills" in the southeastern part of the state. This region, known as *Avalonia,* is one of four *terranes* found in New Hampshire—large blocks of Earth's crust that are of a different geologic character than those they border (figure 2-1).

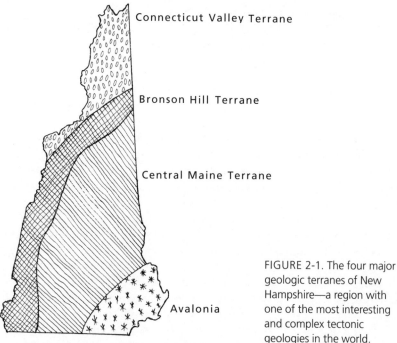

FIGURE 2-1. The four major geologic terranes of New Hampshire—a region with one of the most interesting and complex tectonic geologies in the world.

▧ ➡ ➡ 1:51 A.M. (600 million years ago)   Green algae become the first living things to inhabit the land. Until this time, for 3 billion years, Cyanobacteria (blue-green algae) and other forms of algae were the only life on Earth. Over the next 3¾ hours (100 million years), during the Cambrian period, the diversity of life blossoms. Coastal waters of the future New England crawl with carnivorous trilobites, the ancient ancestors of modern arthropods such as lobsters, crabs, shrimp, insects, spiders, and horseshoe crabs. Like their modern counterparts, trilobites have jointed legs and hard, hinged exoskeletons that are shed as they grow. Trilobites, which range from 1 inch to 1½ feet long, patrol the seabed in search of prey. Other invertebrates that inhabit *Iapetus*—this vast, tepid equatorial sea—include the ancestors of today's molluscs, lamp shells, and ostracods—tiny scavenging crustaceans that are primitive seed shrimps. Ancient sea cucumbers wave their tentacles while a nautilus drifts by (figure 2-2).

At this time, North America and Greenland are part of a continent called *Laurentia*. The equator runs through Laurentia, which, compared with today's orientation, is turned clockwise 90 degrees so that the east coast faces south. New Hampshire lies about 25 degrees latitude south of the equator. Waves lap at the shore of the ancient Iapetus Sea, blanketed by an atmosphere in which oxygen levels are a mere 1 percent of today's levels.

FIGURE 2-2. The ancient sea near the end of the Cambrian Period, which lasted from 2:57–5:32 A.M. (570–500 million years ago): a pelagic melange of seaweeds, sponges, sea cucumbers, brachiopods, worms, trilobites, and crustaceans. *The Field Museum.*

➡ ➡ 3:41–7:01 A.M. (550–460 million years ago)   Calcium carbonate accumulates in these marine sands and muds from the skeletons of countless microscopic ocean animals and from minerals that are precipitating from the seawater. Under pressure, these sediments become limestone and eventually metamorphose into the marble that is now the lifeblood of numerous marble quarries in the Northeast, including the one in Proctor, Vermont.

➡ ➡ 4:48 A.M. (520 million years ago)   New York and most of New England lie beneath the shallow, tropical waters of the Iapetus Sea.

➡ ➡ 6:17–7:34 A.M. (480–445 million years ago)   At about the beginning of this time, deep within Earth's mantle, the ancient flow of magma shifts and forces the overlying crust to move in new directions as the large tectonic plate under the shallow sea splits. On the surface, the continents of Laurentia to the west and another mysterious continent to the east that may have geologic kinship to Avalonia or Africa, are ground inexorably together.

Approaching from the west, Laurentia is eventually driven 600 miles down into Earth's mantle as the African or Avalonian continent, approaching from the east, rides over it. Heat and pressure increase on the subsiding rock until it melts, forces its way to the surface and erupts in a spectacular crescent of volcanos surrounded by the sea[1] (figure 2-3).

As the two plates grind against one another, the dark mud and other volcanic sediments that accumulated along the ancient seashore are compressed, along with other volcanic rocks such as basalt. Under this intense pressure and mild heat, the basalt slowly metamorphoses into greenschists. Other transformations are shale forming schists, limestone becoming marble, and sandstones being altered to quartzite.[2]

Converging further still, the geologic remnants of the ancient volcanic chain, the *Bronson Hill island arc complex,* is squeezed along the margin and pushed up to form an *anticline,* a convex mass of up-folded rock shaped like an "n." (A concave mass that has been folded down into a "u" is a *syncline.*)

The edges of these two plates continue to drive into each other as deep thrust faults form in the Laurentian plate to the west. Pressure causes slabs of this continent to pile up at angles on top of one another until enormous ridges arise and form the Taconic Mountains.[3] In their prime, the jagged, imposing peaks of the nascent Taconics jut two miles into the vapor-thin atmosphere.

As the Taconics are rising, the diverse mix of sedimentary and volcanic

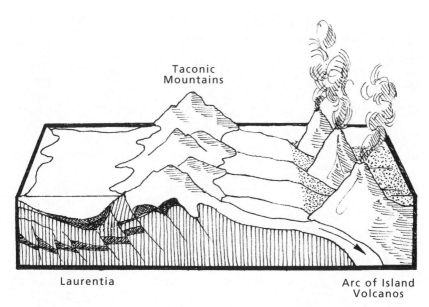

Taconic
Mountains

Laurentia

Arc of Island
Volcanos

FIGURE 2-3. Around 7:01 A.M. (460 million years ago), the continent of Laurentia from the west is forced beneath another continent approaching from the east, possibly a part of Africa, and an arc of island volcanos erupts along the margin. Faults form in the crust to the west, then the sheets of rock buckle and slide upwards, creating the Taconic Mountains. As the continents continue to grind together the ancient ocean sediments and the arc of island volcanos become squeezed in between, forming a band of rock that will one day be known as the *Bronson Hill Terrane.*

rocks that formed beneath the ocean is lifted and mashed onto the eastern edge of the ancient North American continent. This new geologic band, called the *Bronson Hill terrane,* now curves along the western edge of New Hampshire. The 160-mile, north-south expanse of the Bronson Hill terrane starts in the southwestern part of the state east of the Connecticut River, arches northeast through Lancaster, and trends further northeast until it continues into Maine (figure 2-1). Some of the more common rocks here include conglomerates, metamorphosed sandstone, siltstone, and other deposits that reveal ancient volcanic activity.[4]

➡ ➡ 7:34 A.M. (445 million years ago) Small worms now wriggle about on land. Plants have developed roots to anchor themselves and to absorb water and nutrients, as well as stems to transport the nourishment to the rest of the plant. New life appears in the ancient Iapetus Sea amid coral reefs. Snails creep along the bottom from which the siphons of buried bivalves protrude. Both are stalked by primitive seastars.

FIGURE 2-4. Marine life from 8:07–9:25 A.M. (430–395 million years ago), during the Silurian Period. Vast expanses of reef lay just beneath the shallow waters of a rich tropical sea. *The Field Museum.*

➡ ➡ 7:45–8:52 A.M. (440–410 million years ago) Earth is relatively quiet as the dramatic mountain ranges gradually erode and rivers carry the sediments down to the coast of a Silurian Sea (figure 2-4). Somewhere in the middle of this span of time, the first true land-dwelling plants evolve from ancient green algae. The profusion of terrestrial plants that develops over the next hour or so produces forests of giant horsetails, clubmosses, ferns, and the early ancestors of conifers whose crowns reach 40 feet into the warm, humid skies. Creeping amid the greenery of Laurentia are hosts of spiders, mites, and centipedes.

➡ ➡ 8:18 A.M. (425 million years ago) At this time, approaching the middle of the 350-million-year span of the *Paleozoic* era, when sediments from the high peaks of the Taconic Mountains have eroded to the sea, there is a shoreline in western New Hampshire. The rocks and sands of this paleobeach eventually metamorphose into quartzite and a quartz-pebble conglomerate that resembles the "pudding stone" of southern New England. Within the rocks of this *Clough formation,* the original shells of marine animals are replaced over time by metamorphic minerals and preserved. These fossils, which can now be found on Croydon Mountain, Moose Mountain, and in Montcalm, New Hampshire, as well as on the slopes of Skitchewaug Mountain in Springfield, Vermont, include corals, pelmatozoan columnals, and brachiopods that are the ancestors of modern lamp shells. A few rare specimens of trilobites and gastropods or sea snails have also been discovered.[5]

Similar but younger fossils occur within the 400-million-year-old rocks of the *Fitch formation,* which consists of a layer of limestone beneath a zone of metamorphic rock. In addition, these ancient beds, which have been found in Littleton, New Hampshire, and in Bernardston, Massachusetts, contain microfossils called conodonts that are thought to be the teeth of an extinct group of animals that resembled lampreys and were primitive ancestors of chordates.

Also in Littleton, at Slate Ledge, and at Dalton Mountain in Whitefield, numerous brachiopod fossils are associated with the mica schist of the *Littleton formation*—a type of rock that is largely schist and quartzite. The fossils have been preserved in a thin layer of limestone that has metamorphosed into marble where it touches on the granite beneath. These same brachiopods have also been found in Beaver Brook on the east side of Mount Moosilauke.

Somewhat after this time period, the remnants of some early terrestrial plants wash into the sea. Fossils of one of these plants, called *Prototaxites,* are now found in southern Quebec and in sedimentary rocks near Indian Stream in Pittsburg, New Hampshire.

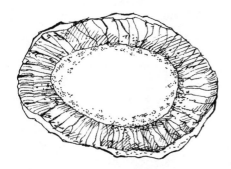

The alga *Prototaxites,* whose fossils are found near Indian Stream in Pittsburg, New Hampshire, was among the pioneer organisms that could survive on land. This shows one of the conductive tubes of *Prototaxites southworthii.*

➡ ➡ 9:14 A.M. (400 million years ago) If you could sail the verge in the ancient sea and gaze into the fertile waters for the geologic equivalent of the next few hours, you would witness the dark flash of a primitive fish—the first animal with a backbone.

➡ ➡ 8:52–11:05 A.M. (410–350 million years ago) Laurentia to the west and the Africa-like land mass to the east are once more on the move toward one another, gradually closing the ancestral Atlantic Ocean. All the while, Laurentia is drifting northward and rotating counterclockwise.

*Paradoxides.* Fossil remains of this species of trilobite, which was several feet long, are common in Africa. They have also been found in New England within the Avalonian terrane.

As these land masses converge, the geologic remnants of the ancient volcanic chain, the Bronson Hill terrane, is again squeezed in between.

Today, the western boundary of the Bronson Hill terrane runs from near Milan on the Maine border, southwest to Lancaster, and on down toward Bath in the Connecticut River valley. The southwest face of the Jefferson Dome, south of Littleton, and the spectacular face on Mount Forest, southwest of Berlin, both offer a dramatic view of the northern portion of the Bronson Hill terrane. Farther south, two spectacular views of the exposed western edge of the Bronson Hill terrane include the steep cliffs on the eastern shore of the Connecticut River next to Brattleboro and the cliffs in North Walpole across from Bellows Falls. The Bronson Hill terrane is exposed in southwestern New Hampshire as a 15-mile-wide zone that can be crossed by driving along Route 9 between Keene and Brattleboro.

The western edge of the Bronson Hill terrane, where it was thrust over the rocks to the west, is now called the *Ammonoosuc thrust fault.* This fault formed a natural path for the Connecticut River as it gradually eroded its course from about Woodsville south to the Massachusetts border. In 1764, when the governments of New York and New Hampshire accepted a royal decree declaring the western shore of the Connecticut River as the boundary between the two states, they inadvertently enshrined and intertwined both the political and geologic character of these distinctive regions. In January of 1777, when Vermont declared itself a free state, its boundary with New Hampshire remained on the west bank of the river.

The Bronson Hill terrane was once connected to another terrane that lies to the east. This, the *Central Maine terrane,* is the spine of New England's bedrock. The origin of the oldest parts of this terrane, which was pushed onto the edge of Laurentia as Avalonia approached from the east, is a geologic puzzle. It may have been a fragment of the African continental plate that got squeezed between Laurentia and Africa as they converged. Sheets of igneous rock, as well as metamorphic rock such as schist, quartzite, and conglomerates, are common in the Central Maine terrane, whose name comes from the rock of Maine's interior that is of similar composition and structure. The Central Maine terrane includes Mount Monadnock, the interior White Mountains, the New Hampshire highlands, and the piedmont that borders the mountains to the east (figure 2-1).

At this time, the land that is to become New England still lies south of the Equator. Soon after the Central Maine terrane is squeezed onto the edge of the North American continent, the final wave of rock arrives when Avalonia is crushed against the southeastern edge of the Central Maine terrane. Avalonia, which was named after the Avalon Peninsula in Newfoundland, contains deposits that formed at 12:00 A.M. (650 million years ago)—New Hampshire's oldest rocks.[6] The state's coast and neighboring inland rocks make up the complex known as the *Avalonian composite terrane.* No one is sure where the Avalonian terrane came from; it may have originated as far as a thousand miles to the south in Africa. Certain trilobite fossils that are unique to Avalonian deposits, including one genus named *Paradoxides* that was several feet long, have been discovered in New England and as far as the Canadian Maritimes, the Carolinas, and the United Kingdom. Fossils of *Paradoxides* have also been found in Africa.

Now the great collision finally occurs. As Africa crashes into the edge of Laurentia, it creates a slow-moving geologic wave from the east that rides over the North American plate. A new range of peaks pushes skyward until the jagged tops of the Acadian Mountains soar a breathtaking 5 miles high. The geologic force of this event folded and altered rocks as far west as the Taconics and the Allegheny Plateau. These forces are responsible, in part, for the steep slopes and folded hills of eastern

The Acadian Mountains as they likely appear at 9:58 A.M. on our geologic clock, 380 million years ago. Their immense summits soar to over 5 miles high—the height of the present-day Himalayas. The massive fields of magma upwelling beneath these great peaks will one day become exposed as the roots of the White Mountains. *Photo by Mark S. Twickler, Climate Change Research Center, University of New Hampshire.*

and central Vermont. Because the tectonic force pushed westward, the hills tend to run north-south and the eastern layers often fold and fault over those to the west.

While these complex events are occurring on the surface, massive fields of magma, the *New Hampshire magma,* well up beneath the roots of the evolving Acadian Mountains. As this rock slowly cools and hardens deep below the surface, the minerals crystallize into mica, feldspar, and quartz, among others. In time, as the overlying rocks erode away, much of this granite—the roots of the White Mountains—becomes exposed. The New Hampshire magma is so extensive that it forms the foundation of landforms that range from Concord to the White Mountains, from the Isles of Shoals off the coast of Portsmouth west to the fine-grained rock now quarried in Barre, Vermont. It even includes isolated remnants that form the bases of Mount Monadnock in Jaffrey and Mount Cardigan in Grafton.

A poetic description of this bedrock springs from the mind of Celia Thaxter as she describes the roots of the land of her childhood, the Isles of Shoals.

> Each island has its peculiar characteristics . . . and no two are alike,
> though all are of the same coarse granite, mixed with masses and
> seams of quartz and felspar and gneiss and mica-slate, and
> interspersed with dikes of trap running in all directions. Upon
> Appledore, for the most part, the trap runs from north to south,
> while the veins of quartz and felspar run from east to west.
> Sometimes the narrow white quartz veins intersect the dark trap, in
> parallel lines, now wavering, and now perfectly straight, and
> showing a surface like that of some vast piece of inlaid work.[7]

The intense heat and pressure generated as the Acadian Mountains rose created a colossal geologic kiln that transformed the rocks of this region. Some of the rocks were folded and the minerals coalesced into bands while they were still partly magma. Because the rock cooled slowly, over millions of years, minerals crystallized into beautiful shapes and colors.

The schist, quartzite, and gneiss that can be seen in road cuts along Route 9 from Brattleboro to Concord are metamorphic rocks from this

Bedrock in many parts of New Hampshire is a melange of different types. Below the Beaver Pond along Route 112, just north of the Lost River gorge, is a kind of granite known as Kinsman quartz monzonite. The large, light-colored rectangles are white potash feldspar crystals. Just to the north is a boundary where masses of this granite intruded into the layers of the bordering Littleton schist. *Photo by Michael J. Caduto.*

FIGURE 2-5. As the Devonian Period came to an end, the ocean was alive with fish. The bottom of the sea was host to a dazzling array of marine life such as corals, crinoids, bryozoans, and brachiopods. A trilobite, cephalopod, and snail crawl along the bottom in the middle of this scene. *The Field Museum.*

time. Bands of gneiss are generally overlain by the quartzite and mica schist. Some of the rocks now common in the Bronson Hill terrane, such as the greenschists that formed from metamorphosed basalt, are from this period. Deposits of schist and quartzite known as the Littleton formation also occur here and throughout the Bronson Hill and Central Maine terranes. Many of the high landforms that define New Hampshire are composed of Littleton rocks, including Mount Monadnock and its satellite peaks of Pack Monadnock and Little Monadnock. Much of the mica schist on the summits of Mount Washington, Mount Monadnock, and Mount Moosilauke is studded with red garnets. Sinuous bands of feldspar, laced with quartz and dark mica, can be seen in the gneiss atop Mount Moosilauke.

➡ ➡ 10:20–10:43 A.M. (370–360 million years ago) Much of the present continent of North America lies quietly submerged beneath the equatorial waters of a Devonian Sea (figure 2-5). In this seabed, to the south and west, sediments created by the erosion of the ancient Acadian Mountains gradually build up to 4,000 feet deep. Over time, these deposits metamorphose into sedimentary rocks whose strata are rich with the fossilized remains of numerous species of fish, seastars, corals, sponges, and other marine invertebrates. These waters are dominated by many colonial invertebrate animals called crinoids that have plates in their stems and arms that are high in calcium. Over eons, the dead remains of crinoids create layers up to 1,000 feet thick.

➡ ➡   11:05 A.M.–12:55 P.M. (350–300 million years ago)   To the west of what is now New England, in an archaic world along the shore, an ancient teleost, walking on rudimentary limbs of fins, emerges from a tidal pool and gulps the first breath of air inhaled by an amphibious vertebrate animal. These first, fish-like amphibians, which have developed lungs, creep through the dense foliage that exists from this time until about 2:00 P.M.—jungles and swamps of spore-bearing, tree-sized horsetails and clubmosses with a lush understory of tall ferns. Some of these ancient arboreal giants—the ancestors of modern clubmosses— have trunks that are covered with deeply textured bark and grow up to 3 feet in diameter, bearing crowns to heights of 100 feet. The remains of plants from this *Carboniferous period* will form the fossil fuels we burn today. The air is filled with the lugubrious drone of predacious dragonflies who patrol their territories while borne on wings that spread nearly 3 feet from tip to tip. These dragonflies, and the cockroaches that scuttle along the ground beneath them, look like identical giant versions of their contemporaries.

Mysteriously, at about the time that the first land animals crawl over the surface, a mass extinction of great proportions befalls life on Earth. Immense numbers of species are wiped out in the tepid seas. For some unknown reason, this extinction does not have a marked impact on the recently evolved ferns and the tree-sized horsetails and clubmosses.

As this hour and 50 minutes (50 million years) ticks away on our geologic time clock, the wind, water, ice, and cycles of heat and cold slowly, inexorably, work away at the exposed peaks of the Acadian Mountains, eroding rocks and sediments at the rate of 1.9 feet every 10,000 years. Sediments that are carried away by streams and rivers and deposited to the west fill in the shallow inland sea there and create the Catskill delta of New York and Pennsylvania. Off to the east, thick layers of sand and silt are deposited as a layer up to 2 miles thick atop the continental shelf, where they bury the reefs and lagoons of the ancient equatorial sea.

➡ ➡   12:55 P.M. (300 million years ago)   Eastern North America still lies south of the equator. Giant, crocodile-sized amphibians, the labyrinthodonts, plod along in the sloughs dappled with shade from the

A labyrinthodont—an alligator-sized, toothed amphibian—basks amid enormous ferns beneath the tree-sized ancestors of horsetails and clubmosses in a Carboniferous forest. A dragonfly with a wingspan of nearly 3 feet hovers above the forest floor that is home to giant cockroaches, spiders, mites, and centipedes.

FIGURE 2-6. *Pangaea, "all earth."*

crowns of the Carboniferous swamp forests. Waiting in ambush, these giants prey on anything small enough to swallow. After a meal, they find a sheltered, sunny place in which, unmolested, they digest their food.

➡ ➡ 1:18 P.M. (290 million years ago) Northwestern Africa, along the edge of the continent of *Gondwana,* pushes into eastern North America and southern Europe. When these land masses meet, their margins fold and buckle; the Allegheny Mountains rise. The southern and central Appalachian Mountains of today are the remaining roots of this once-magnificent mountain range. With the joining of these great continents, Earth's land surface now forms one continuous mass called *Pangaea,* "all earth." Pangaea will remain intact for the next 3 hours and 42 minutes (100 million years) (figure 2-6).

➡ ➡ 2:01–2:46 P.M. (270–250 million years ago) Freshwater fish appear and amphibians begin to decline as the dominant lifeform. Cool, dry areas encourage the growth of conifers on land while seedferns and ferns with broad leaves appear in the southern hemisphere. The giant, spore-bearing horsetails, clubmosses, and ferns of the Carboniferous period disappear and give rise to their smaller, modern descendants, such as our familiar ground pines. The tree-sized ancestors were most successful in the humid, tropical environments of earlier ages because they needed a moist environment in which the sperm could swim to the egg to successfully reproduce.

As this time period passes, the climate gradually dries and conditions favor the evolution of seed plants that do not require a moist environment

*Dimetrodon*

in which to reproduce, because fertilization takes place within the mature plant. The well-protected seeds of the next generation can withstand heat and dryness for long periods of time. Gymnosperms, including the conifers, evolve into the plants that will dominate the land for millions of years.

The drying climate also leads to a decline in the amazing amphibians that populate this period. Reptilian eggs evolve that allow the young to develop and hatch on land, enabling these creatures to increase in numbers and influence. Much like seeds do for plants, eggs provide a self-contained environment in which the next generation can grow. One of the most dramatic reptiles is *Dimetrodon,* which sports a long, tall, fan-like fin running along its back.

➡ ➡ 2:44 P.M. (251 million years ago)   Now comes the time of the Great Dying—the most catastrophic destruction of life in Earth's history.[8] A mass extinction kills off 70 percent of all terrestrial vertebrate animals, most land-dwelling plants, and nine out of ten existing ocean species. Permian fishes, molluscs, and other forms of marine life are laid waste. Trilobites are wiped out forever. This unparalleled biological disaster is most likely caused by the geologic and climatic repercussions that result when a massive comet or asteroid up to seven miles across smashes into Earth. Tectonic upheavals begin a million years of volcanic activity that generates thick, dark atmospheric clouds of dust and ash—the catalyst for prolonged and intense global cooling.

➡ ➡ 2:57 P.M. (245 million years ago)   At this time, the thirteen tectonic plates that compose the world's land mass still consist of the single, enormous continent, Pangaea, surrounded by a giant ocean, *Pantha-*

*lassa* or "all seas." The climate is varied and extreme over much of the surface of this ancient land. In some equatorial regions, the heat and moisture are punctuated by warm, seasonal monsoons. Interior sections are dominated by expanses of hot, dry desert where the temperature frequently rises above 120 degrees Fahrenheit. Far northern regions experience long periods of snow, ice, and cold rains. Seasons are much more extreme than they are today, with scorching summers and white-cold winter months. In interior regions, such as central *Gondwanaland* south of the equator, the average monthly temperatures vary by more than 90 degrees. Here, the continental land mass is so wide that the moderating effect that oceans have on climate is insignificant. The region that is destined to become the Appalachian Mountains and New Hampshire is part of the subcontinent *Laurasia*, where the land mass is not as wide and temperatures are more steady and moderate. Temperatures, though, were much warmer than they are now because New Hampshire's latitude was about that of Texas or Mexico today. The stresses caused by weather near the end of the Paleozoic era force plants and animals to evolve in order to survive. In addition to seeds and eggs, other adaptations probably include strategies for surviving seasonal extremes, such as migrating and becoming dormant.

➡ ➡ 3:17 P.M. (236 million years ago) The evolution of plants continues and the first flowering plants appear in the form of ancestral magnolias. As primitive beetles become attracted to the protective scents and nectars given off by these early flowers, they begin to spread pollen from bloom to bloom. Thus pollination begins: a mutual exchange that is destined to evolve into one of the most intricate and essential of all interrelationships between plants and animals.[9]

➡ ➡ 4:15 P.M. (210 million years ago) A gargantuan meteorite penetrates the atmosphere, strikes Earth, and creates a global dust cloud that leads to a prolonged period of icy darkness. The site of impact could be the 60-mile wide Manicouagan Crater, which lies 500 miles northwest of present-day Nova Scotia. Cataclysmic climate change wipes out 40 percent of the families of animals in existence, including half of all species of amphibians and reptiles. One in every five families of ocean-dwelling creatures disappears.

➡ ➡ 4:37 P.M. (200 million years ago) In time, the tops of the ancient Acadian Mountains erode away and pressure gradually decreases on the igneous rocks below. As these rocks expand, they fracture. Over millions of years, when these fractured layers of rock become exposed, a process called *sheeting* occurs during which the upper layers continually slough off and erode away, forming the familiar dome-shaped tops of the White Mountains.

In some places, isolated mountains emerge because they are composed of rock that resists the erosion experienced by their surroundings. Millions of years later, New Hampshire's Native peoples, the Abenaki, would refer to one of these as a *menadena,* "separate mountain." Today, the 3,165-foot summit of Mount Monadnock or *menonadenak,* "smooth mountain," is so well known the the term "monadnock" is often used to describe any tall, isolated peak. Mount Monadnock is exactly 25 feet taller than *bemapskadena,* "where there is a rocky mountain"—Mount Ascutney—which lies just 40 miles north-northeast on the Vermont side of the Connecticut River. Other well-known monadnocks in New Hampshire include Mount Kearsarge (2,931 feet), Mount Cardigan (3,121), Mount Sunapee (2,743) and, in Massachusetts, Mount Greylock (2,690) and Mount Wachusett (2,006).

➡ ➡ 4:37–9:38 P.M. (200–64 million years ago)  Dinosaurs appear and roam the surface of a violent world. Convective currents again shift as molten magma pushes up beneath the North American plate and the African or European plate. Great changes occur during the next 3 hours and 42 minutes (100 million years). By 8:19 P.M., the giant pieces of the continental puzzle of Pangaea will have drifted apart until the juxtaposition of Earth's continents is similar to what we see today.

Locally, as the exotic plate slides away to the east, it leaves the rocks of African or European origin, of which much of New Hampshire is composed, stuck to the eastern edge of the North American plate. To the north, Labrador is left behind when Ireland, Britain, and Scandinavia pull away from it. With each passing millennium, the rift widens about 55 feet and the Atlantic Ocean flows into this void from south to north.

The crust along this lengthy, widening rift becomes thinner, until earthquakes rend the fabric of the land and hundreds of volcanos erupt. Rivers of lava flow down the steep slopes and the air fills with caustic plumes of acrid volcanic gases that rise into the upper *troposphere,* the layer of Earth's atmosphere that blankets the surface and reaches up to 10 miles high.

Volcanic vents erupt repeatedly over the course of many years. As the magma emerges from these vents, circular sections of the surface collapse into the depleted magma chambers, forming plugs. Magma forces its way up along the edges of each central plug, ringing it with more eruptions and intruding the cracks in the rocks around the plug with dikes of magma. When the volcanos are finally spent, they have formed a circle of peaks around the ridge of the collapsed plug in the center. In some places, this series of events repeats and creates more than one circle, depositing black basalt during the first event and granite-like rock in later eruptions. Over time, granite pushes up into the cracks that form in the central plug, forming a granitic core within the circle. These *ring-dike complexes* form from 5:10 to 7:56 P.M. (185–110 million years ago) (figure 2-7). The picturesque Ossipee Mountains are the remnants of an ancient ring-dike complex that has a diameter of about 9 miles. Another, smaller example, which formed just south of Wolfeboro, is the Merrymeeting ring-dike complex.[10]

Some of the hills and peaks of the White Mountains, as well as numerous hills near Lake Winnipesaukee, are composed of the igneous rock that welled up during these eruptions. Mount Chocorua in the southern White Mountains, and many of the peaks visible along the Kancamagus Highway, are also composed of this granite. These rocks were part of the underground rivers of magma that fed the volcanos of this tumultuous geologic period. As the plates drifted apart, magma rose miles beneath the surface of the ancient Acadian Mountains and covered much of what is now New Hampshire with a subterranean layer up to 9,000 feet thick—the famous *White Mountain magma*. While dinosaurs stalked their prey on the surface, the rocks that would become the Old Man of the Mountains formed deep in the roots of the Acadian Mountains. Another isolated pluton of White Mountain magma would one day be called Mount Ascutney.

The summit of Mount Chocorua. *Photo by Michael J. Caduto.*

**A**

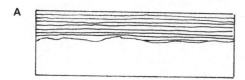

**B**

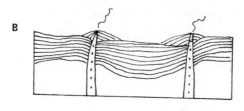

**C**

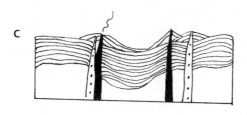

**D**

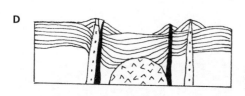

**E**

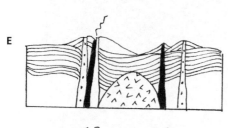

**F**

FIGURE 2-7.

*This page:* The formation of a ring-dike complex of mountains.

**A.** Eruptions occur and layers of volcanic rocks thousands of feet deep accumulate to cover the region of central New Hampshire.

**B.** Magma continues to empty from a chamber deep underground (not shown), causing a large circular block of Earth's crust to sink. Dikes of magma push up through the faults surrounding this sunken block of crust and a ring of volcanos erupts.

**C.** The crust sinks again and another circle of dikes and volcanos forms.

**D.** A massive dome of Conway granite pushes up beneath the ring dike complex.

**E.** Volcanos continue to erupt.

**F.** The upper layers erode over time, leaving the concentric formation of hills and mountains we see today in such places as the Ossipee Mountains, the peaks south of Wolfeboro that encircle Merrymeeting Lake, and in the Chocorua Mountains west of Conway.

*Opposite page:* Overview of the Ossipee Mountain ring-dike complex and neighboring hills.

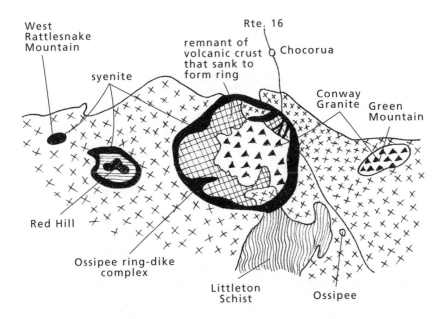

West
Rattlesnake
Mountain

Rte. 16

remnant of
volcanic crust
that sank to
form ring

Chocorua

syenite

Conway
Granite   Green
Mountain

Red Hill

Ossipee ring-dike
complex

Littleton
Schist

Ossipee

During this time of violent subterranean storms, the area that will in time become the Connecticut Valley, up to about Hinsdale, is an ancient rift valley similar to those now found in East Africa. Across this primal landscape and the neighboring lands of the future New England, the footsteps of a 20-foot theropod, *Eubrontes giganteus*, "large true thunder," shake the desert lands where these carnivorous pack-hunters search for prey. *Otozoum*, "giant animal," is a likely victim, even though this prosauropod walks upright on hind feet and uses speed to elude its predators. A still smaller, bipedal, carnivorous dinosaur, *Grallator*, which is about the size of a modern turkey, is in turn preyed upon by *Otozoum*, forming another link in this Jurassic food chain.

At about 8:19 P.M. (100 million years ago), life is a diverse mix of old and new species. Upland forests contain many deciduous trees, including magnolia and sassafras. The deciduous forests are interspersed with grasslands and stands of conifers where ferns wave as a breeze blows through the understory. Seashore environments are much like the estuarine mangrove swamps and bayous of today. Plying the coastal waters are many species of fish, sea turtles, and primitive octopi—animals that often fall prey to gigantic sharks with palm-sized teeth. These daunting predators stalked the same waters as the 35-foot plesiosaurs and 50-foot mesosaurs: rapacious reptiles wielding long, powerful jaws lined with deadly dentition.

➡ ➡ 8:19–9:36 P.M. (100–65 million years ago)  Over the past 7½ hours (200 million years), since the Paleozoic era, the land's surface has risen and tilted upward as erosion has removed the tremendous weight of the ancient mountains. During this period of time, the lofty Acadian Mountains have been worn to a relatively flat plain punctuated by the stalwart, erosion-resistant peaks of the region's monadnocks. The rising of the land has been more extreme in southern New Hampshire and in the interior. In Paleozoic times, the surface now surrounding Mount Monadnock was once buried beneath 7½ miles of rock and sediment, while the land around Mount Pisgah to the extreme north in Clarksville once lay 5 miles beneath the surface. (There are *three* Mount Pisgah's in New Hampshire! Their name comes from the Abenaki *bezega,* "it is dark.")

Near the end of this period, the seas rise so high throughout the world that vast areas of the continents are underwater. New England's monadnocks are islands surrounded by ocean. From atop one of the monadnock islands you see some strange, toothed birds swimming on the surface and diving for fish. These are the ancestors of today's loons and gulls. Off on some distant shore, tiny animals that resemble shrews and opossums scamper through dinosaur tracks as they search for their food. You are witnessing the dawn of the age of modern birds, mammals, and marsupials.

➡ ➡ 9:36 p.m. (65 million years ago)  Burning through the atmosphere as a cataclysmic fireball, an asteroid up to 10 miles wide hurtles down on what is now the Yucatan Peninsula in Mexico and smashes a

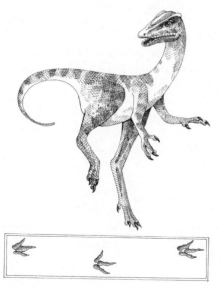

*Grallator*—a turkey-sized, carnivorous dinosaur that walked on two feet and traveled in packs—lived in the Connecticut Valley at about 4:37 P.M. on the geologic clock (200 million years ago).

The 50-foot-long mesosaur *(top)* was 15 feet longer than a plesiosaur *(bottom)*. Both plied the coastal waters 100 million years ago.

hole into Earth's crust as wide as Rhode Island. The force of the impact generates a wave of superheated vapor so intense that fires spontaneously erupt on land hundreds of miles from the site of impact. A mile-high tidal wave radiates out and eventually crashes against the sides of the future White Mountains. Seismic waves cause ruptures in Earth's crust where volcanos spew forth acrid gases and dense plumes of dust. In this dark, sere atmosphere, rain becomes imbued with nitric acid, drenches the surface and taints planetary waters. A dense, smothering aerial blanket of dust blows across the globe and completely blocks out the sun for several months, creating a dark, cold asteroidal winter. Entire ecosystems are wiped out as terrestrial plants die from lack of sun and algae disappear from the base of the ocean food web.

In a few short months, the age of dinosaurs comes to a climactic end. Their demise marks the end of the *Cretaceous* period. Not all life is wiped out, however. Flowering plants, insects, birds, mammals, and marsupials are among those that somehow survive and will one day reign across the land and in the waters of this new world.

*Hesperornis*—an early ancestor of modern loons and gulls that wielded teeth and powerful, webbed hind feet but sported diminutive wings—somehow survived the extinction of the dinosaurs.

Meanwhile, as the continents continue to drift apart, the Atlantic Ocean widens at the rate of about 1 inch each year.

➡ ➡ 9:47–10:31 P.M. (60–40 million years ago)  This is the age of mammals. Giant rodents and pigs walk the land, hunted by ferocious cats and wolf-like carnivores. The ancestors of camels graze the arid regions, while, up from the ocean depths, the first misty exhales of whale spouts emerge and glisten—tiny rainbows backlit by the sun. In South America and South Africa, early primates develop into monkeys and lemurs. Plants closely resemble modern species. From about 10:30 until 11:04 P.M., rhinoceri, hippopotami, and other horned and hoofed animals evolve, along with humpless camels, the ancestors of sabertooth cats, and hyenas. As the climate cools and dries, coniferous forests expand and replace subtropical forests in many regions.

➡ ➡ 11:04–11:44 P.M. (25–7 million years ago)  Grazing mammals roam over the grasslands that have come to dominate vast regions. Great forests of oaks and redwoods appear. Primates continue to evolve.

➡ ➡ 11:42 P.M. (8 million years ago) The ancient plain that existed in southern New Hampshire during the late age of the dinosaurs keeps eroding as the land rises and the surface is worn down by wind, water, and ice. Softer rocks weather down while areas underlain by harder rocks persist as higher points. If you could stand atop Mount Monadnock and scan the panorama of central and southern New England and over to southeastern New Hampshire, the heights of the eroded landscape would stand as peaks of similar elevation—lofted remnants of the ancient plain.[11] During the last 18 minutes (8 million years) leading up to the present time, the land along the coast rises more than 200 feet while inland regions rise to ten times that height. The sediment carried out to sea during this and previous eons of erosion accrues as a layer more than 2 miles thick atop of the continental shelf.

The Androscoggin River cuts its bed down into the rising landscape. Today, this river valley separates the main spine of the White Mountains from the peaks found to the northeast.

➡ ➡ 11:51 P.M. (4 million years ago) Mammals, including mastodons and sabertooth cats, continue to dominate the animal kingdom. Many areas are covered with forests of flowering plants interspersed with large zones of coniferous forest. Humankind's first distant ancestors roam Africa's Rift Valley at this time or, perhaps, even earlier.[12]

➡ ➡ 11:55:34 P.M. (2 million years ago) From this time until 11:59:58.7 P.M. (10,000 years ago), during the *Pleistocene epoch,* the world experiences four significant climatic cycles of cold weather interspersed with warm periods. During the cold intervals, winters in northern Canada and in lands to the immediate south are so extreme that snow and ice build up year-round to a depth of over 1 mile. The hulking weight of each glacier pushes down and causes the ice to creep outward along the edges. Over the course of this 6 minutes and 37 seconds, the Northeast is smothered and uncovered four times by glaciers.

Sea levels rise during interglacial periods and drop during periods of glacial advance when much water is frozen in the ice sheet. Coastal New Hampshire is alternately exposed then submerged during each glacial and interglacial period.

➡ ➡ 11:59:20 P.M. (300,000 years ago) A primate dies and leaves behind what will one day be discovered as the oldest known remains of modern humans, *Homo sapiens.*[13]

A sabertooth cat defends its territory in a time of woolly mammoths, mastodons, and other magnificent beasts.

➡ ➡   11:59.58–11:59.58.4 P.M. (15,000 to 12,000 years ago)   At the end of the most recent, Wisconsinan glaciation, the seacoast is under water, eroded by waves and currents. Sea levels continue to rise as the glacier melts and water is released from the ice. The land gradually begins to rebound after the weight of the glacier has diminished from its surface, but the ocean rises faster and floods the coast. Eventually, the land will rise and a shoreline located close to that of today's will emerge.

Along our present seacoast, fossils of marine organisms can now be found buried within deep beds of sands and clays that were deposited 12,000 to 15,000 years ago at the margin of the melting glacier. These Ice Age sediments, which are now known as the *Presumpscot formation,* range inland to Kingston, Lee, Epping, and Rochester. In this ancient sand and clay, and in the more recent layers of sand and gravel above, some rare fossils have been discovered in New Hampshire and in the Presumpscot deposits of nearby Maine, in which they are more plentiful and well-preserved. Several species of clams, mussels, barnacles, and snails have been uncovered, along with those of sea stars, brittle stars, sea urchins, sand dollars, and a number of other coastal species, including some one-celled protozoans, the Foraminifera.[14]

➡ ➡ 11:59:58.1 P.M. (14,000 years ago to the present)   The climate has gradually warmed and the glacier has retreated from New Hampshire. Animals living in the immediate aftermath of the great ice sheet are well adapted to surviving in a cold climate, including woolly mammoths, mastodons, elk, short-faced bears, and the enormous stag-moose.

In the lee of the waning ice sheet, a cold wind sweeps across a dusty verge of arid grassland steppe. As time passes, the climate warms overall, but summer and winter temperatures become more extreme. For the first .7 seconds (5,000) years of this 1.9-second (14,000-year) period, the mosaic of plant communities in front of the glacier—many growing along the shores of lakes and ponds and the braided streams and rivers—gradually evolves. The grassland steppe becomes punctuated by wildflowers, dwarf shrubs, juniper, and stands of aspen. Increasing rain and snow provide moisture for the lengthening tongues of spruce and fir forest and a multitude of wetlands lush with moss and sedge. Many herbivores cannot adapt as the range of their food plants becomes more restricted and the diversity of habitats decreases. The great grazers and a number of small mammals disappear, followed by the dire wolf, numerous raptors, and other predators from the Ice Age.

Moving north up the valleys and west from the coast, jack pine, red pine, and both paper birch and gray birch arrive as their seeds are carried by animals and on the wind. Mixed forests sprout as new species blend into the woodland mix: ash, elm, balsam fir, ironwood, larch, and oak. Maple arrives ten millenniums ago and white pine a thousand years after that.[15] Hemlock arrives and, in time, the moist woodlands are interspersed with beech, hickory, and chestnut.

New Hampshire now experiences a period of warmth that lasts for .7 seconds (5,000 years). During this period of time, plants and animals form communities that are similar to those found in Virginia today. The diversity of life in this region is far greater than it is at the present time. While the last .5 seconds (4,000 years) passes, the climate undergoes ups and downs as it gradually cools, until the land and the life it supports look and feel much as they do today.

Throughout the duration of the 1.9 seconds (14,000 years) that passes after the glacier has melted, wind, weather, and water are continually refining the surface of the landscape that was forged in Earth's oven and molded by powerful tectonic forces. Coursing through many peaks in the southern White Mountains, the Swift River cuts through joints in the ancient granite, creating a series of magnificent runs such as the one that can now be seen at the Rocky Gorge Scenic Area along the Kancamagus Highway, north of Mount Chocorua. A few miles to the west, over several thousand years, the sand and gravel caught in the swirling spring eddies of Sabbaday Brook carve potholes in the solid rock of the streambed that are as smooth and round as if thrown on a pottery wheel. Water perfects some of its most refined, sensuous sculptures in the Agassiz Basin of the Lost River. About 1 mile west of the village of North Woodstock along Route 112, and just south of the road, the river cuts a sinuous channel down through the local bedrock: an interesting gray amalgam of quartz and large crystals of white feldspar, interspersed with gneiss, schist, and speckles of shiny black mica. Where the water flows over a harder pegmatite dike that cuts across the streambed, it forms a waterfall that plays down the face of this erosion-resistant rock.

➡ ➡ 11:59:59.6 P.M. (3,250 years ago) Growing at this time within a forest of hemlocks, birches, and white pines are some trees that will one day be among the most famous remnants of past life in New Hampshire. Stalwart remains of this woodland persist to the present day in a small cove south of Odiornes Point State Park, one of several archaic forests found along the coast of Maine and New Hampshire. If you visit Jenness Beach and Odiornes Point at low tide, you can still see exposed the prostrate trunks, worn-down stumps, and roots of some venerable white pines. These remains bear silent testimony to a time when the coastal forests were killed as the ice sheet melted and sea level rose, flooding the trees with saltwater. The drowned forest of Odiornes Point is ancient history in human terms but a mere slip in the sluggish sheet of glacial time.

➡ ➡ 11:59:59.9 P.M. (1,000 years ago to the present) As the farming revolution begins, erosion continues to wear down the surface of New Hampshire's landscape at the rate of about 2.3 inches for each millennium. At this rate, it would take more than 5,000 years for Mount Washington's 6,288-foot summit—the highest peak north of the Great Smoky Mountains and east of the Black Hills of South Dakota—to be shorn of another foot.

ఆ٨◉   ఆ٨◉   ఆ٨◉   ఆ٨◉

As wave after tectonic wave of rock washed over this land, each left a new piece of the convoluted, rocky puzzle that we now call New Hampshire: bands of alien terranes crushed onto the edge of the North American plate and left behind by the mother plates from Europe and Africa. Worked and re-worked, folded, uplifted, squeezed, melted, and cooled—New Hampshire's rocks wrack the mind of anyone who would understand their complexities.

Agassiz Basin. *Photo by Michael J. Caduto.*

Sculptured stumps and trunks amid the drowned forest at Odiornes Point are all that remain of a forest of birches, hemlocks, and white pines that lived here 3,250 years ago *(top)*. Amazingly, growth rings are still visible *(bottom)*. *Photos by Michael J. Caduto.*

Hike to the top of Mount Monadnock—the second-most climbed mountain in the world next to Mount Fuji in Japan—and, on any day during the busy season, you may be one of ten thousand people who walks the slopes of this beloved peak. Standing there, at 3,165 feet above sea level, the hard mica schist beneath your feet is not what it seems. Your weight is supported by metamorphic rock that formed from the sediments of sand, silt, and mud that were deposited at the bottom of a Paleozoic ocean.

In order to achieve an understanding of this epic of time, rock, and the elements, of our place in the great scheme, we have to bend our minds around a geologic consciousness. From this vantage, the ground beneath our feet is not the hard, unyielding substance that we experience. It is the surface of a malleable, ever-changing world: a living, pulsing Earth that heaves and sighs as her veins flow with blood of magma. The difference between our reality and that of the rocks is rooted in the limitations of our senses. If we are truly to understand the rocks, we must expand our limited concept of space and achieve an altered perception of time.

# 3. Of Water and Ice

To see landscapes alive, we must turn the key; we must bring
on what scientists think are the main agents of change,
including those that control where the ice domes lie.

—William H. MacLeish,
*The Day Before America*, 1994

                   ᘒ    ᘒ    ᘒ    ᘒ

*A cool dry wind bends the tips of sedge and grass in a dusty clearing. Leaves tapping gently in the breeze, living crowns of aspen are silhouetted against the crystal-blue sky. The midday somnolence is disturbed only by the suckling sounds of a nursing mastodon calf. Sated, the calf begins to mimic its mother, who is grazing on the tender shoots of grass at her feet. They feed unwarily as the calf wanders off. Nearby and unseen behind a thick growth of young juniper, a family of dire wolves is waiting for the right moment to spring: eyes in their broad heads alert, powerful limbs tensed, and tails flicking with anticipation.*

*Lifting her head, the mother faces into the wind and senses danger. She whips her thick, leathery trunk aloft and trumpets a warning that echoes down the river valley. Racing toward one another, mother and calf begin to close the distance just as the wolves sprint from behind their evergreen blind. Reaching the calf at exactly the same moment, the largest, lead wolf sinks enormous canines hard into its haunches and blood spurts from the punctures. The calf's mother charges the canine mass of tooth and muscle until, dodging a deadly stab from her enormous tusks, the wolf is forced to release its grip. Continuing to charge, the mastodon drives the snarling wolves back toward the edge of the tree line, where they slink into the undergrowth. She returns to the calf and licks its wounds until the blood stops flowing. Spent, she prods the limping calf toward safer ground.*

❧  ❧  ❧  ❧

In this seeming mythic time, in a place we now call New Hampshire, countless life-and-death dramas played out in front of the receding glacier. As the most recent glacial period waned some 14,000 years ago, upland areas that were not flooded by glacial lakes lay just beyond the ebbing sheet of ice.

Life in the lee of the glacier was anything but idyllic. North America was inhabited by a surreal cast of giant herbivores and larger-than-life carnivores that could have stepped from our darkest dreams. The herbivores and scavengers spend much of the time with eyes raised, nostrils flared, and ears cocked—the better to catch the sight, scent, or sound of impending danger. Plodding through a riparian copse of aspen is a browsing sloth the size of a small cow while a tapir sniffs the underbrush with its proboscis. Eagles and other raptors hunt from the skies. A magnificent teratorn, the largest flying bird ever to live in North America, soars aloft on a wingspan of 16 feet. Cats seem to be everywhere, including cheetahs, lions, and jaguars, stalking their prey with efficiency and guile. Scimitar cats, although smaller than the powerful sabertooths, have the advantage of incisors sporting serrated edges on both front and back. Even these felines avoid the teeth and claws of the short-faced bear— swift, long-legged, nightmarish predators that stand 7 feet at the shoulder with all four feet firmly planted. Whenever a meal of meat proves more than enough for one of these beasts, the thick-winged teratorns swoop down to pick the bones.

What an experience it would be to fill a backpack with basic survival tools and hike across a mountain pass into a time-warp of Pleistocene New Hampshire, during the time following the glacier. On arrival, you would look down at your feet to notice that the surface of the permafrost has, in places, formed cracks in polygonal patterns that resemble the scales on a turtle's back. Streams of caribou are seen fording a river to reach their food of grasses and sedges on the other shore where a herd of musk ox is already grazing. A stag-moose lifts its head from the shallow water where it is feeding on the submerged plants, now draped and dripping from its out-sized rack of antlers that spread for over 10 feet. Off in the distance, it appears that a black bear, too, is munching on the wetland greenery. On closer approach, you see that it is, in fact, a half-submerged, thick-furred giant beaver, *Castoroides,* an adult that weighs about 400 pounds.[1] The rich, silty soil is exposed in large patches beneath the forest at the water's edge where porcine peccaries have been eating roots, mushrooms, insects, and tubers. One animal's digging has scattered the bleached bones of a careless young peccary that fell prey to a dire wolf.

## A TILT AND A FLUX

Earth is a steadfast traveler, but this satellite we call home wobbles and drifts. Every 100,000 years or so, her elliptical orbit completes a cycle during which Earth moves closer to, then farther from the sun. As she rotates around the sun, Earth's axis is tilted anywhere from 21.8 to 24.5 degrees away from being perpendicular to the plane of her elliptical orbit. It takes 41,000 years for Earth to make one complete cycle within this nearly 3-degree tilt. The angle is now growing smaller from its present 23.5 degrees. Due to these cycles, Earth receives varying amounts of solar radiation at different times, which affects the length and intensity of our seasons.

Exactly how these two complicated patterns of interwoven cycles affect our climate over time is hard to predict, but the effects are extreme. On balance, whenever winters are longer than summers, snow and ice accumulate and glaciers advance. We have warmer, *interglacial* periods when summer melting is greater than winter accretion.

But it takes moisture as well as cold weather for glaciers to form. In addition to the cycling of the sun's energy, large-scale changes in Earth's surface may have been a catalyst that triggered the last Ice Age. One such possibility is the genesis of the isthmus that joins North and South America. This continental connector formed about 3 million years ago when the tectonic plate beneath the Caribbean drove over the plate under the Pacific, pushing the land up and generating volcanic eruptions. When the gap between the two continents closed, the warm current that once flowed through the narrows established a new direction to the north and melded with the Gulf Stream. As this invigorated stream of warm water flowed north, it brought the atmospheric moisture that fed the glaciers.

The *Pleistocene epoch*—the age of the great rivers of ice—commenced perhaps 2 million years ago and transpired over a great expanse of time. The Ice Age started when the climate cooled enough for snow to begin building up in the Laurentian uplands of northeastern Canada. Gradually, the height of the snowpack grew to 30 feet or more and its weight pressed down on the lower layers, causing the snow to form ice crystals. When the nascent glacier was more than 100 feet high, its base transformed into an icy plastic that inched out from the center in all directions.

In fits and starts that spanned tens of thousands of years, immense lobes of the great ice sheet crept farther south by a few feet each day until its margin reached down into the Ohio and Missouri river valleys and half of North America lay beneath its chill blanket. Biological communities migrated before the ice in slow-motion flight as the weather became colder and dryer and the growing season dwindled. Earth's crust was depressed hundreds of feet into the mantle beneath the glacier's hulking weight.

As the Pleistocene wore on, this cycle of glacial advances and retreats repeated itself every 100,000 years. The most recent advance, the *Wisconsinan glaciation*, began about 100 millenniums ago. For 30,000 years or more, the northlands were smothered by the *Laurentide* ice sheet, until the climatological gods turned again and the glacier gave ground.

FIGURE 3-1. At its maximum, the Wisconsinan glacier covered Greenland, Iceland, and the northern half of North America.

By 18,000 to 20,000 years ago, the Laurentide had attained its peak; the ice margin reached as far south as northern Pennsylvania, central Illinois, Wisconsin, the Dakotas, Montana, and Alberta. In the Northeast, the southern and eastern margin of the ice sheet extended to Montauk Point on Long Island, then north to Block Island, Martha's Vineyard, and Nantucket. New York City itself was under the ice. An awesome 2,000 miles of continental glacier stretched north and west from Cape Cod (figure 3-1).

All of New England lay beneath more than a mile of ice—a vast, continuous white expanse.[2] So ponderous was the weight of the glacier that

Earth's crust was forced down into the mantle more than 750 feet in some places. Such a quantity of Earth's water was stored in the glacial ice that sea levels dropped more than 300 feet: so low that Georges Bank and the Nantucket shoals were dry land. The exposed surface of the continental shelf was braided by glacial streams that did not reach the seashore until they had meandered some 90 miles out past where the coastline lies today. Herds of mastodons and other mega-fauna grazed across these windswept plains of waving grasses and forbs interspersed with boreal forest in the lowlands.

Before the Ice Age, New Hampshire's climate was warm and moist and her winters were mild, much like the weather of the Great Smoky Mountains today. After the glacier advanced, the weather south of the ice was wetter and perhaps cooler than it is now, but the seasonal variations in temperature were not as extreme. Paradoxically, the massive sheet of ice split the jet stream and shunted the white-cold Arctic air masses far to the north. As the southern branch of the jet stream flowed before the glacier, it generated violent storms. Heavy winds scoured the eroded landscape and bore thick clouds of fine soil aloft for hundreds of miles to the south. In many places, this aeolian *loess* was deposited more than 30 feet deep.[3] The wind built and sculpted these deposits into dunes whose peaks reached as high as 50 feet in the region that would one day be known as Concord.

By the time the glacier's advance ground to a halt, the geographic ranges of plants and animals had shifted 10 degrees latitude to the south. The weather in Georgia and Florida at that time was like that of New Hampshire today. Dense, cold downdrafts swept from atop the ice. Soil lay in a permanently frozen state as far south as New Jersey. In higher elevations, permafrost reached even farther south, holding the Carolina highlands and the mountains of northern New Mexico in its icy grasp. A diverse, well-interspersed mosaic of ecosystems lay before the glacier; a mix of grassy plains and uplands dappled with low-lying forests and be-jewelled with countless wetlands. In time, expanses of boreal spruce forest, bogs, and sedge meadows would be punctuated with fragments of hardwood forest.

Herd upon herd of Pleistocene animals grazed and browsed across the Southwest: bison, archaic horses, and *Camelops,* which closely resembled the living dromedary. Giant ground sloths munched on desert sagebrush while tortoise-like glyptodonts browsed as they perambulated the shores and wetlands. The sluggish glyptodonts—close relatives of armadillos, sloths, and anteaters—were protected by weighty carapaces of armor that grew to 6 feet long and 5 feet high in the largest species. Massive horns and ominous teeth were everywhere: the enormous ram-like horns of the shrub oxen, the gigantic yet graceful upswept tusks of woolly mammoths, and the razor-sharp, down-curved fangs of *Smilodon,* the sabertooth cats.

How did these colossal animals come to be in North America? During the extremes of recent glacial periods, when sea levels were at low ebb, a wide expanse of land became exposed between Asia and northwestern North America. Some animals, including the mastodon, mammoth, bison, and sabertooth cat, migrated from Asia across this temporary biological link. Other animals that had evolved in the east traveled across this land to the west; among them the horse, camel, ground squirrel, and American fox.

The Ice Age ended when there came a gradual shift in the planetary tilt to its orbital plane. About 17,000 years ago, as the climate warmed, the Wisconsinan ice sheet started to melt faster than it was advancing. Some 3,500 years passed before the ice receded from Massachusetts. Moving at an average rate of 245 feet each year, it took 4,300 years for the glacier to melt back from Middletown, Connecticut, to St. Johnsbury, Vermont.[4]

Beginning more than 15,000 years ago in southern New Hampshire, the glacier slowly, inexorably melted back and uncovered the face of this region.[5] Five centuries passed while the leading edge shifted from Concord to Franklin; covering this 20 miles at the rate of 4 miles every 100 years.[6] A brief re-advance took place in the Littleton-Bethlehem area around 14,000 years ago and the glacier's margin reached Canada about 500 years after that.[7] In time, some remnant, decaying chunks of ice in the high, north-facing valleys of the White Mountains were all that remained in New Hampshire of the great Laurentide.

## THE EARTH POTTER

Where Earth is at once medium and sculptor, her deep heat the geologic furnace, glaciers are the hands of the potter whose icy fingers smooth and etch, pluck and mold the surface of the land. Once New Hampshire's foundation was complete and the basic mold set, the landscape artisans of water and ice went to work and created many of the landforms we see today.

### At the Glacier's Edge

Whenever the temperature reached a particular point of balance, attrition of ice at the margin equaled the rate of accretion. During this period of stasis, the Wisconsinan glacier became a conveyor belt; everything carried within the ice was dropped in the same place at the leading edge, including a jumble of debris from throughout eastern New England and neighboring Canada. This heap of unsorted sand, gravel, and rock—the *terminal moraine*—is more than 500 feet deep in places. The terminal moraine that formed in the Northeast about 18,000 years ago created the aforementioned capes and islands: Montauk Point on Long Island, Block Island, Martha's Vineyard, and Nantucket. These last two locales are composed of moraine that accumulated in between lobes of the glacier.

As the climate warmed, the glacier melted faster than it was advancing and the margin of ice retreated northward. A brief interval of cooling halted the retreat and created a *recessional moraine*. This ridge is marked by Orient Point at northern Long Island, Fishers Island, Watch Hill in coastal Rhode Island, the Elizabeth Islands, and runs up through Cape Cod: Woods Hole, Sandwich, and Chatham.

As testimony to how our knowledge of the landscape grows over time, witness this passage from Thoreau's *Cape Cod* in which he ruminates on how the Cape formed:

> Hitchcock conjectures that the ocean has, in course of time, eaten out Boston Harbor and other bays in the mainland, and that the minute fragments have been deposited by the currents at a distance from the shore, and formed this sand-bank.[8]

## In Front of the Ice Sheet

During the millenniums of climatic warming, the glacier's retreat was marked by stress-releasing creaks, cracks, and moans. Massive blocks of ice calved from its face and raised sizeable waves where they crashed into the sea and dropped into glacial lakes. Icebergs drifted away across the Atlantic.

The streams trickling on, beneath, and within the wasting glaciers grew into deafening rivers that plummeted down crevasses, shot towering plumes of spray from icy portholes, and emerged from tunnels at the glacial margin. Meltwater carried masses of sand and gravel that had been trapped in the ice, and which would transform the antediluvian landscape. Washing off from the front of the glacier, in streams and rivers that ranged from trickles to torrents, the waters fanned out and created deltas and large flats known as *outwash plains*. The burden transported by these waters was gradually dropped and sorted into layers as the water slowed: gravels, sands, silts, and clays.

Many broad, flat plains were formed from this *glacial outwash* or *stratified drift* where it spread out over valley floors. Off the coast of New Hampshire, when the seashore was still much lower than it is today, glacial meltwaters created vast deltas that buried the ancient ocean sediments. These marine deposits were further ground up and sorted by waves to form beaches. Deltas also formed where meltwaters flowed into

As the glacier retreated, lobes of ice calved into the silty waters of New Hampshire's glacial lakes and along the seacoast. The massive ice cliffs would have been hundreds of feet high, similar to those in this photograph. *Photo by Michael J. Caduto.*

glacial lakes. Thinner, less extensive layers of stratified drift were laid down in the uplands.

In places, the valleys of the Connecticut, Merrimack, and Saco rivers are lined with thick layers of glacial outwash. The Merrimack River has cut over 70 feet deep into the outwash east of Concord known as the "Dark Plains." Another impressive outwash plain that is 2 miles wide stretches north of Dover for 9 miles. So consistently flat are the surfaces of outwash plains that many of New Hampshire's airports are built upon them: North Hampton, Claremont, Lebanon, Hinsdale, North Conway, Milan, Twin Mountain, Whitefield, and two in Nashua. The airports at Hooksett, Concord, and Penacook are built atop outwash deltas. Airplanes that land at the Somersworth Airport touch down atop an ancient marine delta.

In many places, the outwash plains and moraines are dotted with *kettle ponds* and pocked with *kettle holes* where large pieces of ice were buried by glacial sediments. Bowl-shaped depressions formed when the ice melted and flowed down into well-drained soils. Wherever these ice blocks lay over an impermeable layer, the melting ice left a depression that filled with water to become a lake or pond. Kettle lakes and ponds are found

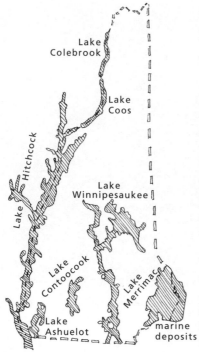

FIGURE 3-2. Glacial lakes of New Hampshire.

throughout the state, including White Lake in Tamworth, Willand Pond in Somersworth, Great Pond in Kingston, and the famous Echo Lake in Conway.[9] Snake Pond in Ossipee is a kettle of the Lakes Region. About six miles to the north and west is the expansive Ossipee Lake, which formed in a depression left by by an enormous remnant of glacial ice. Depending on the size of the pond, the underlying soil, and the drainage conditions, many kettle ponds have developed into bogs, marshes, and swamps over the past 14,000 years.

The surface of New Hampshire was altered on a grander scale by the advent of sizeable *glacial lakes* (figure 3-2). One of the most well known is glacial Lake Hitchcock, which formed more than 16,000 years ago when a ridge of moraine created a dam 7 miles north of Middletown, Connecticut, at Rocky Hill. A stable spillway eventually developed near New Britain.[10] As the ice sheet melted back, Lake Hitchcock crept up the Connecticut Valley until it grew to be over 200 miles long and its two northern branches reached as far as Burke, Vermont, and Littleton, New Hampshire. Lake Hitchcock lasted until about 12,000 years ago when the dam was breached by an outflow that was the beginning of the Connecticut River we know today. Terraces have since formed along the banks of the Connecticut River where the flowing water has eroded down into the ancient bed of Lake Hitchcock in many places.

Even at its greatest extent, Lake Hitchcock was a mere slip of water compared to the immense area covered by glacial Lake Vermont, the predecessor of Lake Champlain between the Green Mountains and the Adirondacks. At the height of the glacier, the level of land in and around the northern part of the lake was depressed as much as 600 feet below what it is today. As the glacier melted northward beyond the St. Lawrence lowlands, sea level rose faster than the land rebounded and salt water backed into the St. Lawrence Seaway. This created a vast estuarine environment that flowed into Lake Vermont, which became a brackish body of water now referred to as the Champlain Sea. Among the marine creatures that plied the waters of this inland sea were whales, seals, and porpoises.

During this same period of time, a considerable amount of New Hampshire lay under the waters of glacial lakes that have been named after today's regions, rivers, and lakes: Ashuelot, Contoocook, Merrimack, Winnipesaukee, Coos, and Colebrook. Glacial Lake Winnipesaukee sprawled out over a vast area of the interior. The Lakes Region that surrounds Winnipesaukee today is a classic remnant of an ancient glacial lake environment. The present outlet is still located near that of the former glacial lake where moraine deposits formed a dam. To the south and west, the city of Keene is built on the bed of glacial Lake Ashuelot where the thick deposits of clay that accrued along the lake bottom are still used for making bricks. Manchester Airport is built directly upon the bottom sediments of glacial Lake Merrimack.

Arms of the receding glacier reached down the valleys toward glacial lakes. The rivers of water melting from a wasting lobe of the glacier flowed along the sides of the ice where it contacted the surrounding slopes. When these rivers reached the margin of the glacier and emptied into a glacial lake, they deposited thick beds of sand and gravel. Over time, as the glacier melted back, these deltas grew and formed continuous terraces along the sides of the valley (figure 3-3). These *kames* and *kame terraces* are common along the sides of rivers and valleys throughout New Hampshire. Some prominent kame terraces are found where streams and rivers flow into the upper Connecticut Valley, such as where the White River enters the Connecticut River across from West Lebanon. Kame terraces can also be found on the shore of Lake Winnipesaukee in West Alton and along the sides of the Soucook Valley, where they run for more than 20 miles between Loudon and Belmont. Other kames are found in the river valleys of the Piscataqua, Lamprey, Warner, Smith, Baker, and Souhegan.

Wherever meltwater streams and rivers first entered glacial lakes, the water slowed and created deltas of sand and gravel. Finer sediments of silt and minute particles of clay eventually settled out in the calm lake waters. Over the course of hundreds and, in some cases, thousands of years, clays formed annual layers or *varves* on the lake bottoms. When the glacial lakes disappeared, many of these bottom sediments became exposed. As the land rebounded, streams and rivers flowing over the old lake bottoms gradually cut down into the sediments, exposing the varves and, in many places, creating terraces along the riverbanks. One well-preserved bank of varved clays near Woodsville shows 1,600 years of accumulation on the floor of glacial Lake Hitchcock. Another excellent place to view varves is along the high bank on the east side of Route 10

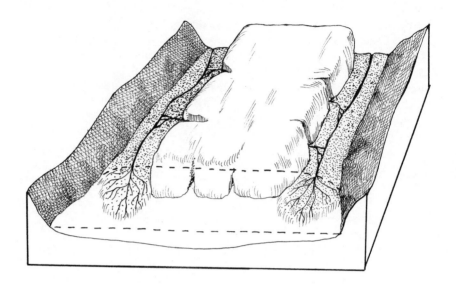

FIGURE 3-3.

*Top:* Kame terraces formed as the ice in front of a glacial lake melted back through a valley. Meltwater streams and rivers flowed along the edges of the ice. When the water entered the glacial lake and slowed, it deposited a delta of sand and gravel.

*Bottom:* These deltas formed strips as the glacier melted back, leaving terraces along the sides of the valley.

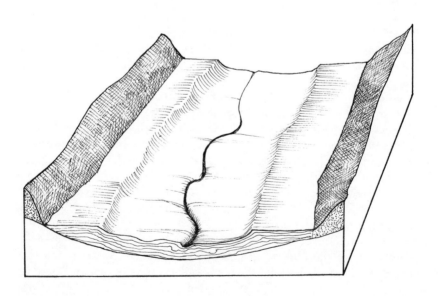

about two miles north of Hanover. The steep sandbanks and varved clay slopes along the shores of the Merrimack River near Concord inspired the Abenaki to refer to individuals from that region as *Benôkoiak,* "Falling Hill People." After their name was anglicized by colonists, the *Benôkoiak* became known as the Penacook and a nearby town was named after them.

One of the most beautiful outwash valleys in New England is the broad expanse of the Saco River Valley from Redstone, New Hampshire, east to the Maine border. The wide plain on this valley floor sits atop thick deposits of sandy glacial outwash and the clays of an old lake bed. It is a place of open sky that frames the silhouettes of striking domed mountains.

Many of the sculptures created by glaciers in the mountain region, however, formed when meltwaters flowed forcefully through narrow passes. Rushing waters filled with abrasive sand, gravel, and rock—the glacier's cutting tools—created a gallery of fantastical shapes in the bedrock under New Hampshire's streams and rivers that are still evolving as you read this. North of the Flume that lies at the base of Mount Liberty, the swirling eddies of the Pemigewasset River have cut circular basins in the bedrock that are the product of 25,000 years of erosion.

The Lost River Gorge south of Kinsman Notch is another dramatic example of the power of water and ice. Lacing through the complex of channels and steep walls that drip with tufts of mosses, ferns, lichens, and liverworts is a creatively designed system of trails and bridges—a life-sized game of chutes and ladders. In many places, the river roars invisibly through rocky channels beneath your feet. The small natural history museum at Lost River explains how this ancient stream valley was broadened, deepened, and rounded by the glacier. While the glacier was melting, the north, Ammonoosuc side of the pass remained blocked with ice long after the Lost River side had melted free. Glacial meltwater surged east through the gorge, washed away the glacial sands and gravels, and scoured the rocks to form myriad curves, arches, and tunnels. The course has been made even more convoluted by numerous boulders that have tumbled into the channel after being forced from the surrounding cliffs by wedges of ice that widened the cracks in the bedrock over thousands of years. A relatively modest stream now tumbles through the gorge and, in many places, plays its sweet song unseen.

## Within and Beneath the Ice

The glacier was a hulking giant. There seems to have been no limit to the volume of soil and size of the rocks it could carry. In places the burden hefted by the ice was deposited as a jumbled layer of clay, sand, gravel,

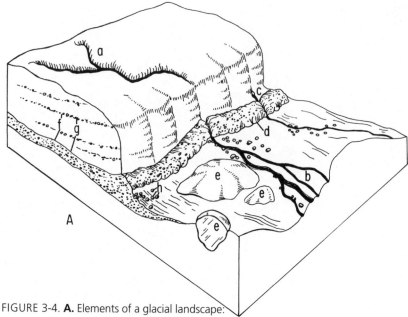

FIGURE 3-4. **A.** Elements of a glacial landscape:
   **a**—meltwater stream over the glacier's surface;
   **b**—meltwater delta in front of the glacier;
   **c**—meltwater stream flowing from beneath the glacier;
   **d**—debris deposited at the glacier's edge;
   **e**—ice blocks stranded in sediments in front of the glacier;
   **f** and **g**—debris trapped within and beneath the glacier;
   **h**—Large boulders transported and deposited by the glacier.

and rock called *till*. Some uplands were blanketed with a layer of this *ground moraine* up to 20 feet thick (figure 3-4).

Large volumes of glacial till were molded between the bottom of the glacier and the underlying bedrock in the lowlands and foothills. These wide, gently rounded hills called *drumlins,* some as thick as 150 feet, are oval shaped, with the longer axis oriented in the direction the glacier was travelling. They tend to be no more than three-quarters of a mile long and half a mile wide. It was discovered that the soil the glacier shaped into drumlins contains more clay than most till that is found around the state; clay that was worked by the ice potter's open palms, that made the soil more prone to being molded into hills shaped like giant, inverted spoons. A few thousand drumlins dot the landscape of southern New Hampshire, including a classic example in Barnstead west of Halfmoon Lake. High concentrations of drumlins sculpt the countryside in Peterborough,

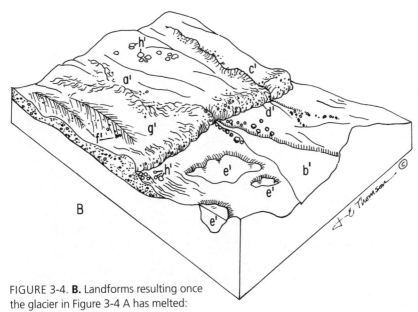

FIGURE 3-4. **B.** Landforms resulting once the glacier in Figure 3-4 A has melted:
  **a'**—kame deposit;
  **b'**—outwash plain;
  **c'**—esker;
  **d'**—end moraine;
  **e'**—kettle holes (kettle lakes shown here);
  **f'**—drumlins;
  **g'**—ground moraine;
  **h'**—glacial erratics.

Rindge, and Jaffrey, as well as Milford, Amherst, and Pinardville (figure 3-5). Numerous drumlins can also be found in and around Canterbury, Pittsfield, Walpole, Kensington, and Rochester.

Robert Frost didn't exactly say "good piles of glacial stones make good neighbors," but that, technically, was his allusion. Many drumlins, and much of the post-glacial landscape, are littered with countless rocks of all sizes that remained when the glacier melted. Ninety percent of these rocks were dropped within a mile of where the glacier picked them up. The glacial stones found in tilled farmland are one of New Hampshire's most abundant crops. Every winter, the frozen ground expands and the rocks rise closer to the surface. By the following springtime, the soil has produced another harvest of rocks.

According to an old tale, a passerby once stopped for a time and stood by a stone wall along the edge of a field to watch a farmer harvesting his

FIGURE 3-5. This drumlin in Jaffrey is one of a few thousand in southern New Hampshire. *Photo by Michael J. Caduto.*

spring crop of rocks. The farmer sweat profusely as he loaded the rocks onto a sledge or *pung,* drawn by a pair of oxen. After a while, the stranger called the farmer over.

> "Where did all those rocks come from?" asked the interloper.
> "They tell me they were dropped here by the glacier," replied the farmer.
> "I don't see any glacier," the stranger observed with great acumen.
> "Nope," said the farmer, "It went back for another load."

Few glacial landforms are more intriguing than an immense *glacial erratic*—a rock or boulder that has been picked up by the ice and plunked down some distance from its source atop bedrock that is different than that from which it came. The famous Madison Boulder is thought to be one of the largest glacial erratics on Earth. Just off Route 113 and 3 miles north of the town of Madison lies this 83-foot-long behemoth that weighs roughly 4,662 tons. The glacier moved it here from a ledge located about 2 miles to the north and west in the neighboring town of Albany. The large Bartlett Boulder, which can be found along Route 302 about 1 mile west of Glen upon a small rise on the left, looks like a wagon propped up on four smaller erratics (figure 3-6). Many a hiker has

FIGURE 3-6. Bartlett boulder is a large erratic that is neatly balanced atop four smaller stones. *Photo by Michael J. Caduto.*

stopped to enjoy the view from Glen Boulder, which is perched on the eastern side of Mount Washington amid the lower cliffs and can easily be seen from trails through Pinkham Notch.

Certain areas where rocks were abundant and where bedrock was easily fragmented became rich veins that the glacier mined on its journey to the south. Because the glacier's path shifted somewhat in response to internal pressures and landforms, the boulders that it carried were dispersed in wide, fan-shaped patterns known as *boulder trains*. Two of the major boulder trains in the state fan out to the south and east of Red Hill and the Ossipee Mountains in Moultonborough and Tuftonboro, respectively (figure 3-7). The origin of these rocks can be traced directly back to the distinctive syenite on Red Hill and rocks of volcanic origin from the Ossipee Mountains. *Syenite* looks like a rough-textured, light-toned granite. Another boulder train, which originates from Mount Ascutney across the Connecticut River from Claremont, flanks the entire southwest corner of New Hampshire as far east as Lempster, then down through Hancock, Peterborough, and beyond.

The glacier was a grinding stone beyond compare. The boulders, cobbles, gravel, and sand that it carried in its bottom layer became the grit that ground away at the bedrock beneath the ice. First the bedrock was

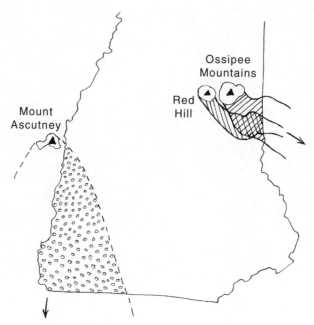

FIGURE 3-7. Three of the prominent boulder trains through New Hampshire. The Mount Ascutney boulder train *(left)* arches through much of the southwest corner of the state. The two boulder trains along the eastern border with Maine include those beginning at Red Hill in Moultonborough and in the Ossipee Mountains. These two boulder trains overlap in the region that is shown in cross-hatching.

scoured clean of soil and debris. Then, depending on the nature of the bedrock, the topography, and the particular localized forces exerted by the moving ice, the glacier wore from 10 to 200 feet off the surfaces of hilltops, valleys, and mountain peaks. Large volumes of fine powdered rock were created by the glacier's pulverizing action. This *rock flour* lent a milky hue to meltwater streams.

Rocks and boulders that were trapped and dragged beneath the ice etched the bedrock with *glacial striations*. These massive scratches are aligned in the direction of the glacier's flow. Although much of New England's bedrock still bears the marks of the glacier, these striations are now covered with soil and are only visible at outcroppings. Walls along the sides of Franconia Notch and the other glacial valleys, for example, are lined with horizontal scratches and gouges. Striations are easy to see atop Mount Cardigan, Mount Kearsarge, and on other peaks where the bedrock is exposed (figure 3-8).

FIGURE 3-8. Glacial striations range from fine lines to deep gouges like the one cutting across the face of this outcrop atop Mount Kearsarge. *Photo by Michael J. Caduto.*

Prominences were either rounded off or sharpened by the glacier. Lake Winnipesaukee formed in a basin created when the weak, friable granite of that region was gouged out. In contrast, the Lakes of the Clouds, New Hampshire's highest bodies of water, are nestled in a few small depressions carved by the glacier high on the slopes of Mount Washington south of the summit.

It is impossible to scan the horizon anywhere in New Hampshire and not see the glacier's handiwork. Look carefully over the landscape and you will notice how, in many locales, the hills appear to be shaped like waves with crests facing in the same direction. Although they are not true drumlins, these hills are sometimes called *rock drumlins*. They are also known as *sheepbacks* and *roches moutonnées*, "sheep-like rocks." As the glacier rode up and over each hill, moving generally toward the south, it created a smooth, gradual incline or *stoss slope*. It then plucked rocks off the *lee slope* as it came down the other side. The wavy crests of these hills, then, point generally to the south, in the direction the glacier flowed (figure 3-9). Whiteface Mountain in Wolfeboro and a number of other hills near the southeast shore of Lake Winnipesaukee are sheepbacks, as is Milliken Hill and other rises in and around Ossipee. Mount Willard, which stands in the Gate north of Crawford Notch, is a classic sheepback that can be clearly seen from Willey House

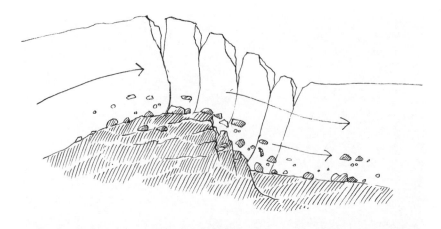

FIGURE 3-9.

*Top:* Sheepbacks are sculpted as the glacier grinds up a "stoss" slope and smooths it off, then plucks rocks from the "lee" slope as it passes over the rise.

*Bottom:* Hills and mountains like this one, with the characteristic sheepback shape, are common throughout New England. *Photo by Michael J. Caduto.*

a few miles south. Joe English Hill in New Boston is among the famous roches moutonnées.

Sheepbacks, however, are mere trifles when compared to the grandeur of the glacial valleys of the White Mountains. Even the great Laurentide had to yield when it was squeezed down and through the curves of these valleys, its north-south direction forcibly altered. Enormous pressures and abrasive forces built up as the ice gnashed against the valley walls and floors. Over time, the Laurentide ice sheet and the glaciers that came before it removed eons of accumulated talus and ground off as much as 500 feet of bedrock from some valley floors. In their wake, the glaciers left broad, sweeping, U-shaped valleys with steep walls. The larger and most familiar of these "notches" include Franconia, Pinkham, Crawford, Dixville, and Kinsman (figure 3-10).

When the climate cooled enough for the most recent glacier to accumulate in the north, numerous glaciers also formed in New Hampshire's mountain valleys. These glaciers flowed down the sides of the mountains, out through the mouths of the valleys, and removed the rocks and sediments from the V-shaped valleys that had been shaped by streams and rivers. Rocks were also swept away that had broken from the valley walls as water froze and expanded in the fractures along the cliff faces. When the main body of the glacier arrived, it further sculpted the valleys. Broad, steep-sided, U-shaped bowls called *cirques* are the magnificent result. One of New England's most famous cirque landforms, the Knife Edge on Mount Katahdin in north-central Maine, runs along the ridge of the Great Basin. Here the ice gouged so deeply into the mountain that the top of the cirque met with the steep south slope, honing the Knife Edge.

Roughly twelve glacial cirques were carved in New Hampshire's mountain valleys. Among those in the Presidentials are Huntington Ravine, King's Ravine, the Ravine of the Castles, and, largest of all, the Great Gulf. Another cirque, named Jobildunk Ravine, lies east of the summit on Mount Moosilauke. Tuckerman Ravine, a well-known glacial cirque on the east slope of Mount Washington that is famous for its late-season skiing down the headwall, is still among the coldest spots in New England. Some millenniums past, up in a high, north-facing crevice of this ravine, one of the last, crumbling pieces of ice melted during the heat of a summer's day. Here, too, one day, snow and ice will again begin to accumulate; a harbinger of the next Ice Age (figure 3-11).

One of the most fascinating glacial landforms was created as the aging ice sheet waned. Some streams and rivers of meltwater cut sinuous channels beneath the ice and built up beds of sand, gravel, and cobbles. When the ice melted, the sides of these long deposits, called *eskers,* collapsed and formed steep-sided hills as high as 100 feet that snake over the land.

FIGURE 3-10.

*Top:* The expansive Crawford Notch today.

*Right:* A view of how Crawford Notch may have appeared in the aftermath of the glacier, as seen from the wide southern verge of the Notch looking north. *Photos by Michael J. Caduto.*

FIGURE 3-11. Tuckerman Ravine is a spectacular glacial cirque. *Photo courtesy New Hampshire Historical Society.*

Eskers are also known in some places as *horsebacks* and *whalebacks*. New Hampshire's most prominent and famous example is the serpentine Pine River esker that follows the Snake River for about 5 miles to the south and east of Ossipee. As it wends east of Route 16, its distance from the road varies from about 1 to 3 miles. Another esker nearby lies east of Route 16 in North Rochester. Far to the west, fragments of an esker run along the east side of the Connecticut River from Lyme, and south through Hanover to West Lebanon. Pieces of esker stretch for 20 miles along the Soucook River northeast of Concord. A busy traveller along Route 93 can view a portion of an esker in north Manchester where it goes under the northwest end of the Merrimack Bridge by exit 10. The meltwaters did the work of sorting the sand and gravel in this esker, which is now being mined.

After the glacier melted, 14,000 years of freezing, thawing, heating, and cooling of the surface of the bedrock in the White Mountains arranged the rocks into patterns. On steep talus slopes where the incline is greater than 7 degrees and exceeds the *angle of repose*, rocks have formed drooping, necklace-shaped bands. Where the angle of the slope is from 3 to 7 degrees, rocks became aligned into evenly spaced stripes (figure 3-12). On many peaks, and on the haunches surrounding them, where the ground is nearly level, time and ice have set the rocks into irregular polygons. All of

FIGURE 3-12. Rock stripes, such as these on the slope of Mount Washington, form where talus slopes are inclined at an angle of from 3 to 7 degrees. *Photo by Hugh Raup, courtesy Harvard Forest Archives.*

these patterns can be seen from the hiking trails that cross mountain peaks, traverse steep talus slopes, and overlook the precipitous sides of cirques and mountain valleys.

A few of the more interesting and popular post-glacial landforms are found in Franconia Notch at the north end of Profile Lake. The granite cliff on the east face of Cannon Mountain is a good example of *exfoliation,* where rock weathering, combined with freezing and thawing, has gradually loosened the face of the cliff along even, parallel joints that formed when the rock cooled and contracted deep underground. Layer after layer of these massive sheets of rock have separated from the cliff face, plunged to its base, and piled up there as a talus slope. If this cliff were turned on its head, the even, angular ridges that have formed where the layers of rock sloughed off would make a giant's staircase (figure 3-13). Watching from atop this cliff is the face of the Old Man of the Mountain. The slabs of granite that compose his icy visage jut out over the edge of the cliff. In recent years, the Old Man has kept his chiseled good looks due in no small part to careful cosmetic surgery that involves numerous stays, cables, and turnbuckles.

FIGURE 3-13. Sheeting or *exfoliation* of rocks along the haunches of Cannon Mountain in Franconia Notch. *Photo by Michael J. Caduto.*

The Old Man of the Mountain. *Photo courtesy New Hampshire Historical Society.*

## The Earth Rises

Released 14,000 years ago from the imposing weight of the ice sheet that covered New Hampshire, Earth's crust moved little at first, then began to heave a slow-motion sigh of relief that lasted until 8,000 years ago.[11] The farther north you travel, to where the glacier was more than 2 miles high at its center in the vicinity of Hudson Bay, the greater the rebound of Earth's crust. New Hampshire's northernmost territory has risen 700 feet more than the land bordering on Massachusetts.[12] Major rivers cut deeply into the ancient lake beds and glacial outwash plains as the land beneath the waters lifted up. In many places, terraces along the riverbeds mark the levels of ancient floodplains that lie well above those of today. Tributary streams cut steep-sided, V-shaped valleys through these terraces as they made their way to the main river channels.

Oceans swelled, flush with the tremendous volume of water that flowed from the melting glaciers. Released from the ponderous weight of the ice sheet, Earth's crust rebounded, but more slowly than the rising ocean that flooded the coast as it followed the retreating ice. This marine invasion pushed the New Hampshire shoreline some 20 miles inland from where it is today. Layers of marine clays, such as those in Exeter and Epping, show that fingers of the ocean penetrated well up into major river valleys and created long, winding estuaries. In some places along the Maine coast, brackish water stretched some 75 miles farther inland than it does at present, all the way up to Millinocket and Moscow. In time, as the land continued to rebound, the coastline slowly retreated to about the same place where the land now meets the sea.

## THE FINAL ACT

Pleistocene seasons in front of the glacier were cooler overall but lacked the extreme temperatures that we presently experience during summer and winter. The late Pleistocene climate supported a melange of biotic communities far more diverse than those now found in the Northeast: from grassland steppe to forests of spruce, fir, larch, birch, and poplar interspersed with species that these trees do not commonly associate with today, such as oak, elm, ash, jack pine, and ironwood.[13] Warmer environments to the south and west harbored oak, maple, hemlock, and white pine, as well as beech, hickory, and chestnut. Within this quilt of habitats, mastodons and grazing herds of caribou lived alongside wild turkey. Giant beavers plied the waters of lakes and ponds that were home to ducks and amphibious reptiles, including painted, spotted, and snapping turtles.[14] Newts and northern water snakes wriggled through these waters and, in their seasons, the serenades of spring peepers, green frogs, and bullfrogs were overheard by the great beasts.[15]

We can only imagine the wonders and marvels of the Ice Age: the grazing woodland musk ox, great-racked stag-moose, and the hulking mastodons standing 10 feet tall at the shoulder. But the reign of the mega-fauna was brief, for change is an inescapable constant in nature. Soon after their kingdom had attained its full expression, it started to eclipse. In the first two millenniums after the glacier's retreat, two out of every three species of big mammals that flourished in North America during the Pleistocene disappeared, as well as many small mammals that lived out their secretive lives amid the giants.[16] By 10,000 years ago, the bellowing of woolly mammoths was silenced. No more did the gleaming fangs of the sabertooth and the howl of the dire wolf strike fear into the hearts of vulnerable young sloths. Never again would the enormous antlers of a stag-moose rise up from the morning mist dripping with moss, while, nearby, the giant beaver, *Castoroides,* cut a wake through the marsh. Such was the fate of the walking eagle and the short-tailed bear. Perhaps the carrion-eating teratorn was among the last to go, gorging on the rotting flesh of its contemporaries while the sun set on a magnificent period of this continent's past.

Why did they perish? Was it not possible for these great beasts to endure the changes of the last 2,000 years of their time, to co-exist with the black bear, turkey vulture, mountain lion, chickadee, and cottontail? Their demise may belie the adage that might makes right. Theirs was an age of poorly adaptable specialists who had particular needs for food, space, and climate. Once the glacier was gone, the blustery cold Arctic air masses again blew across this land, shortening the growing

The flightless *Diatryma* is among the magnificent Pleistocene birds and mammals that will never be seen again. The horse-sized head of this carnivore stood over 9 feet tall and was equipped with an enormous hooked beak. When caught out in the open, few of its prey could have escaped the "Terror-Bird," whose long legs powered it swiftly across the South American grasslands.

season and creating intense winter storms of deep snows. Although the weather was warmer than it had been on the whole, the highs and lows of summer and winter temperatures were more extreme and the ranges of plants constricted to where they could tolerate this new climate. Eventually, the open grassland steppe in front of the glacier became interspersed with stands of poplars and birches and expansive areas where a dense forest canopy of spruce, jack pine, and balsam fir sheltered a wet blanket of inedible mosses. As this forest spread, the diversity and nutritional value of food for the grazers and browsers decreased, forcing them to seek alternative sources of nourishment.[17] Malnutrition and disease felled entire populations of weakened animals. Carnivores cannot survive for long without prey to chase down, kill, and consume. Finally, the scavengers began to scavenge on themselves, until few were left.

Some say it wasn't the changes in the land and the cold blasts of Arctic air that bled the life from the Ice Age beasts, but the cold stone of a hundred thousand fletched spearpoints. Climatologists and archaeologists tell us that humans came across the land that now lies beneath the Bering Strait more than 30,000 years ago, when sea levels were at their lowest ebb during the height of the glacier. At that time, the sere Arctic air of Siberia and Alaska lacked the moisture to generate the snow that feeds the glaciers, so this breadth of land lay exposed.

But another story has been handed down through the millenniums. It is the story of those who were created in this land and from this land; who simply returned in the wake of the glacier and were powerless to change the inexorable course of the world around them. It is a story of hunters who knew that a spear thrust into the heart of a prey killed more than a source of meat; who mourned the passing of the great beasts just as we sense the loneliness that would come if we were to one day witness the last sounding of a right whale beneath the waters of the Atlantic, never to rise again.

# PART II

# Spears and Bows, Seeds and Hoes

# 4. People of Stone and Bone

❧ ❧ ❧ ❧

*H*igh on a terrace above a mountain river, several families sit on the sandy ground hunched over their work. The staccato of stone against stone punctuates the steady rush of the roiling waters below. One man, his fingers bent and tired from fashioning spear points of stone, looks up across the spread of the valley. He sighs, says a few words to one of his companions, and continues to put the finishing touches on a long, fluted projectile.

A handful of rough, low dwellings huddle nearby, fashioned from caribou skin stretched over saplings that are lashed together with sinew. Lazy smoke drifts from holes atop each lodge and carries the scent of cooked meat down into the valley on the cool, summer evening breeze.

After eating her fill, one of the women picks up a small pouch, crawls from the lodge, and walks to the dark edge of the plateau. Untying the satchel of soft elk hide, she unrolls the bundle to reveal a beautifully crafted spearpoint made of clear quartz crystal: a gift from the animal spirits. She takes the point in hand and stands caressed by the evening breeze. Holding the crystal up to the moonlight, she begins a low, methodical incantation that calls on its power to grant success in finding and catching game on the forthcoming hunt. She cradles in her hands a fallen child of the stars that flicker overhead, themselves born of the Great Light that brightens each morning and journeys across the sky.

*At the sound of a stag-moose trumpeting in the distance the woman falls silent. An owl calls from the opposite bank and another responds from a stunted spruce tree that protrudes from a swale amid the dusty expanse of grass, sedge, and juniper. The woman stands alone, trembling in awe before the nocturnal terrors and powers that speak and frighten, wrapped in splendor beneath the twinkling arch of the sky dome. Tears well up and slide down her cheeks, tears of ecstasy that come to those who step outside the circle of light that protects the familiar comforts of family and lodge, who dare to gaze beyond into the unknown.*

—Jefferson, New Hampshire,
11,000 years ago

ᥫᩙ   ᥫᩙ   ᥫᩙ   ᥫᩙ

This primal woman stands on a terrace 200 feet above the Israel River in Coos County. Her family arrived along an east-west route that wove through the north country, then completed their journey by walking to the south and east, moving upstream along the banks of the Israel River. They came to be near the large, streaming herds of caribou and to have access to sources of good stone that lay to the east and west.[1] Their tools were basic. It was an age of stone and bone. We could call them *paleo-peoples,* after the Greek *palaio* for "ancient." One day, when they appear in the imaginations of those from a distant future, these old ones will come to be known as *Paleoindians.*

When the Jefferson woman's people came here to hunt, they discovered an abundance of boulders plucked by the glacier from a nearby vein of granite-like, volcanic *rhyolite.* With an enviable expertise, they fashioned raw stone into long, fluted *Clovis* spearpoints. They looked up occasionally while working upon an elevated perch to take in an inspiring view of the river valley and surrounding mountain peaks. Over the next millennium, paleo-peoples occupied at least four different sites—the largest over 10 acres—in pursuit of their prey and to work this friable rock that lay interspersed in the glacial till.[2] They also brought stone here that originated from as far away as western Vermont and northern Maine.[3]

On certain days, when the wind blew out of the north, this ancient people huddled against the icy sting of Arctic breath. But 3,000 years earlier, in the lee of the melting glacier, this was a different world. A cold, heavy wind settled down off the tongue of ice and raised the rich, dusty silt of an arid grassland steppe. Standing on a hill in this broad swath of landscape 14,000 years ago, brushing the dust from your eyes, you would thank the merciful wind that blew away the clouds of biting in-

Clovis spear point.

sects. All around your feet, sprouting from the rich, sandy soil, are patches of grass and sedge interspersed with elfin shrubs, herbs, wildflowers, and crowberry. A meadow vole emerges from the door of its grass house, sees you, then shoots back inside. The cry of a golden eagle rings out overhead.

Now your gaze shifts across the nearby valley and off to the far hills. A long, ribbon-like copse of quaking aspens, balsam poplars, and white birches lines a sinuous, silty river that drains into a lake rich with shrubs and young trees along its shore where a stag-moose is feeding, belly-deep in a thick bed of aquatic plants. Somewhere in the distance, herds of caribou and musk ox drape up and over the hillsides and a small family band of mastodons perambulates down toward the river for a drink. These grazing herds of the late Pleistocene feed on a wide range of nutritious plants whose seeds arrived borne on the wind, stuck to fur and feathers, and plopped down in the rich droppings of herbivorous birds and other animals. It is a fertile land in which plants only grow wherever there is enough water for them to sprout and survive. Look off still farther to the distant mountains in the east and there is no forest to hinder your line of sight, only a haze that occludes the farthest peaks and turns the rising sun into a ruddy pastel that evokes a glowing hearth.

On this day, you are going to begin a journey through four thousand years of late Pleistocene time. Hiking the first steps down the hill and toward the south is easy and the going swift, sidestepping only the thick clumps of grasses and forbs and fording an occasional stream.[4] Beneath these warming, dusty summer silts and sands, deposited years ago by a spring flood of glacial meltwater, the ground is frozen year-round. Spartan though it appears, the soils of this grassland steppe grow such a richness and variety of plants that they support a greater diversity of large animals and a larger biological mass than the boreal forest you will encounter farther to the south.[5] More than fifty times the living mass of plants grows here than in the tundra.[6] Each winter, the tops of these grasses die back, energy is stored in their roots, and the nutrients contained in this year's growth are quickly returned to the soil.

As the wind picks up, it whistles in your ears and blows swirling clouds of dust. Even though the temperature is mild, you shiver suddenly and can only imagine the windchills of mid-winter, especially those that would accompany the many clear nights. In the springtime, snow melts quickly from these hills, swept clear of snow. During the summer, this expansive, open landscape is usually drenched in sunlight beneath clear, blue skies.

In many places, the broken, ground-up bones of the land itself lay bare: expansive slopes strewn with boulders amid rugged hills and banks of sand, gravel, and clay. Plants that produce windblown seeds and spores have been the first to arrive in the land in front of the retreating ice sheet. Bending down to look more closely at a rock, you wonder about the hard, thin, colorful scale that encrusts its surface. Lichens, which spread by aerial spores, have colonized the bare rocks and gravel left by the glacier. These rugged organisms are an association of a fungus that provides the growth environment and mineral nutrition for an alga, which, through photosynthesis, contributes the carbohydrates that feed the fungus. Fungal acids slowly dissolve the surface of rocks to obtain minerals for growth. As generations of lichens grow, die, and slough off from the rocks, their remains accumulate as small pockets of organic matter in the interstices between grains of sand amid the pieces of rock and gravel, and in cracks and hollows atop the rocks themselves. Lichens are already thick on the exposed rocks of taller mountain peaks, which were the first places to become exposed when the wasting ice sheet started to thin. The ancient pollen that has been preserved in the bottom, earliest layers of acid bogs shows that fireweed, wormwood, and plantain were among the first plants to populate the mineral-rich soil.[7]

Your study is interrupted by a struggle through a swale of thick bushy willows. Soon you enter a small clearing on the shore of a large body of water. The vegetation has been consumed all around. You stoop down and run a finger around the edge of a track pressed into the mud that was made by an animal with webbed feet. A shiver runs along your spine as you realize the track is farther across than the full length of your hand. You would be even more frightened if you knew that the track's creator has enormous down-curved incisors that measure a full 4 inches. Glancing nervously around, you quietly make your way through the willows and hide behind a small boulder that sits alongshore. Gingerly you climb onto one of the rocks and look out across the water, only to see a dark brown animal the size of a mature black bear just 10 feet away, cutting a deep, V-shaped wake across the lake-sized pond. When the giant beaver notices you, it dives and its long, thick tail throws up a spray that sprinkles the front of your clothing. The substantial waves of its wake wash over the shore and lap at the base of the rock upon which you stand in open-mouthed awe of this great aquatic herbivore.

Something else is moving in the shallows on the far side of the pond. It looks like a moose but like the beaver, its size is extraordinary. A moment ago, the half-submerged stag-moose was contentedly munching on some aquatic plants. Now, having been alerted by the beaver's sudden dive, the stag-moose lifts its head to reveal a breathtaking rack of antlers that span 10 feet from tip to tip, draped with sheets of dripping aquatic plants.

The stag-moose of North America, *Cervalces scotti,* and other giant members of the deer family abounded during the Pleistocene. Some males among the Irish elk shown here, *Megaloceros giganteus,* rivaled the stag-moose in size and had antlers that spanned over 12 feet.

Quickly, as fast as you can, you scramble down the dam, cut back along your trail, and start along a new course that marks a wide berth around the pond.

In time, you walk uphill and enter a wide, grassy break in the aspen forest that is ringed with young birch trees and dotted with islands of juniper. The resinous scent of the evergreens spices your nostrils. On the way to the hilltop, you encounter an animal trail of large round tracks a good distance apart that have pressed deep into the earth. As you walk alongside this trail, you notice a gathering of the tracks in a place where two piles of fresh, fibrous dung buzz with flies. One of the pungent piles is over a foot high. A second set of hand-sized tracks surrounds the smaller heap of droppings: a sign that a younger animal is accompanying an adult. As soon as the trail reaches the edge of the wood, you find a tree where great sheets of bark have been stripped off to about 20 feet up the trunk. Just as you're pondering this latest find, a rich bassoon-like baritone call rings out across the barrens. A fleeting moment of intense excitement and curiosity leaves you torn between moving toward or away from the sound. Your skin feels tight and flushed as you break out in the cold sweat of fear as an image flashes through your mind of a living, territorial hill of flesh, covered with coarse black hair and deftly wielding 8-foot tusks. Quickly, you double back along the animal trail in the opposite direction from which a mother mastodon and her calf plodded as they cut across the clearing earlier that day.

Following a river valley as it winds its way southward, you are coming to a time and place where the climate is wetter and seasonal temperatures more extreme. Encountering a mosaic of habitats, you realize that plants and animals are moving quickly on your time-lapse journey. Normally, without time shifting, we cannot notice the movements they make in response to changes in the environment. Moss and sedge are appearing in low wetlands that course through the drier, well-drained sites of the upland grasslands. On the average, depending on the length of their life cycle and how they disperse, plants are able to respond to the changing climate by shifting their range by as much as a few hundred meters each year.[8] Winged creatures, including insects and some species of birds, can move into a newly habitable climate within a year. Ospreys and snowy owls are adept at moving in response to climate. Certain mammals, such as white-footed mice, can shift their range by a few kilometers each year, while larger animals with longer lifespans take many years or even decades to take advantage of a new environment.[9]

Now it is 12,000 years ago, and you have walked through two millenniums of late Pleistocene time. New Hampshire's weather is wetter and temperatures are more variable than when your journey began, much like the climate of Labrador's interior today. Slowly, over time, the open steppe is being invaded by fingers of spruce and fir forest reaching up the valleys from the south and inland from the coast.[10] The geographic ranges to which plants are now restricted has much to do with the extreme temperatures that come with the seasons. It also depends on which plants can better compete for root space, sunshine, and water in the harsh, nutrient-poor world of the advancing boreal forest.

You are slogging through a dense, wet ground cover of mosses and sedges that is not as productive as the grassland steppe. A masked shrew, one of the smallest animals, darts across your path in a blur. The thick, boggy mat of this creature's home insulates the soil and keeps the ground frozen and wet. But there is little browse for animals to eat and many plants contain compounds that are toxic to discourage grazing animals. When the deep winter snows arrive, it will be impossible for the surviving large mammals of the grassland steppe to get around.

Passing through the extreme land of the boreal forest—where surprisingly hot summer days are followed by shivering nights—you notice that the patches of black spruce and white spruce take up more and more of the landscape. This ecosystem is as fascinating as it is challenging to navigate. It is an ecological amalgam of mosses, lichens, juniper, alpine plants, and dwarf alders, willows, and birches. A multitude of insects swarms here for the little brown bat to feed on after sunset, and the pine marten finds no shortage of prey.

You pick your way through dense stands of spruce while swatting at a maddening hoard of biting insects. Each time you reach a clearing, you look up and notice, longingly, that portions of the higher hills and mountains are still covered with open grassland where strong winds drive the insects before them. Your heart leaps when the bright, clear sound of a white-throated sparrow rings out from the forest depths.

While you are staring up at one of these hills, you see something move far in the distance. Training your eyes on that spot, you discern the branch-like antlers of caribou bobbing up and down where they graze in a gray field of lichens. After watching for a time, you walk on through the lowland evergreen forest.

The steady, trancelike motion of your feet causes your mind to wander as you drift through the sun-dappled spaces in the understory. Then, at the far reaches of the peaty soil, the land rises. You climb through the edge of the forest past winterberry, dwarf huckleberry, and swamp highbush blueberry, moving as quickly as you can away from the biting insects into an open, relatively parklike forest of poplar, jack pine, and paper birch.[11]

Walking by day, camping in makeshift lean-tos each night, feeding on the berries, roots, large insects, and small animals that you can find, you gradually make your way south, traveling through space and time. Dense forest is interrupted less and less by open grasslands. Many streambanks and wetlands are lined with stands of poplar along the edges of alder swales. You climb the north-facing slope of a small mountain, passing through a diverse forest of jack pine, spruce, balsam fir, red pine, larch, and poplar. You notice some long claw marks etched into the smooth bark of an aspen and realize that you are walking through a black bear's territory. Picturing the bear in your mind reminds you of other large animals that live in these hills and valleys, including the moose and white-tailed deer.

Reaching the rocky summit, you look across the valley to a south-facing declivity that is a lacy tapestry woven from the crowns of birch, elm, oak, and white pine. Here, in the hollow of a tree, a deer mouse has left the gnawed husks of acorns behind. The lowlands harbor pockets of sugar maple, ash, and ironwood.

From the perspective of ten millenniums ago, standing atop this exposed peak that affords a panoramic view, you scan the northern horizon. You have traversed 4,000 years through time and space, up and down a temporal landscape, through heaving swells of green. Looking toward where you began your journey, you scan the mixed broadleaf and evergreen forests and beyond to the distant hills thick and dark with conifers, journeying through eons of cooling and drying climate, riding the crests and troughs, beyond the verge of a verdant sea whose waves lap on the shores of the grassland steppe, ebbing and flowing on the tide of ecologic evolution as you sail back through the last millenniums of the Pleistocene.

ೕ೦   ೕ೦   ೕ೦   ೕ೦

*A chill autumn wind snakes down the river valley from the north and drives golden leaves up the funnel of a dust devil, lifting them toward the treetops where they were hanging just days before. Dust rises up and speckles the eyes of a woman and two children who are scraping a caribou hide by the fire. She rubs the grit from the corners of her eyes with the soft hair on her left forearm, then continues to scrape fur from the tough hide with a black, curved chert blade.*

*The twin six-year-old boy and girl, who are helping their mother prepare the skin that will later be fashioned into clothing, suddenly drop their scrapers, jump up and shriek when a young, dark-gray wolf bounds into their midst. With its powerful legs working and tail lashing, with children hugging its neck, their pet wolf barks at some leaves twirling down from overhead. It chases the leaves across the campsite and drags the children with it, clinging to its fur.*

*Two Spots, the wolf pup, had been out hunting with the children's father, so they know he can't be far behind. When he emerges from the edge of the forest into the clearing along the riverbank, the children rush over to greet him. He gives their hair a playful tug, walks over to the fire ring, and drops a blood-spattered snowshoe hare onto a flat rock near the fire stones, its fur already showing splotches of the white that would have helped it blend in with the deep winter snows.*

*The children's mother looks up at him and nods her approval. She wishes there could be more meat to feed the family on that evening, at the end of a day when the Great Light had not stayed long in the sky and the air felt as sharp as the blade of her scraper, but she knew that it was hard for her husband to spear any of the larger game animals from a distance. Last summer, as he and a group of other hunters stood over a wounded caribou, ready to thrust the last spears that would end its life in order to give its flesh to feed the clan, the beast jerked its head so violently that the lance-like tip of an antler punctured her husband's left eye. Now, when she looks at the man who has fed her and her children for as many turns of the seasons as she can remember, only one eye stares back to express the warmth he feels for her and the little ones gathering by the fire.*

*—On a terrace above the Ashuelot River,*
*West Swanzey, New Hampshire,*
*10,800 years ago*

The barren ground caribou.

These hunters and gatherers of the long past were adaptable and intelligent enough to create a protective bubble of culture and security; a place that was sufficiently safe to enable their families to survive in a world fraught with dangers that are now unimaginable. Understanding the value of cooperation and cohesiveness to survival, and the severe repercussions of violence and aggression toward one another, they formed communities of necessity. As with many contemporary hunter-gatherer societies, individuals most likely possessed a great degree of independence, equality, and freedom from domination by others.[12]

The community's survival depended on its ability to travel without restriction, so those who became badly injured and extremely ill were often left behind to fend for themselves. This seeming paradox of familial and community compassion at the occasional expense of certain individuals has been cited many times as proof that early indigenous peoples were cruel, heartless barbarians. But one can imagine painful scenes of separation when the larger group was torn between their connection with an ailing individual and the drive to stay alive.

Even though we have no evidence that human beings were on the regular menu of mountain lions, wolves, or black bears, a giant moose cow defending her calf easily could have killed someone who presented a threat by wandering between them. And many a powerful, carnivorous predator that is driven upon the penetrating lance of starvation is capable of eating a human being in order to survive. But the toll taken by these large mammals paled when compared to the number of people incapacitated and even killed by internal and external parasites, the tiniest predators of them all. A paleo-hunter who had distinguished himself in the hunt would have been at a loss to explain the fever, swelling, intestinal pain and insomnia visited upon him by trichinosis.

As paleolithic peoples throughout the world have taught us, few families or communities of hunters would *prefer* to face death on the tusks of a mastodon, musk ox, or woolly mammoth, or by the fangs of a dire wolf, when they were surrounded by a bounty of other plant and animal foods that were easier and relatively safer to hunt and collect. The large herds of barren ground caribou that congregated in wetlands, along rivers, and in fields of lichen were hunted with long, lance-tipped spears and were an important game animal that provided a great deal of meat for families. Ranging throughout the diverse habitats of the late Pleistocene and early Holocene, the ancient peoples of New Hampshire encountered moose, white-tailed deer, beaver, caribou, elk, ducks and geese, squirrels, hares, and other small mammals, trout, turtles, and the eggs of ptarmigan, tortoise, and snakes among other species. In time, and in season, the waterways were fairly choked with shad, alewives, and other *anadromous* species—those that live in the ocean and run or race *(dromos)* up *(ana)* streams and rivers to reproduce in the freshwater places of their birth. Like their contemporaries in western New England, New Hampshire's coastal communities of paleo-peoples likely hunted and partook of the abundance of fish, seals, porpoises, the odd stranded whale, and even walrus meat.[13] Plant foods were prolific: berries, roots, herbs, nuts, and other seeds as well as an abundance of greens.

Although paleo-peoples were powerful, agile, and skilled hunters, even at the beginning of the *Holocene epoch* 10,000 years ago, big-game hunting was likely an occasional act of necessity to help their omnivorous communities survive a drought, a long winter season, the aftermath of a fire, and times when other, more easily obtained sources of food were scarce. The tracking down of a mastodon may also have been a rite of passage into adulthood. Relying on the variety and abundance of plant and animal foods available in each season was the best way to ensure survival and limit the energy that had to be expended to live.

For much of the time in the rich, ecologically diverse paleo-environment, enough food was available in spring, summer, and autumn that these warmer seasons would have allowed ample time for activities beyond mere subsistence. People had time to nurture a culture: they crafted tools of stone and bone, practiced early forms of art and medicine, and trained gifted individuals to heal both body and spirit. Their connection to the natural world went as far as rescuing young orphaned animals, including gray wolf pups—the first wild dogs that were domesticated into faithful companions. Even so, paleo-people quickly would have starved if their numbers grew beyond the *carrying capacity* of their rich environment, so they were subject to the same constraints of ecological laws as the plants and animals that sustained them. Probably no more than a few dozen people occupied every hundred square miles of vast wilderness. When the number of people in a region grew beyond the ability of that environment to sustain the population, some families migrated to new habitat in search of food and other resources.[14]

Adults among the paleo-peoples needed to eat roughly 3,000 calories each day.[15] During the summer months, as much as two-thirds of their diet may have come from plant foods, but meat and fish were the winter staples. Today, almost all of our plant foods come from a mere twenty crops, including corn, wheat, rice, and rye. Ancient peoples consumed a wide variety of local plant species in season and they drew upon every edible plant part for their nourishment: fruits, berries, tubers, roots, flowers, sap, gum, nuts, and other seeds. In addition to providing far more nutrition than the foods we eat today, including greater amounts of energy, fiber, and essential vitamins and minerals such as vitamin C, calcium, iron, and folate, these wild plants contained an array of necessary trace elements. Food plants that were foraged in the wild also contained more protein and less starch than modern agricultural varieties.

The ancient hunter-gatherers ate two to five times more protein from both plant and animal sources than is found in the typical contemporary American diet. They most likely ate more calories than they needed when food was plentiful and stored this energy as fat to burn during times of scarcity. The proportion of their diet comprised of meat varied from 20 to 80 percent depending upon the foods available in different seasons and locations.[16] On the whole, meat from deer, mastodon, and other animals contained 13 to 16 percent of the total fat content and five times the polyunsaturated fat of the farm-raised meat we eat today. It also contained about 4 percent more eicosapentaenoic acid, which helps to prevent arteriosclerosis. Paleo-prime cut provided enough fat and fatty acids, iron, and vitamin $B_{12}$ for their diet, but it contained more protein and less calories than that of today. Overall, the paleo-diet was healthier than ours and it would have prevented many of our diet-related diseases.

ളඌ      ളඌ      ളඌ      ളඌ

*A crystal spring morning breaks clear and bright. Wisps of early haze drift in ghostlike arms that reach across the still surface of the lake. Well out from shore, a hunter stoops atop a smooth granite rock, motionless and intent upon seeing beneath the lake's dawn-light mirror. His taut, muscular arm—a cocked spring drawn back to the top of its full arc of power—stands ready to thrust the spear held tightly in his hand.*

*In the shallows alongshore, a great blue heron holds its beak aloft and at the ready, as if teaching the fisherman its venerable craft. A loon's yodeling penetrates the stillness from a nearby cove where the male defends its territory from an intruder.*

*The polished dome beneath the hunter's bare feet rises from the surface in a narrows between a vast lake on the north side and a prominent adjoining bay to the south and west. Flashes of light and dark—migrating shad—are darting past the hunter's rock, so close that he can see their silhouettes against its pale gray submerged granite base. He waits until a pattern appears in the movement of their passing; wave after wave of silvery shad. Many of the fish are swimming over an underwater ridge that was cut into the rock as it was dragged beneath the glacier and ground along the bedrock a mere 4,000 years ago, before it fell from the decaying ice along the shore of a glacial lake as vast as an inland sea.*

*Shifting his weight, the hunter aims the spearpoint a fraction below where the ridge in the rock appears to be, knowing instinctively that the fish always seem to be closer to the surface than they really are.*

*A large shad slips by, then another streaks past in a sudden burst of speed. In the blink of an eye, as fast as a frog's tongue snaps at a fly, the spear cuts through the still surface without throwing up a drop of water, its long yellow quartz lance tip cutting through tough scales and deep into the soft flesh. Pulling up the writhing shaft, the hunter sees that the shad is nearly as long as his arm and lets out a triumphant cry that echoes across the valley until it is swallowed by the surrounding hills.*

*Back on shore, a woman looks up from the hide she is scraping with a curved, sharpened piece of flint. The families in their lodges know that their morning meal has just been caught, and that it is an impressive catch. Someone readies a knife that has been honed from the tines of an antler especially for gutting fish. Bigger sticks are thrown on the fires and mouths begin to water in anticipation as the hunter half wades, half swims back through the bone-chilling waters, leaving a wake of drifting fog that curls behind him like the embracing fingers of the morning spirit.*

*—Weirs Beach,*
*9,600 years ago*

This community, between Lake Winnipesaukee and Paugus Bay in Laconia, was inhabited by New Hampshire's *ancient* people, the ones who came "before." Like the rich schools of fish that drew them here each springtime and kept them alive, they came with the hope of fecundity, of creating the next generation. Most likely theirs was a sizeable gathering of related families. Their encampment along this lakeshore was part of a large home range in which they lived year round, migrating to take advantage of the seasonal sources of food. Within this territory were riverside and upland camps, game trails and paths trodden by human feet that connected seasonal community sites.

Who were these ancient peoples whose lives and the world in which they lived still occupy a primal niche in our own ancient memories; a place of stories born of events so venerable that they rise in our unconscious like wakeful visits to the land of stone and bone? When the last tongues of ice melted and ran into the sea, leaving most of New Hampshire's surface exposed more than 14,000 years ago, the arrival of these ancients was imminent. Anthropologists tell us that the families of New Hampshire's first people migrated here from the south and west soon after the most recent glacier receded.

At the height of the Wisconsinan glaciation, as well as the glacial periods that preceded it, when sea levels were some 300 feet or more below where they are now, a land "bridge" formed between Siberia and Alaska. An engineering term does not aptly describe this transcontinental passage whose breadth was more than 1,000 miles measured north-to-south; this expansive subarctic grassland steppe was a continent in its own right. In this environment, entire ecosystems and human communities thrived for tens of thousands of years during glaciations. This subcontinent, *Beringia,* was exposed time and again during the 2 million years of periodic Pleistocene glaciations. Most recently, this bioregion emerged about 80,000 years ago, lasted for 70,000 years, and was widest during the last 13,000 years of this time before being swallowed by the sea.[17]

Woolly mammoths and sabertooth cats moved into North America in this distant past while horses, camels, and other Pleistocene animals migrated from here into Eurasia. Mammoths and mastodons evolved from their elephant ancestors to the south, growing heavier fur coats and trading their large, floppy ears for smaller ones that could withstand the arctic freeze. Ancient steppe bison with horns that spanned 6 feet made their way here from Siberia, crossing Beringia during an interglacial period 300 millenniums ago. These were the ancestors of today's *Bison bison,* which have a comparatively small horn span of only 18 inches.

The most recent ice sheet, a grinding behemoth like those that came before, removed much of the north country's overburden down to the bedrock and erased any traces of earlier inhabitation by humans, plants, and animals. If paleo-peoples returned to southern New Hampshire with the first wave of plants that colonized that rugged land, they could have come back no sooner than 15 millenniums ago. Even in other regions, archaeological findings have traditionally been interpreted to mean that people first came to North America about 12,000 years ago. This date, however, which is based on findings of ancient tools of stone and bone, the remains of human communities that lived beyond the glacier's reach, is gradually being chipped away by a number of discoveries.

Projectile points that are smaller and more rudimentary than those made by Clovis peoples were unearthed on a rise called Cactus Hill, which lies east of the Nottoway River about 45 miles from Richmond, Virginia. They are believed to have been made 15,000 years ago.[18] Stone tools and evidence of basket-making found at the Meadowcroft Rock Shelter along Cross Creek, a tributary of the Ohio River in Pennsylvania, date back as far as 19,000 years.[19] Bones that were shaped by humans

40,000 years ago have been found in the Old Crow Basin of the Yukon. Some paleolithic peoples lived in South America as far back as 32,000 years.[20] A 25,000-year-old piece of an ancient hunter's projectile point, still protruding from the foot of an extinct horse, and some ancient hearths that may date back 35,000 years, were found in a cave not far from Orogrande, New Mexico.[21] And in some cave dwellings under the ancient rocky brows of cliffs in northeastern Brazil were found some stone age tools and paintings of ancient people and animals who once lived in this region, reminiscent of the setting and style of cave paintings in the Dordogne region of France. Charcoal that is encircled by soot-stained rocks in the oldest fire hearths in the Brazilian caves date back to 47,000 years ago, nearly three times the age of the venerable art of Lascaux.[22]

During their search for food and for new hunting territories to exploit when their numbers grew, and with the unending human urge to explore new horizons, ancient peoples were constantly expanding across the landscape. Over time, scientific evidence continues to push back the oldest known date of human presence in the Americas. It is not likely, however, to bridge the gap between anthropological tenets and indigenous beliefs that these ancient peoples had their origins here, in this land.

Why did the ancients settle where they did when they reclaimed this land from the conquering ice? Weirs Beach and the rivers Israel and Ashuelot—wherein lies the link? Early peoples were students of their surroundings, stone-age seekers of the necessities for survival. Food and water were abundant in river valleys and along the shores of glacial lakes. Over time, as the dams of glacial moraine were breached, the location of these small family groups shifted down with the receding lakeshore. Others remained on the old, elevated terraces that afforded good lines of sight and protection from predators. Shelter and security were found on river terraces, alongside lake outlets, streambanks, wetlands, and near the deltas where rivers flowed into lakes and the ocean. Seashores, as now, were rife with food and all forms of flotsam and jetsam that could be used to build. Bones of a stranded whale became lodge poles over which seal skins were stretched, imbued with the smoke of cooked whale meat and burnt ambergris.

With its rivers, lakes, and seashore, this region was, as it still is, rich in life-giving resources. Many other paleo-sites have been found in addition to those in Jefferson, Laconia, and south of Keene in West Swanzey, including sites along the shore of Lake Sunapee, on the shore of a kettle lake near the Merrimack River in Thornton's Ferry, in Manchester atop terraces overlooking where the Merrimack River has cut down into the floor of an ancient glacial lake, atop an ancient delta in Ossipee, at Intervale in the Saco River valley, in Randolph, Colebrook, and, possibly, in Newbury, Vermont, across the Connecticut River from North Haverhill.[23] Paleo-tools found at another site, in a cave on Mount Jasper near the confluence of the Androscoggin River and Dead River, are on display in the Berlin Public Library.[24] These are merely the Stone Age sites that have been found; others are yet to be discovered. In addition to sites on land, some coastal settlements lie beneath the ocean waves, having been flooded when sea levels rose as the glacier melted.

Numerous sites consist of layer upon layer of cultural history preserved in stone, bone, and ash; earthen connections that record the presence of a cultural continuum through time. Findings at Wadleigh Falls in Lee date back to 8,630 years ago, a time of transition between paleo-times and the changes to come.[25] Ancient sites in Sunapee, the Saco River valley and the Merrimack River valley are composed of vertical layers that have preserved the remains of people who lived over a period of 10,000 years or more, starting in paleo-times, through the Archaic and Woodland periods and, in some cases, continuing after contact with Europeans.

Throughout ancient times, plants, animals, and people responded to an ever-changing climate in the land that would be New Hampshire. A dry, arid steppe dominated the landscape after the glacier melted back, followed by forests of birch and aspen, then the spruce forest born of a wetter, more variable climate. Temperatures began to moderate about 11,000 years ago, and gradually, over the next millennium, the treeline crept up the mountainsides. At the end of that time, temperatures had warmed to such an extent that, by reading the existing evidence of wind-and-ice-stunted *krummholz* fir forest near the Lake of the Clouds, we can see that the ancient treeline had advanced higher than it is today on the summits of the White Mountains. Remnant plant communities are still found in the alpine zone atop the higher peaks and in the extreme habitats of lowland bogs.

Cottongrass blooms in lowland
bogs and in pockets of peat
atop higher peaks. *Photo by
Michael J. Caduto.*

By about 9,000 years ago, the land stood at a threshold of a long period of warmer, drier weather that would last for nearly five millenniums.
The upland forest was a patchwork of poplar, spruce, fir, and jack pine
interspersed with birches. The raucous cries of crows and melodic trills of
juncos played amid the branches. Lower slopes—interspersed with ash,
ironwood, maples, and stands of larch—were home to robins, gold-
finches, and evening grosbeaks. Southern regions were a mixed forest of
oak, elm, and white pine laced with streams and interspersed with wetlands and clearings where phoebes, cardinals, and house wrens courted
with song, nested, and taught their fledglings the art of flight.[26] Down in
the understory, American toads stood motionless near mushrooms and
woodland flowers, waiting for the next meal to alight.

These natural communities were among those that flourished in the
aftermath of the glacier, when New Hampshire was a cascade of late
Pleistocene and early Holocene environments and peoples. Living
through these changes was not just a matter of tooth and claw, fur,
feather, or tusk, nor of bulk and strength; survival was determined by a
force unseen. Those organisms that possessed it survived; others did not.

As the great wave of change bore down on this land long ago, human clans moved and learned how to survive on the plant and animal food, the fuel and material resources that presented themselves, doing without those that passed away. Caribou, musk ox, and others migrated north or died off. Wolves were among those that stayed and adapted to the changes occurring around them, while some species, like the white-tailed deer, returned. But many of the archetypal Pleistocene fauna did not live to see the full flowering of the new land. About 9,200 years ago, the last trumpet of a mastodon, who was persisting in the highlands, echoed across an ancient world, diminished in the verdant valleys below, and passed forever into the land of memories and dreams of the great beasts of antiquity. Traveling by cloven hoof on its final journey was the stag-moose, whose cumbersome rack of antlers and competition with the moose may have weighed it down into the inescapable quicksand of extinction. By the final days of the Pleistocene, over one hundred species of large mammal had passed into oblivion.[27]

Among the thirty-five genera of North American mammals that disappeared at this time were some of the most exotic herbivores and rapacious predators that ever stalked this continent.[28] No longer were giant elk, sloths, and the young of mammoths, shrub oxen, moose-elk, and primitive horses chased down, torn apart, and consumed by the two species of cats that expertly wielded their giant canines and serrated teeth. Never again was an agile, 1½-ton short-faced bear to ambush a beaver caught unaware on land, only to have its neck crushed and spine severed by one bite of the massive ursine jaws. The land witnessed the demise of the armadillo-like, hippo-sized pampatheres and the sluggish, 20-foot giant sloths whose mass rivalled that of the mammoths. At some point in the dusk of Pleistocene time, the last howl of a dire wolf sounded and struck fear into the heart of its prey, perhaps a herd of Pleistocene antelope that raised their four-horned heads, cocked their ears, and nervously snorted at the breeze. The range of herbivores that would graze no more across the North American landscape included many that resembled animals whose relatives we now find only in Central and South America, Africa, and Asia: gigantic tapirs, capybaras, and one-hump camels reminiscent of the dromedary.

What caused these venerable beasts to disappear? Why did they find the changes occurring around them to be inexorable, whereas other species did not? Were the climatic and environmental shifts too swift and extreme, as some believe?[29] Did the adaptable gray wolf out-compete the dire wolf? Was the short-faced bear, despite its size, speed, and ferocity, simply no match for the opportunistic and ubiquitous black and grizzly?

Or, as some would argue, was the intensity of human predation so great that it pushed their struggling populations over the brink, just as herds of *Bison antiquus* later were driven en masse over western cliffs?[30] It is unlikely that the ancient hunters would have exterminated the largest and most perilous prey, and those that were not known to be staples in their diet, when immense herds of their preferred food of caribou and bison were there for the taking. And even though these animals, which were among the most common Pleistocene prey, faced the greatest hunting pressures, they endured.

What of the multitude of smaller Pleistocene animals that became extinct even though they were not hunted? Among those were fully ten genera of birds, ranging from jays, eagles, and cowbirds to a shelduck and condor. As a proportion to the entire spectrum of species that both survived and became extinct at that time, the same percentage of bird species disappeared as of mega-fauna.[31]

In light of the clear more-recent extirpation of the dodo, the passenger pigeon, the Carolina parakeet, and a host of other species, it is a small step to imagine the ancient hunters as heartless, relentless killers to the end. And, perhaps, it is a little too easy to transfer a bit of our own guilt onto those who lived thousands of years ago, to take the buffalo jumps and other limited examples of those hunters' profligacy and apply them with a broad moral brushstroke, rooted in hindsight enfeebled by a distance of ten millenniums, across all paleo-peoples and places. Perhaps the well-preserved specimen of a woolly mammoth that recently was cut from a block of frozen Siberian tundra and flown out over the Arctic landscape, aptly dangling by a single thread, may, in its silence, begin to flesh out the final chapter of their tragic tale.

Giant short-faced bear.

# 5. The Warming Time

In the natural order man invests himself in the landscape
and at the same time incorporates the landscape into his
own most fundamental experience. This trust is sacred.

—N. Scott Momaday, 1976

Time flows along the millennial arc while ripples of change
swirl and roil in the stream of years. At the end of the extinction of the great mammals, more than 9,000 years ago, the climate began
to moderate. For the next 4,000 to 5,000 years, the *Warming Time,*
weather in the land-that-would-be-New-Hampshire became warmer and
drier than it is today. By 5,000 years ago, the average summer temperature was nearly 4 degrees Fahrenheit warmer than it is now and the climate was similar to that of modern-day Virginia. Hemlock and white
pine were growing as much as 1,300 feet higher in elevation than where
they are found today.[1]

During this time, when evaporation was greater and precipitation was
less than it had been, countless glacial lakes and kettle ponds became
drier and gradually succeeded into marshes, swamps, and bogs. As the
plant communities of the region were altered by the warm, dry weather,
the last havens for remnant populations of Pleistocene flora became the
coldest alpine summits above treeline and bogs with their poorly drained,
acidic peat. In these few remaining extreme environments, boreal plants
formed *relict* communities.

Paleo-peoples were malleable. As the environment changed and their
cultures evolved, they adopted new tools and technology, hunting tech-
niques, and behaviors that allowed them to endure. Many of these inno-
vations likely arose from regions with large populations. In this way, the

ancient peoples who lived in the rich environments of the Merrimack and Connecticut River valleys, in the region surrounding Lake Winnipesaukee, and along the coast had a strong influence upon family groups of the uplands and regions of the deep interior.

Early peoples were just the beginning of a cultural continuum that stretches back to soon after the glacier's retreat. Each new thread of knowledge, every strand of wisdom that survived as a legacy to the next generation, was incorporated into the fabric of life that would again be transformed by the children to come. Although it is impossible to show a direct linear archaeological and cultural connection through time, peoples of this vast region evolved, like their environments—with fits and starts. When viewed through a temporal lens, the lives of these ancient peoples come into focus as having a clear trend and a character whose expression was molded by the land around them.

  ᘓᘓ  ᘓᘓ  ᘓᘓ  ᘓᘓ

*A family wades into the swirling waters of an early summer stream. Standing in the pools and riffles that they know to be the homes of some unusually large trout, the mother and father unfurl a length of net between them, stretching it the full breadth of the waters. Along its length, the children pull down and straighten the bottom edge, which is weighted with pebble sinkers that are notched where the net cord is tied around them.*

*Once the net is in place, two of the younger children walk upstream along opposite banks. When they reach a good distance from the net, they begin to wade slowly downstream, systematically rousting the trout from their quiet haunts in the shady lee of large rocks and logs and beneath overhanging mossy banks. Inexorably, the trout are driven toward the mouth of the net.*

*After the fishing has begun, the father and his oldest son pick up their spears, knives, and spear-throwers and say goodbye to the rest of the family. The hunters walk in the direction of a marsh where they saw an old bull moose feeding the day before. Reaching the shore of the marsh at midday, each arranges a spear and spear-thrower or "long-arm" so they can be picked up and employed quickly if the moose appears.*

*The older man performs a brief ceremony to cleanse his spirit. He offers his prayers to the spirit of the moose, expressing his honor and respect, then tells the moose of his family's hunger and their need for food. He removes from a skin bag tied to his belt a small wooden effigy carved in the shape of a moose, places it on the ground, and asks the animal to offer its life so that they may have food to eat.*

Once his father has prepared for the hunt, the young hunter pulls a small crescent-shaped stone weight from the deerskin pouch that is tied to his waist. With expert loops of sinew lashing, he deftly attaches the weight to the shaft of the spear-thrower in a position that experience has taught him works best with the particular spear he has brought. He stares at the fine spearpoint he fashioned two moons ago, proud of how the two well-made ears at its base hold the lashings snugly in place.

Both father and son reach inside a small bag they have brought and begin to chew on some dried caribou meat, something that has become a rare delicacy since the prey known as "head of many spears" has mostly moved farther to the north. As the man watches, he remembers how his own father once threw a spear at a caribou not more than five times the elder's height away. He had watched, both excited and saddened, as the speartip passed through the animal and emerged from the other side.

The young man stops chewing and looks up when he notices that his father's gaze has frozen and he is staring out over the marsh. As the old bull moose moves alongshore, munching on the buds of some low shrubs, the hunters turn their heads until their eyes meet. With a silent thrust of his head in the direction of the moose, the father gives his son the signal that means he has permission to throw the first spear. The young man's heartbeat quickens and his mouth suddenly feels dry.

Slowly, quietly, with motion barely perceptible, he steadies the spear in his left hand while he firmly grips the long-arm in his right hand and rises to his feet. Hooking the end of the spear in a notch on the far end of the long-arm, the young hunter reaches well behind his head with his throwing arm, puts his weight back on his right foot, and takes careful aim. In one quick, seamless motion, he arches forward, shifts his weight to his left foot, releases his hold of the shaft of the spear, extends his throwing arm forward, and flips the long-arm. He senses the flex of the spear's shaft as it springs from the thrower that has become an extension of his arm.

A bit off the mark, the spear penetrates the moose's haunch and the animal bellows in pain. Its cry is instantly cut short when the elder hunter's spear finds its true mark. The long legs crumple as the moose drops, then begins kicking. By the time the hunters reach their prey, it lies motionless in the shallow water.

—*In and around Pequawket Brook,*
*Madison, New Hampshire,*
*8,000 years ago*

ৎ৹   ৎ৹   ৎ৹   ৎ৹

A hunter uses an atlatl to throw a
spear at an elk or Wapiti.

The pebble-weighted fishnet and the implement now known as the *atlatl,*
which comes from the Aztec word for "spear-thrower," are tools that
symbolize the evolution of ancient peoples in the Northeast, subsistence
cultures that are known as the "old" or *Archaic* peoples. In what kind of
world did the long-arm hurl the spears that rent the thick hides of their
prey?

Small groups, probably made up of extended families, lived mostly
along lakeshores, at the mouths of rivers, and on riparian terraces. They
used these locations for homesites, campsites, and bases from which to
hunt, fish, and both prepare and cook their meals. Some far-ranging sites
were located in the hills and mountains near sources of quartz, rhyolite,
and other kinds of stone that made good raw material. These quarries
were visited by day or for short-term overnight stays in order to fashion
and repair tools and hunting equipment. Children, who came along on
these visits and were taught the secrets of fine stone work, made mini-
ature versions of the points, stone knives, and other tools being created
by their parents.

From about 9,000 to 7,000 years ago, as the climate grew warmer, the
forests of spruce and fir had retreated to the higher slopes and remnant
bogs. Pure stands of aspen were common, whose cottony, windblown
seeds made them the first trees to invade clearings created by fires and forest blowdowns. The ancient peoples of this time subsisted in an ecological
mosaic that included forests of white pine, oak, gray birch, and hemlock.[2]
Balsam fir was also found in cool uplands, and, in moist, rich soils,
maple, elm, ironwood, ash, and both white and yellow birches grew.

Maples and oaks both migrated from southwest of here during the early Holocene. Oak trees had few means of moving their substantial, meaty seeds, which often traveled no farther from the tree than the distance that hungry squirrels would scamper before burying their stash. Oaks may have had some help from the ubiquitous blue jays, which have a propensity for gathering the nuts in their throats and caching them up to a mile or more away from the source.

Seeds of maples and birches, too, could not travel as fast and as far as those of the aspen, but their whirligigs and fleur-de-lis fluttered down a good distance from the parent trees to continue the generation-by-generation march northward. Even though the seeds of beeches are too heavy to be carried by the wind, the pollen of this smooth-barked tree shows up in the layers of peat from this region that were laid down over 6,000 years ago when forests of hemlock, birch and beech covered large expanses. Since beech seeds are hardy, it is possible that some may have survived being carried long distances in the crops of passenger pigeons who dropped the seeds along their migration routes, complete with a coat of fertilizer.

Passenger pigeons were an important food for people during the spring and autumn hunt at this time. Families continued to live on the shores of lakes and major waterways, along the banks of rivers, high on river terraces, and into the uplands along perennial streams. These homesites were near an essential food—the fish that were seasonally abundant in great quantities: anadromous species such as shad, salmon, and alewife that migrate from the ocean to fresh water to spawn, as well as *catadromous* eels that live in freshwater lakes and "run," *dromos,* "down," *kata,* to the ocean to multiply.

One thousand years later, forests of yellow birch, beech, and sugar maple had come to dominate the north country, and hemlock was generally restricted to cooler, wetter slopes. Eventually, the changing land harbored a biodiversity even greater than that of today. It wasn't until about 5,000 years ago that the first hickories arrived in the Northeast from the Mississippi Valley, while chestnut didn't appear until around the birth of Christ.[3] These diverse forests were punctuated with openings frequented by deer, elk, and turkey. Rabbits, squirrels, birds, and many kinds of small game abounded. Over time, the Archaic peoples' diet grew to include a greater variety and abundance of smaller animals as well as foraged plant foods, including many berries, nuts, roots, and greens.

Pollen records preserved in layers of bog peat tell us that stands of black gum and forests harboring the tulip tree or yellow poplar once grew here in warm low-lying areas and along the coast. Pockets of habitat containing warm temperate species are still found in locales where a particularly mild climate has created a small haven. The near lack of

Some stone tools used 4 to 5,000 years ago: *(clockwise from top left)* gouge, adze, and hammerstone.

hemlock pollen in the layers of peat that date back 4,800 years tells us that this once-abundant, widespread tree had been virtually wiped out by disease in eastern North America, most likely by the hemlock looper.[4]

By the latter part of this period, as long as 5,000 years ago or more, New Hampshire's ancient peoples were paddling canoes down riverways, across lakes, through marshes, and out upon coastal waters.[5] In addition to foraging for plants and eating prodigious amounts of shellfish, hunters along the seacoast were so proficient at plying the waves of the open ocean in quest of food that they were able to catch a variety of marine animals, including swordfish, which was one of their staples.[6]

Rugged craftsmen used stone gouges, adzes, and celts to fashion whole logs into dugout canoes. Stone for making these tools was obtained or traded for other goods and often came from great distances: New Hampshire's Ossipee Mountains, Maine's Mount Kineo, and several locales in Massachusetts, including Attleboro, the Blue Hills, and the North Shore.[7]

Descendants of the earliest paleo-families to venture into New Hampshire, and who now ranged well up the northern valleys and beyond into the foothills and mountains, provided a significant quantity of the stone that was an essential raw material throughout this vast region. Quartz was found on the slopes of the White Mountains and hornfels in the Ossipee Range.[8] Trails wound their way through the passes to connect seasonal mountain sites and year-round homes in the foothills and valleys. Some sites on the mountain slopes were occupied as places to obtain raw stone for tools and to manufacture both crude and finished projectile points, knives, and other implements on site.

In this moderate environment rich in flora and fauna, the people of New Hampshire would likely have been a society of leisure similar to other Stone Age cultures, requiring as little as four or five hours of work each day to meet their survival needs.[9] Their lifestyle was so efficient that they were able to live within smaller home ranges than the earlier peoples of this region. Unlike the big-game hunters of previous times, these families consumed a greater diversity of foods. They relied increasingly on "smaller" animals such as beaver and muskrat, bear, moose, and deer. These animals did not gather in large herds like caribou, so hunters had to adapt new skills and more efficient weapons. The fish that teemed in rivers and bays made up a larger proportion of their diet. In this warmer climate where a variety of wild plants proliferated, many were gathered and eaten.

Imagine travelling back to that era and walking upstream along the banks of the Merrimack River. As long as 9,000 years ago, especially in spring and early summer, you would encounter families fishing at Amoskeag Falls and other falls and rapids where the river narrows made it easier to come home with a good day's catch.[10] Wolf-like family dogs are waiting patiently nearby for someone to throw them a morsel as the fish are gutted and cleaned.

Continuing upstream to where the river flows through and beyond what are now called Franklin and Bristol, you eventually come to Newfound Lake. Here, along the banks, a family is standing in water waist-deep, casting their net to enclose the mouth of a small cove. Wading back toward the shore, they are careful to hold the top of the net above the surface and to keep the small stone weights scraping along the bottom. When the net is hauled in, it teems with dozens of fish. Looking closely, you see bass, pike, perch, and pout or catfish.

As you follow the family back to their homesite, you are surprised that one of the children has a dead loon slung over her shoulder. One of the boys is carrying both a wood duck and a mallard in a similar fashion. You approach their home and pass a pile of refuse that contains some recognizable feathers, including those of the Canada goose and snow goose, turkey, grouse, and even a kind of gull. After the child hunters have plucked their prey, they use stone skinning knives and scrapers to cut the skin and meat and prepare it for use. With expert hands, they deftly wield stone-ground blades whose sharp edges cut easily through skin, muscle, and connective tissue. Once the children have portioned the meat, they hang the strips on drying racks near their lodge. In different seasons and environments, this process will be repeated and strips of the meat from many other prey will hang by their fire, and by countless fires throughout this region: trout, catfish, sucker, shad, eel, and turtle.

For several days you are engrossed in the fascinating lives of this family, intrigued by how they employ virtually every possible resource. Thick-furred bear hides are used as door flaps and for blankets on one of the colder nights spent sleeping inside lodges that are made of moose or deer hide stretched and sewn over bent saplings. Hats and vests are of the nearly waterproof furs of beaver, muskrat, and otter. Fingering a small pouch, part of a shirt, and other articles of clothing that come into contact with their skin, you are struck by the soft, smooth feel of brain-tanned deer hide. One of the breech-clout style articles of clothing has a long, tough belt made from the skin of a water snake. Tucked into a dark, disused space inside the edge of the lodge, you find some children's mittens that are perfectly fashioned from the soft, warm, chocolate-brown fur of mink. Although some of the moose-hide moccasins and skin bags are sewn together with tough sinew, many of the clothes are made with thin, soft deer-hide thongs. The fur of many animals, including that of fisher, marten, and fox, is sewn into other kinds of clothing.

Dried meat, fish, berries, nuts, roots, and greens are among the family's most important staples. Looking around the lodge, you notice that beechnuts, acorns, butternuts, blueberries, elderberries, and a variety of other plants are used. Every part, including flowers, roots, leaves, stems, and seeds, seems to have its own particular purpose as food or medicine, or as a raw material from which to fashion other things. Meat is sometimes eaten raw but mostly when broiled, smoked, or dried. It seems that every part of the animal is used. Antlers have been cleverly made into hooks, needles, awls, weapons, and even headgear. Bones are used for scrapers, rhythm instruments, and the playing pieces for some simple games. Hooves serve many purposes, from glue to rattles. Food, water, and personal effects are stored in simple, elegant containers made from wood, bark, and hide. Rugged bowls of stone stand next to simple, delicate bark baskets.

Spying some small items fashioned with seashells, you discern by the careful, reverent manner in which they are arranged that they are used for spiritual rites. Coming from the coast, the shells were obtained by trading with families that live as far away as present-day Boston. Some of the stone tools lying nearby come from the volcanic rocks of the Ossipee Mountains to the east.[11]

What kind of spiritual and social life did the Archaic peoples live? No matter how carefully we thread the archaeological needle and interpret the physical signs, it is a challenge to understand families and cultures from the vantage point of this vast temporal distance. One way to glimpse the ancient world is to use existing and recently extant Stone Age peoples as windows to the past.

For millions of years before the dawn of agriculture throughout the world, people relied completely and intimately on their natural surroundings for every aspect of life. If enough stone and bone, bark and wood, skin, flesh, and water was available to support a family or group of families, they would remain in that place. In order to make sure that competition for the most basic needs was at a minimum, families dispersed over wide areas. Whenever a group of families began to grow so large that they might outstrip the land's ability to sustain them, they would split into two smaller groups and move apart. This fluid way of life meant that each group was small enough to live within the limitations of the surrounding land. It also lessened the social strains that come with crowding and competition.

Since the essentials of life were plentiful and available to everyone, there was little incentive to stockpile, trade, or hoard goods. If an *affluent* community is one that supplies everyone's material needs equally, then the peoples of New Hampshire's Warming Time in all probability were truly affluent.[12] Even though the hunter-gatherers of the past were at the mercy of the vicissitudes of nature, the needs of each family group would have been met.

Many existing pre-agricultural, hunter-gathering cultures are so successful at getting food and meeting their other needs that they are societies of leisure, virtually at a loss for how to use their time. Among the Australian Aborigines in Arnhem Land and the Dobe section of the !Kung Bushmen of Botswana, each person works an average of four to five hours per day at most to meet their basic needs.[13] Most of their time is employed sleeping, relaxing, resting, and socializing. These peoples choose to live with the fewest possessions possible, a life that is considered a virtue, a mark of freedom. Following this tenet, the strongest leaders are those who have the fewest belongings, who are unburdened by wealth, and who are truly free to put the best interests of the family group and community first.

The climate of the proto–New Hampshire region, however, has never been like that of Australia or Botswana. Peoples here have always experienced seasonal extremes and shortages of food. In those times when the surroundings could no longer meet the needs of a family, they would simply move to a new area. Mobility was crucial—tantamount to survival.

Too many possessions were an unnecessary and at times life-threatening impediment. Among many existing Stone Age peoples, it remains impractical and undesirable to be burdened by physical possessions and attachments beyond the necessities of life. Many acts that seem heartless when viewed through our cultural lens, such as killing or abandoning a newborn with birth defects and leaving the aged to fend for themselves, were designed to reduce the burdens on a family group and to enable them to pick up and move as quickly as possible, ensuring that the family would survive. The common act of practicing sexual restraint and even abstinence when a mother was nursing was a means to this same end.[14] As traditional Stone Age family groups and societies made use of the available resources, they continued to grow, develop, and co-evolve with their surroundings, responding to changes in the environment.

ༀ  ༀ  ༀ  ༀ

*The young woman touches her mother's shoulder and gives a parting glance, then follows her father down toward the bank of the river; he looks back with satisfaction at her willowy frame fluid along the familiar trail. He is proud of his daughter and marvels at how her hunting skills have developed over the past two seasons.*

*He had always pictured his son at his side during the hunt: The boy was once equally alive and vibrant. They did not usually seek out the great cats, but one had attacked, killed, and eaten a child from a nearby family. Something was not right with this particular "silent walker." Its mind was crooked and it had developed a taste for human flesh, so a group had set out to stalk and kill it. They could not have known, but should have anticipated after they had wounded their dangerous prey many moons ago, that the limping mountain lion, its haunches still searing with pain, would circle around behind them and stalk the smallest, most vulnerable hunter at the end of the column. At the instant his son's cry reached his ears, the hunter had known it was already too late.*

*But when father and daughter reach the marsh on this peaceful evening, the sun is setting behind the downslope of the mountain named "stands alone" that towers above the land to the west. The warm glow of the late-day sun paints the horizon with fire, as if the forests to the west were bursting into flame.*

*The two hunters motion their dog to sit beside them and give it the sign for quiet. It sits obediently while they stroke its thick, coarse fur. As he looks over at his daughter before him, crouched there at the edge of the cattails, her reflection mingling with the gentle arches of marsh grasses upon the still evening waters, he can see the girl's mother in her hair and in her eyes. He is grateful for her prowess and for the eagerness that she shows on their forays to find game for the family.*

*They each untie a long cord from around their waists and lay it over the palm of their throwing hand. A disk-shaped stone with a small rounded stem on top for attachment is lashed to both ends of the long pieces of sinew. In anticipation, the hunters hold the cords loosely while causing the ends to sway gently, presaging the moment they will wind up and throw.*

*When they both nod the mutual signal that they are ready, the young huntress points the dog toward the edge of a thick growth of cattails that surrounds a large bay and pats it firmly on the rump. Quietly, with all the stealth it can muster, the dog creeps forward and disappears amid the thick stems. A few moments later, the quacks of several large ducks rend the stillness as the dark feathers of fowl explode from the water's surface.*

*Standing now, with arms cocked and ready, the hunters let their bolas fly as soon as they see the ducks rise above the cattails. Aiming just enough in front of their prey, they sling the weighted cords with one arching motion of their arms. Turning end over end, one of the cords finds its mark and wraps around the neck of a duck, which fights to continue flying as it gags and struggles to carry the extra weight. While its companions rise and veer off over the forest on the other bank of the river, the one doomed fowl arches lower and sinks until it lands, flopping on the surface at the far end of the bay.*

*In an instant, the dog, which had been running along the riverbank following the aerial path of the wounded duck, launches from the bank, splashes down, and swims out to retrieve the bird. By the time the hunters have run up the bank parallel to where the duck floundered, the dog is loping toward them, tail wagging, carrying the prize in his mouth.*

*He drops the dead bird at their feet. The girl pets and praises him, then pulls a piece of dried meat from her bag and holds it in an outstretched hand. The dog gently snaps up its reward and begins to chew. As she watches the dog gnawing its treat, the young woman begins to imagine the rich smell of duck meat upon the cooking fire when they arrive back home, drops of its aromatic grease falling onto the coals and bursting into flame.*

—At the mouth of the Sugar River,
Claremont, New Hampshire,
5,500 years ago

℘ ℘ ℘ ℘

During the 5,000 years of New Hampshire history that began with the Warming Time nine millenniums ago, people continued to add to the

Hunting waterfowl with bolas stones.

existing settlements throughout the region as they migrated up the waterways and landforms that oriented them generally north to south—the
valleys of the Saco and Piscataqua Rivers, the Connecticut and Merrimack rivers and their tributaries, including the Winnipesaukee. Many
homesites in these valleys, which were carefully chosen to be close to food
and water, were located on the rich, flat, well-drained soils of river terraces and floodplains. Most sites were found less than 60 feet above the
water level and within about 300 feet of the water's edge. Brooks, wetlands, rapids, and areas below waterfalls within about one-third of a mile
from major waterways were preferred.[15]

Some locations offered ideal sites with abundant food, water, and shelter under the umbrella of a mild climate. Wild plant foods, fish, and game
were plentiful at the mouth of Paugus Bay along the shore of Lake Winnipesaukee. Families lived at the site of present-day Weirs Beach starting
9,600 years ago, through the first 2,500 years of the Warming Time, and
again near the end of this period nearly four millenniums ago. They left
behind a well-documented record of their lives, including the locations of
lodges and hearths and rich layers of stone points, chippers, scrapers,
hammerstones, whetstones, a carved stone effigy, and even the charred remains of ancient seeds from plants that rooted along these shores and
reached for the sun more than 7,000 years ago.[16]

Ten miles south in Lochmere, on the west bank of the Winnipesaukee
River between Lake Winnisquam and Silver Lake, at an ideal site atop
well-drained sandy loam, some of New Hampshire's early families lived

a subsistence life based on hunting and fishing.[17] Beginning about 6,000 years ago and continuing down through the millenniums, families and travelers frequented this and other sites in the region. They feasted on the prolific runs of salmon and shad in late spring and eel in the late summer and early autumn. The deep, cold waters of the Winnisquam to the north were home to a bountiful supply of trout, pickerel, and bass. Silver Lake's warmer waters also harbored pickerel and bass as well as perch. Four thousand years ago, these astute hunters and fishermen were using the atlatl to take deer and and other game in the nearby uplands. Later, with great skill, they whirred the cords of bolas above their heads and let fly the deadly stones to bring down the waterfowl fleeing above the marshes.

The people of Lochmere and of the dozen or so sites found along the Winnipesaukee River corridor were rarely alone. They likely exchanged visits with families at another site that was active at this time on Clark's Island in Silver Lake. In time, an interconnected chain of sites formed along the riverbanks, linked with other settlements and seasonal sites along the Winnipesaukee River a few miles south where it flows out of Silver Lake, then east through Tilton and Franklin on its way to the Merrimack River.

It is likely that some families lived in this region year-round while others came in season to partake of the abundant fish. This corridor between the lakes became a major route of travel between the Lakes Region and the Merrimack Valley. Through this region passed stone for trade that was important raw material for fashioning weapons and tools: volcanic rhyolite from the hills and mountains to the west and volcanic stones and hornfels from the Ossipee Mountains and other hillsides in the east.

As families sought out their most basic needs, this region became a focal point for the evolution of the people of New Hampshire's interior; fueled by a mutual hunger for fish and a need for stone. Here the shape of a budding culture was determined by the ancient paths of rivers and the routes of migratory fishes. Stones that were formed by geologic events of great age—the upwelling of White Mountain magma and the volcanism that created the Ossipee Mountains nearly 200 million years ago—were now a dynamic force molding the very movements, the shape of the future for the people who walked the land. In this way, the sites in the interior corridor of rivers, lakes, and islands grew to become one of New Hampshire's most important gathering places during the Archaic period and in later times for the sharing of society, culture, technology, and spirit.

Other ancient sites reach southward to near Amoskeag Falls along the Merrimack River in the vicinity of current-day Manchester and as far south and east as the drainage basin of the Little River in Plaistow and

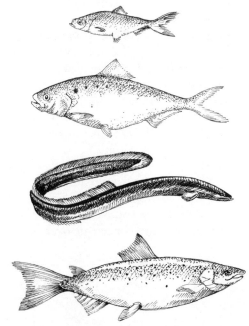

Alewife, shad, eel, and salmon *(top to bottom)* have attracted people to Amoskeag Falls for more than 8,000 years.

Kingston, New Hampshire—a waterway that flows into the lower Merrimack in Haverhill, Massachusetts. Six sites have been discovered on the sands and gravels of the glacial outwash in the Little River area that date back as far as 6,000 years.[18]

The vicinity of Amoskeag Falls has been inhabited throughout most of the last 8,000 years and, in particular, was heavily populated from 6,000 to 2,500 years ago.[19] Further north along the Merrimack River, located above and below Concord, two more recent sites were first used for fishing just before the end of the Archaic more than 3,000 years ago: Sewall's Falls south of Penacook and Garvin's Falls downstream from Bow Junction. The rich alluvial sites along the banks of the Merrimack River nearby would one day become the soil to grow the seeds of the next great revolution in the lives of the people of New Hampshire's interior.

Many sites that date back to the Warming Time have also been found in the watershed of the Connecticut River. These are not as abundant as those of the Merrimack Valley, perhaps because the Connecticut does not link up to a vast inland system of lakes and interconnecting rivers or, more likely, because many are yet to be discovered. Beginning 11,000 years ago and continuing until 7,400 years ago, families lived along the banks of the

Ashuelot River in West Swanzey at the site that was brought to life in chapter 4. A few thousand years later, another group of families lived at the edge of Ash Swamp Brook along the border of Keene and Swanzey.[20] Ancient peoples also lived on a sandy knoll along the banks of California Brook in Swanzey during the middle to late millenniums of the Warming Time. Two more sites have been found in the town of Winchester: one along the shore of Forest Lake and the other on the banks of the Ashuelot River that was occupied more than 3,000 years ago. Just east of Winchester on the shore of Meadow Pond in Fitzwilliam are more remains of the period that likely go back more than four thousand years.[21]

Well to the north and west is the settlement at the mouth of the Sugar River in Claremont that was described earlier in this chapter. Follow the Sugar River to its source in Lake Sunapee, then travel to the north shore, and you will come to another inveterate site in George's Mills. This rich lakeside locale has been occupied nearly continuously for over 9,000 years.[22]

Families lived along the Connecticut River by the Horse Meadow Oxbow in North Haverhill more than 6,000 years ago. *Photo by Michael J. Caduto.*

Move farther north to one of the most beautiful, expansive places in the Connecticut River valley, and you come to the Horse Meadow Oxbow above the town of North Haverhill, in a part of the Connecticut

River watershed that is also known as the Lower Coos. Remains of settlements here tell a story of occupation starting more than 6,000 years ago.

Near the very tip of the arrowhead-shaped entity that makes up the present-day New Hampshire, in the northern reaches of the First Connecticut Lake in Pittsburg, are some remains that date back as far as 5,000 to 6,000 years ago. Along this lakeshore, at the level that is now submerged when this dam-controlled lake is at high water, were found the remnants of an ancient site as scant as this rugged country is spartan: a single, impressive, nearly 6-inch-long by 2-inch-wide stemmed spearpoint from the middle of the Warming Time.[23] Two other ancient sites have been found in this region whose exact time of activity is unknown. One is located in Berlin at 1,500 feet above sea level near York Pond in the foothills of the Pilot Range of the White Mountains, in the watershed of the Upper Ammonoosuc River. The other site is at the Nash Bog Pond along a mountain pass in Stratford, at 1,700 feet, near the source of Nash Stream.

ϾΘ　　ϾΘ　　ϾΘ　　ϾΘ

*The old woman looks down as she stops the rhythmic grinding of the pestle in her hands. The cooked, dried acorns in the hollow of her mortar stone have already taken on the texture of fine meal. Leaf shadows dance across her face as the wind sways the branches of the hickory above where she kneels. She tilts her head toward the sky and sees the lacy crown of a nearby cherry tree silhouetted against the deep blue of summer. Tousled from this sudden, pungent breeze off the marsh, she picks up the comb she has fashioned from a piece of the long jaw of a swordfish and smooths her graying black hair. Still, she is glad for the wind as it drives away a small swarm of biting gnats.*

*She turns to her two grandchildren, who are fighting over who gets to eat the last mussel that is boiling in a hide pot on the cooking fire. "Stop!" cries the old woman. "If you are going to fight, no one will eat the mussel. Bring the shells to the shell pile and place them there, then each of you take a mussel and bring it back to the rocks where we gathered them. Give them back to the mussels and offer thanks for the food they gave you."*

*"Yes, grandmother," they say sheepishly. When the children reach the shell pile, which is interspersed with the remains of sea urchins, they place the remains of the mussels upon it. Nearby, they notice the pit in which the bones of the many animals they have eaten that winter and spring have been placed: bones of many a muskrat and deer, some from the black bear and a few from the bobcat, elk, porpoise, and seal. They see the bones of a cod, some marsh turtles, and the jaw of "many-teeth," the shark. Bones of "crab*

*eater," the gull, lay side-by-side with those of the geese, "those who fly
together." There are many bones and feathers from ducks, shore birds, and
other sea birds that the children have not yet learned to recognize. Off to
the side, placed neatly in the hollow of an old tree trunk, is the complete
skeleton of the "large-beaked one," the Great Auk.*

*The children turn and walk toward the rocky shore. "We have to go
around this place," the young girl admonishes her brother as they approach
the family burial ground. As they quietly and gently step around the outside
edge of that place the girl asks, "Do you remember when Grandfather died?"*

*"I remember the seal skin he was buried in. It was painted with the red
clay to protect his spirit on the long journey to the next world."*

*"Yes," she says, "and we gave him his favorite spear so that he could
hunt when he arrived."*

*They both stand in silence at the edge of the burial ground, staring at the
plot of ground they are discussing, when a hollow "thump, thump" rings up
from the shore where their father is working.*

*Hurrying down to the rocks where they harvested the mussels, the two
children leave their gifts and give thanks. Then they run over to where their
father is working. The familiar, comforting sound of his gouge drumming
against an enormous white pine log mixes with the aromatic scent of the
burning wood. For a time, before he notices their arrival, the children stand
behind their father and watch him work. They can see by the length of this
log, which is three times their father's height, that this canoe is meant for the
men of several families to paddle out beyond their sheltered cove into the
deep, rough waters in search of swordfish, cod, skates, sharks, seals,
porpoises, and perhaps even the "grandmother porpoise that sings."*

*Away from where he is working, their father has spread glowing coals
from the fire in a shallow groove that runs along the top of the log. Heavy
smoke rises from the wood as the coals burn into the upper layer. On the
near end, where the top has already burnt, the craftsman is wielding a fist-
sized beach cobble for a hammerstone to strike the end of a stone gouge.
Flakes of charcoal and burnt wood fly up. As their father changes the angle
of his tool and shifts his line of sight accordingly, he notices the children,
stands to greet them, and smiles.*

*"Father," says the boy, "the water is calm and the sky is clear. It would be
a good day to go fishing."*

*The man looks up at the sky and studies it as if he is noticing the fine day
for the first time. As he does this, his son and daughter glance around at the
exciting collection of tools and weapons neatly arrayed on the site: fishing
spears with rough quartz points; well-made nets with stone sinkers tied to
one edge that have been carefully grooved and notched, bola cords hanging
from the low branch of a tree with their ends weighted by small stones tied*

*on by a carved neck of small protruding stems, a spear with a long shaft and
a point similar to the fishing spear but larger, a "long-arm" with which to
throw the spear leaning against the trunk of a tree with its crescent-shaped
weights attached, and the adze that their father used to fell the tree that he is
now carving.*

*"Yes," their father finally replies, "the waves will be small and the fishing
good. While we are gone, the coals can burn into the log."*

*He places the hammerstone and gouge on an old stump, then walks
downhill toward the shore while the children trail behind. There he
uncovers a cache of several spears for landing fish from the canoe, sharp
bone knives as long as his hand for gutting the fish, and handlines fitted
with curved bone hooks. He picks up some of the heavier fishing gear and
motions the children to gather the rest.*

*When they reach the tidal river where their canoe is tied off to some
bushes that contain thorns and sweet-scented flowers, their father wades
into the channel with a spear and begins to stalk some of the palm-sized,
blue-shelled crabs that frequent that place. He spears several crabs and
wraps them in a skin pouch, then they all load the canoe with this fresh bait
and the fishing gear.*

*"Get in," he says as the children look on impatiently. They scramble
aboard and are careful to walk only down the middle of the tipsy, hollowed
log. The girl takes a paddle and sits up front while her younger brother sits
in the bottom, mid-beam. Finally, with one strong fluid motion, their father
pushes the prow down the channel toward the harbor and leaps into the
back of the canoe. As their paddles silently ply the smooth surface, drops of
water drip from the tips each time they raise them and push them forward
for another bite into the brackish river. The familiar and faintly unpleasant
smell of rotting seaweed stranded above the high tide line rises to meet them
and heightens the anticipation of the adventure to come.*

*—The shores of Browns River and Hampton Harbor,*
*Seabrook, New Hampshire,*
*3,500 years ago*

ᙦ     ᙦ     ᙦ     ᙦ

New Hampshire's peoples have lived on and near her coast since antiquity. More than sixty sites have been discovered here in coastal habitats,
dating back nearly 9,000 years.[24] In addition to living along the Atlantic
shore, families who settled in the drainage basins of rivers near the coast
usually located their homes next to or near streams and rivers, wetlands
and lakes. Rivers were provident, particularly near coastal estuaries.

These nutrient-rich wetlands where fresh and salt water mingle in the tidal flow, and the ecologically diverse uplands that surround them, are home to a variety of plants and animals used by people.

One ancient site was discovered in the upper coastal region at Wadleigh Falls Island along the Lamprey River where it passes through what is now the town of Lee. This meandering waterway eventually flows past Newmarket and into the Great Bay, an extensive estuary near Durham that drains into the Piscataqua River and out to sea through Portsmouth Harbor. Beginning 8,600 years ago and for about 2,000 years thereafter, people lived continuously at Wadleigh Falls. The site was then occupied intermittently until 1,000 years ago.[25] This river community thrived in a rich environment; the people ate a variety of plant foods, many kinds of fish, numerous small mammals, and even turtles. They left behind a story buried in the soil, recorded in the remains of ancient hearths, fire pits, and lodge post holes as well as remnants of bone, projectile points, other stone tools, and pits that were used for storage and refuse.

Well to the south and east of Wadleigh Falls, 4,000 years ago, some families built their homes in a forested site that is now found on the southwest bank of Browns River, which flows between Seabrook and Hampton Falls. This was the very end of the Warming Time, when meltwater from the polar ice caps was still swelling the seas. These resilient peoples lived here for 500 years, until the area was finally engulfed by the ever-rising tides. The Seabrook salt marsh has been developing atop the old homesites ever since. Covered by waterlogged sediments for thousands of years, the ends of some of the ancient wooden posts that held up these lodges that once bustled with life have been preserved, buried under 5 feet of rich marsh soil.[26] Although the remnants of the Seabrook settlement now become exposed during low tide, many other ancient homesites along the seacoast and lakeshores are constantly underwater.

Speaking to us from the Archaic site beneath the Seabrook marsh are the oldest remains of a great auk ever discovered in New Hampshire. This venerable phoenix is nearly four thousand years old.[27] Were the Seabrook hunters capable of imagining that in several thousand years someone would kill an auk—the last of its kind—and drive the species into the abyss?

As late Archaic peoples hunted, fished, gathered plant foods, and chiseled and ground raw stone into weapons and tools, their lives in turn were sculpted by the plants and animals, the soil and rocks. Their fate dangled at the end of a line wielded by the inescapable hand of nature; a future caught up in a sweeping net of elements and events particular to that time and place. Forced to leave their homes by the rising waters, the Seabrook families rode one of the last waves out of this ocean of time.

Exactly where these ancient peoples resettled cannot be known, but they lived at the cusp of historic change. The Warming Time drew to an end about 4,000 years ago, when the mean temperature began to drop, yearly rainfall increased, and weather patterns became more erratic. This shift in the cycles of the seasons was followed by a revolution borne in the germ of a seed. It was the dawn of an era when the balance was tipped and humankind joined nature as a force that co-determined the fate of the world.

Great Auk.

# 6. A Land of Plenty

Tribal land was divided into family hunting territories with
definite boundaries. The proprietors of each territory knew
intimately the plant and animal inventory therein, harvested
the supply carefully with rituals of atonement and
thanksgiving, and rotated their activities in such a way as to
conserve the supply."

—Gordon M. Day, 1953

ᥫᩣ    ᥫᩣ    ᥫᩣ    ᥫᩣ

*"This is a good place to camp," says one of the travellers. "We have a
clear view up and down the river."*

*The four young men stand quietly as they scan the riverbank in both
directions. They appear to be related, with the same round head, broad
nose, and strong muscular build. Satisfied, they take off the deer-hide bags
that hang from straps slung over their shoulders and put them down near a
small ring of firestones that someone has built on the upper terrace about 30
feet above the river.*

*The oldest of the young men, who stands about 5 feet, 6 inches tall,
bends over the fire ring and holds his palm over the ashes. He wears a shirt
woven from milkweed fibers and adorned with a flowing, floral design that
is painted with colors obtained from the pigments of roots, flowers, and
berries. He is the only one in the group wearing a shell necklace. A small
bag woven from Indian hemp hangs from his neck, tied with square knots
to a cord spun of fibers from the inner bark of a basswood tree. Inside this
medicine bag are several small bundles of healing plants that are bound with
strands of bark from the slippery elm and symbols of his animal emblem:
some claws and a small wooden carving of a black bear.*

*"It is still warm," he tells the others. "Someone camped here last night."*

*The traveller places several pieces of thin birchbark atop the warm ashes, then completes the fire set with succeeding layers of twigs and larger sticks. He rearranges the firestones into a neat circle, twisting each one and pushing it down into the dark-brown, sandy loam. He then unties a clamshell from his waistband and removes the sinew that binds the two halves. Reaching inside the shell, he removes a clump of peat in which a small ember still smolders. Carefully, he places the peat under the birchbark and blows gently into the mass. After several lengthy puffs, smoke begins to rise from the peat. With a bit more encouragement, the nascent fire bursts into a small flame that quickly spreads to the birchbark.*

"I have a bit of meat for everyone" *says another man as he scrambles up from the riverbank with a sizeable painted turtle in each hand. He takes the turtles off to the edge of the forest where he speaks kindly to each, asking permission for the sacrifice as he prepares to kill them for the meal.*

"Here are some acorns from the oak that has leaves with round fingers," *says a third, who then sits down near a flat rock and uses a quartz cobble to crack and remove the shells.*

*As the men work, they chew on slices of dried venison from the provisions they brought for the journey.*

*The fourth member of the group pulls a heavy pot from his pack. The clay is thick, coarse, and dark. A cord-like pattern that is imbedded in the pot runs from the rounded lip of the rim, along its rotund belly, and down to the pointed bottom. A small ring of triangles, with their points up, adorns the upper rim just below the mouth of the pot.*

*This man scrambles down the bank, fills the pot with water, and pours the entire contents back into the river.* "Thank you Grandmother," *he says to the river.* "Thank you for carrying us upon your back to this place and for this water that we now take." *He fills the pot again. As he climbs back up the riverbank, he slips and nearly tumbles on some of the acorns and slick reddish leaves that litter the ground. The familiar, pungent scent of decay rises up.*

*By the time he gets back to camp, the fire is going strong and some coals have begun to glow from the hearth. Moving quickly and carefully, he places the pot at the edge of the fire and turns it back and forth a few times until the point nestles into the coals. Once the water begins to boil, he places the shelled acorns into the pot. After a time, the water turns brown with tannin. Using some deerskin gloves that he made for use around the fire, he lifts the pot from the hearth. He pours out this water and brings fresh water from the river to refill the pot. After repeating this process, he adds the turtle meat to the acorns and leaves it to boil.*

"Look, over there, another camp," *someone exclaims as he points upriver to the north and west.*

"Go ahead," *says one of the men.* "I'll stay here and watch the pot."

*Three of the young men reach excitedly into their packs and pull out some fine, palm-sized pieces of volcanic stone that they brought back from the coastal region to the south where they spent a full turn of the moon. They hike upriver toward the distant campfire.*

*Just as the turtle and acorn dinner is about ready to eat, the three traders appear back in camp. Each holds forth a piece of dark gray chert; the result of some hard-won haggling. "Look at these fine pieces of point stone!" one exclaims as they hold their prizes out toward the one tending the fire.*

*"It was a good trade," he agrees.*

*While they are eating, the three traders take turns telling of how they outwitted the men in the other camp to get the better end of each trade. Although a few of the young men habitually chew their food so as to avoid the space where they have lost a tooth to a gum infection in the past, caries cannot be found among any of their teeth.*

*After they are done eating, all four travellers take the bones that are left from their meal and walk down to the riverbank. The one who caught the turtles shows the others where they were found. The four young men kneel down there, place the bones back in the water, and thank the turtles for their sacrifice and gift of life.*

*For the rest of the night, and anticipating more trades to come in the morning, this small party hones the stone tools and points they carry in their packs, using careful pressure to remove small flakes and create the best possible edges. Some of the projectile points are a bit less than 2 inches long and are notched along the bottom for tying to a spear shaft. Other points, which are nearly 2 ½ inches long, are rounded at the base where they narrow down to a neck that leads to a flared, fishtail-shaped end for attachment. An impressive array of other tools that are ground and flaked from slate and greenstone lie on the ground in the midst of the group, including a chisel, scraper, digging tool, and adze. A portable hammer made of a hard quartzite sits next to a large granite boulder that has a hollow on top where it is used for grinding and, sometimes, as an anvil. One of the men is wearing an elegant pendant—a flat, egg-shaped piece of slate that has been chipped into shape and ground to a fine edge, and that is small enough to cradle in the palm.*

*Every so often, someone stops working, looks across the river to the northwest, and admires the striking late day sky ablaze with a fire that backlights the orange leaves of a maple tree whose branches overhang the bank.*

—Near the mouth of the Nashua River,
3,000 years ago

ᘓᖆ   ᘓᖆ   ᘓᖆ   ᘓᖆ

For 8,000 years, a river has cut a channel to the north, flowing from its source in the upper corner of east-central Massachusetts. *Nansawi,* "between," carried countless generations of people on its back as they traveled northwest from the coastal region, then headed north and east into the Merrimack Valley of New Hampshire. During this great expanse of time, traders from many Native cultures have moved up and down the contrary Nashua River between the ocean and the interior.[1]

Around the time that *Nansawi* reached half its present age, the climate began to cool, a trend that would continue for the next 3,300 years.[2] It was 14,000 years ago, however, in the depths of the glacial meltwater that covered vast regions of this land, that the raw material for a technological revolution was created. Lakes that were dammed by glacial deposits covered much of the Connecticut River valley as well as the expansive interior regions surrounding the rivers that now bear the names of Winnipesaukee, Merrimack, and Contoocook. Glacial Lake Ashuelot covered the entire Keene Valley. Year after year, the layers of extremely fine sediments settled out of the still waters on the bottoms of glacial lakes, composed of the smallest particles washed into the lake by streams and rivers as well as the microscopic remains of the shells of countless diatoms made almost entirely of silica.

The first use of this sedimentary handiwork of the glacial waters began more than 10,000 years later, soon after the Warming Time ended, when these ancient lake beds were braided by streams and rivers that had cut down into the clays of antiquity and exposed them to the eyes of New Hampshire's original peoples. They called themselves *Alnôbak,* simply, "the People." This is how they distinguished themselves from others, from neighboring cultures, from the giants and monsters, from those individuals who dwelled in the land of the spirits, and from the *Manôgemasak,* the Little People who lived in the rivers and lakes.

In the lapping flames and glowing coals whose heat and light reflected off the warm skin of their venerable hands, the legacy of clay left by the frigid glacial waters was fashioned into the vessels that wrought the first of many changes that were to sweep this land. Well before the twang of a bow cord sent an arrow forth to find its mark, and earlier still than the first seeds of maize sprouted from this soil, the People began gathering clay, forming it into vessels, and firing the first of New Hampshire's pottery. This innovation began the most recent era in the history of New Hampshire's original peoples, a time that is often called the *Woodland* period.

Myriad ways of cooking and storing food had been employed even before the advent of pottery. Meals were boiled by placing small stones to heat in the coals of the cooking fire and then dropping the hot stones into

Among the first clay pots
fashioned by the Alnôbak,
3,000 years ago.

a wooden trough or stone bowl filled with water. This time-consuming method of preparing meals required hard work and tremendous patience. Stone bowls made of steatite were placed directly on the fire for cooking, but making these vessels called for long, dedicated periods of labor and they were too heavy to move between sites. Buckets made of hide or bark were easy to make and, when filled with water, could be placed directly on a small fire for cooking in a pinch. But high flames burned away any material that stood above the water line, so the life of these vessels was brief. Clay bowls were simply more practical and long-lived than those made of other materials, such as the wood, birch bark, and soapstone or steatite used by the peoples of the southern Connecticut River valley near Hinsdale at the end of the Warming Time.[3]

Pottery was better than all of the best attributes of early vessels combined. Clay was easy to find and gather. Substantial deposits are found in many areas, including Concord, Bow, Pembroke, and Hooksett. Once clay had been formed and fired, the vessel could be used over and over again and it was sufficiently lightweight to be portable. Soft, pliable, and pleasant to work with, it was the perfect substance for the work of human hands; an ideal medium on which the imagination could make its mark.

Clay from the riverbank was gathered, the River and the Creator were thanked, and an offering of a small gift was left in gratitude. Before it was molded, the clay was mixed or tempered with the small particles of mica and quartz that are frequently found in river gravels. Other kinds of fine grit were also used for tempering, including burned feldspar and granite particles from fire-cracked hearth stones as well as shell fragments from along the coast. Although pots were sometimes made by molding a depression in a large ball of clay, the most common technique was to build up the walls with layered, snake-like coils. The sides were then smoothed with the fingers or by using a paddle-like instrument made from wood or bone to form a consistent surface about one-third of an inch thick. Before they were fired, many pots were adorned by scoring the outer surface with simple, elegant designs: impressions of scallop shells, cordage, and even fingernail crescents. Some pots were decorated with serrations around the edge of the rim or with short vertical and diagonal etchings bordered by horizontal lines that encircle these just below the mouth of the vessel.[4]

As time passed, the Alnôbak created pottery of many different designs. Remnants of these vessels have been found in abundance at New Hampshire's ancient fishing grounds, such as Sewall's Falls and Garvin's Falls along the Merrimack River in Concord and Bow. The remains of more than 750 individual vessels have been discovered farther to the south, a venerable fishing place along the Merrimack River above Amoskeag Falls in Manchester. This site has been used for much of the past 10,000 years and the Merrimack Valley's first pottery was created here more than 3,300 years ago.[5]

Expertise in making and decorating pottery was not the only knowledge growing with each new generation. The number and diversity of plants encouraged in the wild garden around homesites and campsites was increasing. Many of these plants grew in the floodplains and were frequently encountered on forays in search of clay for making pottery. When a desirable plant for food, medicine, or material was found, these early gardeners-of-the-wild often weeded around it to reduce competition for sunlight and soil nutrients from neighboring plants. During times of drought, they may have watered certain patches of wild plants to help them survive, and, perchance, even picked seeds as they matured and spread them around to enlarge the stand.

Groundnut was one of these important staples. If you have ever spent time poking along a riverbank on foot, or meandering by the shoreline in a canoe, the delicate pea-like leaves of groundnut have presented themselves, and you may have whiffed the sweet scent of the beautiful purple flowers that are tinged with brown. Often, after a heavy rain or the spring thaw when the rivers have run high and eroded their banks, the large cord-like roots become exposed, bearing strings of groundnut tubers the size of a husked butternut. Nearby, in the rich dark soil, you may discover a lush patch of wild leeks that can be harvested for the tasty, tender scallion-like roots with their intense onion flavor.

These are just two of the edible and medicinal plants that the People both picked and propagated around their homesites. Hemlock bark was boiled to make a medicinal tea used for treating respiratory ailments.

The leaves and tubers of groundnut. *Photo by Michael J. Caduto.*

This denizen of cool, moist slopes, which had been wiped out by disease 4,800 years ago, was once again abundant in many forests following an absence of nearly two thousand years; its seeds borne upon the wind from distant, surviving populations.[6]

As time went on, the plants that were cultivated and encouraged around home grew to include nut-bearing trees and shrubs. Sometimes the natural gardeners of the forest were invited to help. When they moved to a new homesite, the People placed piles of acorns, butternuts, chestnuts, hazelnuts, or other favorite foods of people and squirrels alike around the lodges. Squirrels soon discovered this largess and buried the nuts in secret caches throughout the area. Those stores that were forgotten became the seeds of orchard-like groves of "wild" nuts that surrounded many homesites.

ლຄ    ლຄ    ლຄ    ლຄ

"*This is a good year for* mkwamagw. *I have never seen so many leaping the falls.*"

*A fisherman stands* namaskik, *"at fish land" on the bank of the "deep
water,"* molôdemak, *where the runs of shad, alewife, and salmon or "red
fish,"* mkwamagw, *have begun. The nearly full orb of the moon that is just
touching the horizon casts its cold light on the small, white petals of
shadbush blooms. He and the others who line the falls and ledges, who
wade out into the shallows of the river channel, who fish the narrows and
eddies, seem as abundant as the prey that struggle against the current to
reach their spawning grounds. Many are scooping fish from the rushing
waters with dip nets hung from bent, bow-shaped rims attached to long
handles. Others wield clubs, stone-tipped spears, and leisters—fishing spears
with two flexible, gripping prongs on the end and a hard, sharp, penetrating
point in between. Below the falls, in one of the small bays, a family sweeps a
purse of exhausted fish from the still waters where they have stopped to rest.
Like the strands of the dip nets, the mesh of their seine is woven of fibers
peeled from the inner bark of spruce and elm and twisted into cord.*

*Throughout the day, fish that are freshly killed, and many that are still
alive, flapping, line both banks of the river. Women, children, and elders use
stone knives to gut the fish. They rinse the filets in the shallows and lay them
out in the sun to dry. The scent of death, entrails, and scales wafts over the
shore where others are tying the filets onto ropes.*

*Later, in the long shadows, the dark water seems to deepen and the arms
of trees reach across dusky banks. Strings of fish are carried back to the
village and hung from the drying racks. Some strings contain ten or fifteen
smaller fish while others hold the filets from a few large* mkwamagw *that
weighed close to twenty pounds when pulled from the water. After cooking
a delicious stew of fish, wild spring greens, and groundnuts, all boiled in
pots stamped with distinctive geometric designs around the rim, the families
begin to sing and tell stories. When the fishing season is over and large
stores of dried filets line the walls of the* Alnigamigw, *the "wigwam," the
families will gather together to dance and feast, to celebrate their bounty,
and to thank the fish and the Creator.*

*After eating, some of the fishermen grab their bows and arrows and
several small skin bags, then they light their torches and walk out into the
darkness, eagerly looking forward to* wassawôgan, *"fishing with a torch
light." When they reach the riverbank, they stand the torches up by pushing
the sharpened handles into the ground. Each one takes the bones that
remain from their family's meal out of a skin bag and places them into the
water. "Thank you for your gift of food," says one. "I return these bones to
you and your children."*

*Afterward, each pair of fishermen pulls a canoe from the bushes and slips
it into the deep water above the falls. They place the paddles and bows
quietly inside, careful not to cause any sounds that would resonate across*

*the valley in the still, moist, evening air. One of them yanks a torch from the
ground and both step inside. Shortly after they have pushed the canoes off
into the river channel, one of the fishermen leans over the prow and holds
his torch out above the water. The other takes an arrow from his quiver and
sets it in the bow string.*

*Dark, sinewy shapes begin to congregate in the luminous, watery glow of
the torch. Watching a particularly fine mkwamagw, the fisherman sets his
arrow, draws it back partway, aims, and waits. The fish moves off beyond the
ring of light. The fisherman continues to wait and sees the fish glide along the
edge of the torch light, once, and again. He watches the fish meander around
the margin of the reflected light and envisions how far below it he must
shoot to hit the mark. Finally, Mkwamagw noses directly into the brightness,
only to enter the long darkness that comes at the end of an arrow aimed true.*

*—In and around Amoskeag Falls,*
*Manchester, New Hampshire,*
*2,000 years ago*

A run of water below Amoskeag Falls. *Photo by Michael J. Caduto.*

Mkwamagw, "red fish," is the name given to salmon by the People. Two
thousand years ago, salmon, shad, and alewives began their migration
in early May and made their way up the rivers *Molôdemak* (Merrimack), "deep water"; *Gwenitegw* (Connecticut), "long river"; *Beska-*

*tegwa* (Piscataqua), "a branch river"; and
*Msoakwtegw* (Saco), "river of standing
dead trees" that were killed by beavers.
Fish weirs were used along the branch of
Gwenitegw that is now known as the
Ashuelot River, a name that may come
from *azwalak*, "place to carry (transfer)
someone," or *azowlagik*, "place to change
canoes." Amoskeag Falls along the Merrimack River was a popular spring fishing
ground, as were Garvin's Falls and
Sewall's Falls. *Zigwaniwi*, "in spring,"
many nearby tributaries teemed with fish,
including Salmon Brook in Nashua and
the mouth of Turkey River in Bow where
fish passed on their way to spawn.

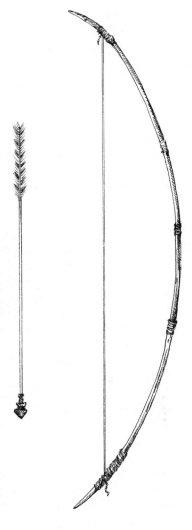

Although the spear and atlatl were still
being used, a new weapon appeared
about 2,000 years ago that possessed
both power and grace. The bow and
arrow did not completely replace the
spear and the long-arm, but it was the
most efficient short-range weapon when
stealth, speed, and accuracy were essential. Bows were fashioned from long,
slender pieces of hickory if possible, but
ash and maple were also used. When it
was drawn back, the tightly strung animal sinew of a bow cord stored tremendous energy that could be harnessed and
released with a small amount of steady,
deliberate motion that would not alarm
the prey.

Arrows were carried in a quiver that hung over the hunter's shoulder.
Some arrow tips were small, simple triangles. The bottoms of other
points were gently contoured or contained small notches or ears on
which to catch the sinew that fastened the point to a shaft. Arrow tips
were sometimes made from bone, but stone tips lasted much longer. A
deft, expert hand could fashion good knapping stone, such as chert, into
a fine point within fifteen or twenty minutes. The back of each arrow
was carefully fitted with directional feathers. These were aligned at a
very slight angle in relation to the arrow's shaft. This design caused the

This dugout canoe lay submerged in Lake Ossipee for over 450 years. *Photo courtesy New Hampshire Historical Society.*

arrow to fly straight and to spin as it sliced through the air, a motion that prevents the shaft from wobbling and helps an arrow to fly true. Each hunter was known for creating a unique arrangement of feathers and a particular design along the length of the shaft. These patterns were individual variations on a larger theme created by hunters from a certain region.

Stone was also fashioned into the tools needed to practice some of the more remarkable skills that were essential for living in ancient times. Two thousand years ago, when birchbark canoes began to appear, New Hampshire's original people had already been making dugout canoes for more than three millenniums. Using fire as an ally, along with the adze, gouge, and hammerstone, dugouts were made from the logs of white pine, oak, and chestnut. These craft could be seen in various stages of completion near homesites throughout the land, whether high on a terrace along the banks of the Connecticut River near Woodsville, by Mirror Lake in Derry, or along the shore of Lake Ossipee, *Awasibagok,* "beyond the water."

When dugouts were not being used, they were often submerged with rocks to hide and help preserve them. These canoes were sometimes forgotten or abandoned and their oxygen-deprived environment often preserved the wood for centuries. One ancient canoe that was submerged for over 450 years was discovered in recent times along the shore of Lake Ossipee.[7] This canoe is now part of the collection in the Museum of New Hampshire History in Concord. Several dugout canoes have been found submerged along the shore of Shelburne Pond in northwestern Vermont, including one in 1979 that was about the same age as the Ossipee canoe, and another that was about 510 years old when it was raised in 1985.[8] From Hopkinton to Kingston and from Londonderry to Wolfeboro, more than a dozen dugout canoes of various size and age have been found preserved in the sediments of lakes and wetlands around New Hampshire.[9]

Imagine that you are going to visit a site in the pine woods by a small gathering of *Alnigamigol,* wigwams, near the edge of a shallow harbor at the mouth of the Piscataqua River along the coast. It is the heat of summer two millenniums ago and the long, lazy days have arrived. If you have the patience to watch for several weeks, you will see the practice of a venerable, painstaking craft.

Two young men, friends, are standing next to an ancient white pine, *goa*. They face the tree, ask permission to use its wood, and place a gift of pine seeds at its base where the large roots flare out from the rough, dark bark of the main trunk. Using stone axes and working from opposite sides of the trunk, they cut away the bark and inner wood just above the ground. After working all day, they build a fire around the base of the tree and bank the freshly cut wood with a thick bed of glowing red coals. The coals burn down during the night but they leave a thick belt of charred wood around the tree.

When the sun rises the next day, the young men return and chop away the blackened wood. After working hard until sunset, they open a deerskin pouch and pull out a compact meal of some dried meat and roasted chestnuts. Although the chestnut tree only arrived in this area some ten generations ago, their village has already adopted many uses for both its wood and the delicious, substantial nuts.

After another day of chopping and a second night of charring, they return for a third day. On that morning, when the last bits of the previous night's charred wood are cut away, a groan emanates from deep within the pine. The branches quiver. A sharp cracking sound resonates up the length of the trunk as the great tree lists to one side and falls to earth with a roar of wind and a deafening, ground-shaking crash. During the next few days, the men use the same, tedious process of chopping and charring to remove the branches from a section of the tree and to then section off a 20-foot length of trunk. Then they roll the log up onto four posts that they have planted in the ground nearby at just the right height and distances apart to provide access to the entire outside edge of the nascent canoe. Once they have removed the bark, they build an intense fire along the top edge of the log. By charring and chopping with an adze, then scraping with a gouge that is often driven into the wood with a hammer of stone or hardwood, they gradually create a trough down the center of the log. Whenever necessary, controlled amounts of water are used to wet the edges and prevent the fire from burning through the sides. The outside and ends of the canoe are also trimmed and shaped. Over a period of three or four weeks, the craftsmen squeeze time for working on the canoe into their other tasks of hunting and family responsibilities.

At last, using fine stone chisels and shell scrapers, the persistent builders create a smooth finish inside the well-formed dugout whose sides are now several inches thick. They use the same tools to refine and smooth the surfaces of the four paddles that they have fashioned of wood from several of the larger branches. When the day comes that the canoe is completed, it weighs about 300 pounds and measures 18 feet long, 30 inches wide, and 16 inches deep.[10]

That evening, the craftsmen solicit two friends to help them carry the craft down to the shore. Together they take two strong ropes and slip one under each end of the canoe to create slings. Wrapping the ends of the ropes around their wrists and forearms, the four young men lift the canoe and work their way down toward the harbor. It is a warm, still night and the familiar smell of the ocean stings their nostrils as they heavily inhale the night air. When they at last reach the shore, the team puts the canoe down and gazes in awe over the harbor. A gentle fog rises from the glassy surface of the water. The reflections of dozens of torchlights drift eerily through the mist. Their families and neighbors are using torches made from knots of burning pitch to attract lobsters, flatfish, crabs, and other prey for the spearing.[11] Carefully and quietly, the four friends slip the canoe into the ghostly pall to proudly display their handiwork. They paddle through the liquid sky and the torchlit stars dance atop the ripples in their wake. A male loon, sensing that its territory is about to be invaded by this stray canoe, yodels in the late-day shadows and mist.

The ancient forest of white pine, hemlock, and birch in which these two young men cut and crafted a fine dugout canoe was long ago swallowed by the sea. New Hampshire's coast began to submerge about 4,000 years ago and the shoreline has continued to creep inland to this day.[12] If you visit the cove at low tide, you can still see the stumps and reclining trunks of white pines that died over 3,000 years ago in the drowned forest of Odiornes Point.

In their dugout canoes, however, the People plied the waters of rivers and lakeshores that would appear familiar to us, allowing for the eel-like slip of oxbows and the gradual shift of shorelines over time. Their environment contained many of the same species that now populate New Hampshire. The highest mountaintops harbored alpine meadows amid large expanses of lichen-dappled, windswept outcrops and slabs of rocky slopes. Stunted forests of spruce, fir, and wizened alpine birches grew below treeline. Moving downhill into a gradually milder vertical climate belt, the spruce-fir forest came into its own, then graded into the upland hardwoods of birch, beech, and maple. In this fashion, these two forest types covered the mountainous regions, much of the north country, and higher elevations in the south. In the middle and southern reaches of this land, and in the expansive lowlands, milder temperatures cultivated forests of white pine, oak, hickory, chestnut, elm, and ash. Hemlock thrived in the cooler valleys and on cold, damp, north-facing slopes. Reaching up into the vast areas covered by this mix of temperate hardwoods and softwoods were remnant species of warmer climes that grew in the southern

Pine marten.

reaches of the Connecticut and Merrimack River valleys and inland from the coast.

Two millenniums ago, the lowland forests abounded with three seasons of abundant foods: the spring greens of fiddleheads and of budding sassafras leaves; the blackberries, raspberries, elderberries, cherries, and wintergreen snowberries of summer; the autumn harvest of staghorn sumac berries, acorns, and the nuts of hickory, beech, butternut, black walnut, and hazelnut. Seeds of these plants were sown around the homesites, along with those of other plants that were useful for weaving, cordage, matting, and insulation, such as bullrush, chairmaker's rush, and bedstraw.

In addition to the many anadromous fish and the catadromous eels that were a major food source during their respective spawning seasons of spring and autumn, brown bullhead, northern pike, sturgeon, bass, perch, and many other familiar fishes swam the lakes and broad river valleys year round. Herons stalked the shallows where ducks dove and dabbled, while grebes and rails hid in the surrounding skirts of cattails and reeds. Gulls and terns soared and dipped above coastal waters.

The fauna from this period ranged from white-tailed deer, cottontails, porcupines, chipmunks, and both gray and red squirrels and foxes, to woodchucks, beavers, minks, muskrats, black bears, raccoons, snowshoe hares, and skunks. But bobcats were common then, as were pine martens, otters, fishers, and gray wolves.[13] On occasion, hunters returned with a game bag full of meat from one of the elk that lived in these parts until at least 1,000 years ago. Hunters often returned from a hunting trip with the meat, antlers, and thick-furred hide of a moose. And occasionally, when hunger stalked the homesites, a dog found its way into the cooking pot.

No one knows when New Hampshire's original people began purposefully to clear land close to their homesites in order to create habitat for animals. Trees had long been used for firewood, food, medicine, and raw materials, such as the fibrous inner bark that was twisted and braided into rope and the outer bark that was fashioned into canoes, houses, utensils, and even weapons. Perhaps hunters noticed that deer, elk, cot-tontails, and other prey frequented the open land created when a section of forest had been cleared by a blowdown, burned by a lightning fire, or transformed into a wet meadow on the exposed bottom of an abandoned beaver pond after the dam had been breached. The animals were at-tracted to the young, vigorous growth that sprouted when the understory became exposed to sunlight. White-tailed deer, bear, moose, and other grazing animals thrived when their environment included openings of lush growth where they could find food amid the grasses, greens, berries, and the buds of shrubs and young trees.

In time, guided by the animals' attraction to these clearings, the People began to encourage wildlife by purposefully killing sections of forest; by girdling the bark of trees with stone knives and axes to sever the flow of sap to the tree crowns. Trees were often burned after they died on the stump. Along with the natural forces that created openings in the forest, such as disease, insects, heavy winds, and lightning caused by fires, this pattern of land use created a regional mosaic of habitats in various stages of growth ranging from fresh clearings to mature forest—a landscape of diverse food and cover that attracted many of the animals that were hunted. Large clearings eventually developed around many homesites and families moved when the forest and the populations of game animals needed time to recover and replenish.

In the simple act of starting fires in their surroundings, the People formed a relationship with an immensely powerful ally. Lighting *skweda,* "a fire," was an act of creative destruction, of making something new—a thing that had been imagined—by incinerating what already existed. In addition to being used as a tool to create and improve wildlife habitat, fire was used in the spring and autumn to encourage the growth of berries and other foods around homesites, although large stands of nut-bearing trees were protected from the flames. Burning increased the size of open grasslands near homesites to improve views and the visibility of anyone approaching. Fire-cleared areas that were free of underbrush were easier to travel through and harbored fewer biting insects, reptiles, and other animals that were not wanted close to the *Alnigamigol.*[14] Regular burn-ing also prevented fire from spreading into the tree crowns and causing an intense conflagration that would devastate the forest ecosystem and alter the hydrology of a region.

As time passed, regular burning formed large, open intervals along the banks of many New Hampshire rivers. Expansive, prairie-like grass-lands were created along the coast as far north as southern Maine.[15] Some of the larger New England grasslands eventually grew to a few hun-dred acres.[16] Open, park-like forests and large grasslands attracted bison into Massachusetts and, likely, southern New Hampshire, sometime after they crossed the Mississippi about 1,000 years ago.[17] Coastal grasslands were home to the once-abundant heath hen.

At some point in time, fire also became an important element in the interaction of friend and foe, hunter and prey. Signal fires and smoke were used to communicate over long distances.[18] Fire also became a weapon that was used for both offense and defense in times of war, for driving enemies into the open and for burning their sources of food, wood, and other materials. In southern New Hampshire, up the river valleys and along the coast, fire was used as a tool for hunting. The fires of autumn drove white-tailed deer and other game animals toward hunters in wait.[19]

The scale on which hunting occurred did not mean that the People simply took what they could get from their environment regardless of the consequences. Each family had a specific territory under its care and protection. Families observed the plants and animals within their territories closely and gained an intimate understanding of the members of each species.[20] Among animals in their immediate surroundings, hunters could tell which animals were weak or healthy, which were young or old, and even whether or not a doe was pregnant. This detailed knowledge enabled each family to maintain a strong breeding population. Archaeologists have discovered that some families hunted mostly male deer: the remains of white-tailed deer at some ancient homesites show a nearly complete lack of bones from females.[21]

Special care was taken to leave animals alone when they were raising young during the summer, a time when fishing was the main activity. One exception may have been made when hunting waterfowl. During the summer, when mature ducks were molting and unable to fly and young ducks had not yet developed the power of flight, ducks were sometimes herded into small coves, then up narrow creeks where some were caught with nets. The meat was smoked and added to winter stores.[22] It is most likely that only the adults were taken because there was a strict taboo against killing young birds.[23]

The number of animals was watched carefully and hunting was practiced with concern for the fecundity of each species. Wasteful killing was not allowed among the People. Within their belief system, animals had their own individual lives, families, and spirits. Similar to humans, animals formed communities and cultures with their own fates and destinies.

# 7. Seeds of Change

⟳  ⟳  ⟳  ⟳

"Nonon," *cries the little girl as she spreads her hands wide,* "Mother, will this little seed grow into a pumpkin this big?"

"Yes, but we have to give it water and make sure that the crows, mkazasak, *do not eat that seed of the squash,* wasawa."

"I will chase them away!"

"Good, and your father will help you. That is why he and your brother are building the small Alnigamigw *in the middle of the field. They will wait there and surprise the mkazasak. Mkazas is good and is close to Dabaldak, the Owner who created everything you see. But mkazas will eat most of our seeds,* kikaimenal, *if we let him. Now, we must get our planting done before the sun goes down."*

"What is brother doing?"

"Ôptakahiga, *he is hoeing. See how he makes the mounds for me to plant in? He is using a hoe,* lakahigan, *that he made by lashing a handle onto the shoulder blade of* moz, *a moose. Your other brother made a hoe from a flat rock that he sharpened on one side like an axe."*

"Your seeds are not the same as mine, Mother. What are you planting?"

"I am planting the seeds of maize, skamonal, *which are different colors. Around skamonal, I plant beans,* adebakwal. *These seeds were first brought to us by mkazas from the south,* zowanakik, *and from where the sun sets in* nakihlôdakik, *'the land where it goes down.' That is why we do not kill mkazasak, and why we let them eat their share of the seeds and crops."*

*"How do you know when to plant the garden, Mother?"*

*"When the leaves of the white oak,* wacilmezi, *are the size of the ear on the mouse, the little one that gnaws,* alezawad, *that is when we plant kikaimenal. It is the time of the Corn Moon, Skamonkas."*

*"Will mkazasak eat those seeds too?"*

*"Yes, and when the plants begin to grow, then* nolka, *the deer, will come and eat her share. That is why we plant much more than we need."*

*"I like working in the garden, Mother."*

*"Why do you like coming here?"*

*"Kwôgweni, because."*

*"Because of what?"*

*"Because all of the families work together in the fields and I see my friends here. And because I like to watch* zogelônihlak, *rain birds; the way they dip down and touch the top of the river when they are flying."*

*"Yes, they are very beautiful. And so are you. I am going to call you* Biwi Zogelônihla, *Little Rain Bird."*

—East bank of the Merrimack River,
Concord, New Hampshire,
800 years ago

       ལྡ    ལྡ    ལྡ    ལྡ

Later that day, Biwi Zogelônihla and her mother returned to the main village that was built on a high escarpment overlooking the Merrimack River, a place that is known today as Sugar Ball Bluff. The steep sandbanks and varved clay slopes below the village inspired the Alnôbak name *Benôkoiak*, "falling hill people," after which the nearby town of "Penacook" is named. Biwi Zogelônihla's village was surrounded by a palisade of tall, upright logs. Two other large villages were located nearby: at the north end of Concord near Sewall's Falls and at what is now called Fort Eddy Plain on the west bank of the Merrimack River. These villages, like others of their time, were composed of extended families whose members were related to people in nearby villages by both descent and intermarriage. The word for family bands or communities among the Alnôbak, *gôgassigamigwzoak*, means "they are many families."

In her village, Biwi Zogelônihla was raised by a community of relatives. She spent much of the time with her mother, *nonon*, and her grandmother, whom she called *nigô*. Years ago, when Biwi Zogelônihla's grandfather, her *gicinemahôm*, was killed by a bear during the autumn

Steep riverbanks by the homes
of the *Benôkoiak,* "Falling Hill
People," the Penacook. *Photo
by Michael J. Caduto.*

hunt, her grandmother served as *zôgemô,* the village chief.[1] This old
woman, whose name was *Sibes Lintowôgan,* "Singing Bird," was known
as a *manigebeskwas,* a "lively, unconventional woman."

Heart of the Penacook culture lay at the confluence of the Merrimack
River and the *Bagôntegok,* the Contoocook or "Butternut River," near
the present-day towns of Concord, Bow, Boscawen, and, of course, Penacook. Their homeland stretched west to the watershed of "rock water,"
*Seninebik,* Lake Sunapee; east to the rough mountain, *Gôwizawajok,*
Mount Kearsarge; and as far north as the Winnipesaukee River, a river in
the "land around lakes," *Wiwninebesakik.* The territories occupied by
other family bands among the Alnôbak, who were related to the Penacook by culture and beliefs, stretched vast distances to the four directions. Ever since those early days long before Biwi Zogelônihla was born,
this greater homeland has been called *Gedakina,* "Our Land."

Each year, before the fishing began in earnest, the Penacooks hoed and
planted the sandy loam of the fertile floodplains and fields along the

*Benôkoiak* (Penacook) axe and grub hoe.

riverbanks and on the islands midstream. Hoes were often made from adze-shaped heads of granite or slate with a sharp edge ground or chipped into one end. A groove encircled the stone near the opposite end around which the split ends of a branch were wrapped and lashed with sinew to form the handle. One of the "gardens" covered at least 40 acres of an island in the Merrimack River and some of the fields in the floodplains exceeded 100 acres. Gardens, like fishing grounds, were shared by everyone in the community.

After the seeds were sown, near the end of *Kikas,* the Planting Moon, the village moved for a time to a high bluff east of the fishing grounds at Amoskeag Falls where they stayed for two to three weeks while catching and curing thousands of salmon, shad, and alewives.[2] By the middle of the next moon, "the Hoer," *Nokkahigas,* the fish runs had ended. The dried fish were then brought back to the village and placed in storage pits lined with bark. Dried corn and beans would later be stored in a similar way and all of these stores were used in the winter village.

On that long ago day when Biwi Zogelônihla and her mother moved among the mounds of their garden, they sowed the seeds of a new relationship between the People and the Land. With every new planting year, this nascent revolution grew along the fertile floodplains of New Hampshire's rivers as far north as the Saco. These rich valleys were the Mesopotamia of Gedakina; these rivers her Tigris and Euphrates.

At roughly the same time that wheat, rye, barley, peas, and other crops were becoming staples in the Fertile Crescent, maize was first cultivated in Middle America in the vicinity of Teotihuacán, Mexico. Mayans were among the earliest horticulturalists to grow and adapt maize from a native wild grass called teosinte more than 7,000 years ago. *Teosinte,* which means "mother of corn" in the language of the *Nahua* or Aztecs, still grows wild in southern Mexico, Honduras, and Guatemala. To this day, patches of teosinte that are interspersed in the fields of maize cause the crop to be more vigorous and productive. It is no wonder that the Lacandon Maya still tell their children how people were first created from a dough made of cornmeal.

Teosinte, "mother of corn," a wild grass, is among the most ancient ancestors of maize.

Throughout the Americas, foraging plants for wild foods, medicine, and materials continued even as cultivation gradually became a greater part of the Native diet. The first wild seeds of the familiar bottle gourd, *Lagenaria siceraria,* were probably carried on the ocean waves to the east coast of Florida from Africa or tropical America more than 7,000 years ago.[3] At about this same time in eastern North America, sunflower, chenopod, and marsh elder or sumpweed were among the first foods whose growth was encouraged in the "wild" by Native peoples. As long as 4,000 years ago, true domestication of plants began in the East when the seeds of individual plants that were the most productive and fast-growing were first saved and planted. Other sources of food indigenous to eastern North America that were gradually domesticated include the summer squashes, such as scallop and crookneck squash, acorn squashes, fordhooks, sunflowers, and an ornamental gourd, *Cucurbita pepo,* subspecies *ovifera.*

When new crops were introduced from the West, they supplemented the rich harvest of domesticated foods that were native to the East. Over time, corn, beans, peanuts, peppers, tomatoes, and certain varieties of squash, such as pumpkins and marrows, gifts from the Incas of Peru, the Aztecs of Mexico, and the Maya of Central America, spread to the North and East. Maize first appeared in the native gardens of eastern North America, in Illinois and Tennessee, around 2,500 years ago.[4] Another 1,500 years would pass before maize was the dominant crop in the gardens and diets of Native peoples in eastern North America. At roughly this same time, an eight-row flint corn that could mature in short, northern growing seasons first appeared in the Ohio Valley, Great Lakes region, and in the Northeast. The development of this variety allowed maize to spread throughout northern North America.[5]

Around the turn of the first millennium, the northeastern climate grew warmer. For the next two hundred years, there was a brief shift northward of people, plants, and animals. Families of cultures to the south pushed northward: the Pocumtucks came up the Connecticut River valley into the lands of the Alnôbak and the *Msiwajok* or "Massachusett," those who lived "at the big mountain," moved up the Merrimack River. Seeds of corn, beans, and squash rode these warm winds into the homeland of the Alnôbak almost 1,000 years ago.

Nearly 9,000 years earlier, a number of different crops had sprung forth in the Fertile Crescent, the lands between Asia Minor and the Arabian Peninsula east of the Mediterranean Sea. There, the Caucasians responded to this new-found ability to grow crops by rapidly exceeding the numbers the land could support. They began a long, dark history of expanding outward and taking land from their neighbors on which to grow more food as fuel for further expansion. In a twist of irony rooted in a seed, farming among the Caucasians set in motion a tradition of aggressive growth and exploitation that would one day scatter their distant progeny across the continents and seas and lead them to confront the People in the heart of Gedakina.

But the Alnôbak adapted to their rich new source of indigenous foods in an entirely different way than the cultures of the Fertile Crescent: a response as contrary as a temperate forest is to a desert plain. In Gedakina, horticulture augmented the hunting and gathering that had supported the People and their ancient ancestors for over 12,000 years. While the wielding of *skweda,* a fire, had already given the People a powerful tool to alter the land, it did not greatly change the carrying capacity of their environment. With the coming of the *kikawinnoak,* the "planters," however, the People sowed the seeds of a future in which they enabled the land to support more families than it ever had. With the advent of farming, the People had to adjust their stewardship practices and adapt ways of living that re-established a new bal-

Blossoms of the native common sunflower, *Helianthus annuus.*

ance in their relationship with each other and the land. They responded to horticulture by transforming a time-honored tradition of living sustainably and deepening their reciprocal relationship with plants.

The Alnôbak drew strength from nurturing deep roots in this land. Generations learned the secrets of growth and renewal from a venerable story. Through the cycle of the Corn Mother, the past speaks with a tongue of fire, the future rests with the quiet sprout of a gentle seed.

&#x25AA;&#x25AA;&#x25AA;&#x25AA;

In the deep woods, when the world was young and the dew of spring glistened from the wild strawberry leaves, a youth emerged from his lodge.

"Every day is the same," he thought to himself. "I go into the wild to gather food. I am tired of nuts, roots, and berries."

This young man had been alone ever since he was born. He had no friends or family; not even a dog. His days were long and winter was especially hard because he did not even know of fire. In the years when the heart of a youth is often alive with wonder and adventure, his heart was heavy with the weight of solitude.

On this morning, the young man began to walk along the familiar trails that led to the best patches of early spring greens in a sun-dappled clearing amid the trees. For most of the day, he idled up the trail, feeling neither hunger nor desire to go on. When he at last reached the clearing, he was weak and light-headed. He leaned back against an ancient tree at the edge of the clearing and fell asleep.

The fatigue that he felt was so deep it touched his spirit. For several days he lay against the wizened tree until the land of dreams became his world. Then, something caused him to stir. A soft sound came from in front of him, as if the wind itself was playing on the grass before his feet. From beneath closed eyelids he saw the dull fire of the blood-red sun. When a shadow fell over his face, a shiver of fear ran down the nape of his neck.

He opened his eyes to the blue haze that comes from staring at the sun with eyes closed. When it faded and his vision cleared, there stood before him a breathtaking young woman. Her eyes were the color of the mid-day sun and her thick hair was the pale green of fresh spring grass. She was tall and lithe and his heart went out to her.

"Are you the daughter of the sun?" he asked as he rose to his feet. "I have never seen anyone or anything so beautiful as you. All my life I have lived in these woods alone and I hoped that some day my loneliness would end."

With those words the young man stepped toward the woman. She slid away, just enough to keep him at bay. He moved forward a few more steps and again she moved back to match.

"Please, come closer so that I may see you and we can tell of what is in our hearts."

In a voice that soothed like a gentle breeze, she replied, "If you want to be with me, listen well and do exactly as I say."

"Yes," he replied eagerly, "please tell me what I must do."

She led the young man into the middle of the clearing where some tufts of dry, brown grass from last year's growth had been shredded into fine matting and left at the opening to a mouse tunnel.

"Take these two sticks. Rub them quickly and press them together like this," she instructed. "Do this in the middle of that dried wad of grass."

The young man did as he was told. In time, some smoke began to rise from where the sticks were rubbing. He began to sweat, but he kept working the sticks against one another. At last a small ember fell into the grass. The young woman bent down with her face next to his and blew upon the ember until it erupted.

He jumped back as the flames singed his eyebrows. "Ayee!" he cried. "What is that?"

"It is fire," she replied. "Now come with me to the edge of the clearing and we will let the fire do its work."

For some time the tongues of flame spread and danced across the clearing. The young man had never seen a creature so hungry and quick to consume its food. By the end of the day, the grass, wildflowers, and small shrubs in the clearing were reduced to a blackened, smouldering carpet.

"Now what do you want me to do?" he asked her.

"Do exactly as I say. After the fire in the sky travels below the tops of the trees, I will lie down at the edge of the clearing. Take the ends of my hair in your hand and drag me across the clearing until I have touched all of the burned ground."

"But I do not want to do what you ask," he said in earnest.

"You must. When you are done, night will have fallen. Leave me there in the clearing. When the fire rises again in the sky, I will be gone."

"Please!," he implored her, "do not leave."

"If you do these things, I will come back and I will be with you always." She then told him what else he must do.

When she was done speaking, they waited together at the edge of the clearing, seeing in each others' eyes their worlds completed. As the sun slowly set, he noticed the spark in her eyes begin to fade. By the light of dusk he gently pulled her back and forth across the clearing until he saw that every spot of ground had been kissed with her beauty. When he was done, he lay her motionless body next to his and watched the fading daylight through a cloud of tears.

The next morning, as the fire rose again in the sky, he awoke to the bittersweet feeling of what had passed. He jumped to his feet and looked out over the clearing.

"Where are you?" he cried to the young woman. "Please come back."

As he stood alone in the silence he tried to remember her face and the rich color of her wonderful hair. Then he began to recall what she had told him he must do to assure her return.

All that day, he filled a bark bucket at a nearby stream, brought water back with which to wet the field, and returned to fill the bucket again. In a few days, small grass-like plants began to grow wherever the young woman had touched the earth. He kept the plants watered and weeded around them. As the days passed, the stalks grew tall and their leaves bent over and swayed in the breeze, singing a sweet song that reminded him of her gentle voice.

In time, small tufts of shimmering green strands the color of the young woman's hair began to grow in places where leaves emerged from the sides of the stalks. He knew, then, that she had not forgotten him. One day, he noticed that a tiny, leaf-covered head of seeds had formed beneath each tuft of hair. Just before the leaf-falling moon arrived, he picked the first ear of maize, *skamonal*, placed it at the base of that corn stalk and said, "Thank you for your beauty and for your generous gift." Once he had harvested the garden, he pulled back the husks and hung the corn from the poles of his lodge to dry it as he prepared for the winter months.

Keeping his word to the young woman, he saved some seed for the following spring. When the leaves of the white oak tree grew to the size of a mouse's ear, he planted a new garden and cared for it. From that time on, whenever the People see the silken hair growing from their cornstalks, they remember to thank the young woman, who has never forgotten.[6]

എൻ  എൻ  എൻ  എൻ

The story of Corn Mother has been told among the People for more than a thousand years. Within it are found the lessons and simple wisdom necessary for growing crops: the need to plant and harvest in tune with the moons and seasons; to water, weed, and nurture the growing plants; and to maintain a reciprocal relationship with the crops, one of giving and receiving.

With the coming of horticulture and an increasingly sophisticated stone technology, the People experienced changes that were common to other cultures, including the peoples known in the Eastern Hemisphere as *neolithic,* coming from the Greek words *neos,* "new," and *lithos,* "stone." Community life took on a larger scale in some places as small family bands blended into villages of extended relations centered around the rich, fertile lands. These population centers, which grew from sixty to one hundred people or more, brought gradual changes in local economies, regional trade networks and social relationships. Many families continued to live around the villages and in outlying areas, maintaining their own garden plots of about an acre or more.

Always resourceful, the People now survived along a horticultural continuum that ranged from simply gathering wild plants, to harvesting from the cultivated patches of plants and nut orchards near homesites, to planting seeds in their gardens. Families that lived in northern New Hampshire and at higher elevations where soil and seasonal extremes are not as suitable for gardens continued to rely mostly on hunting and gathering, but crops became a vital part of the diet among villages in the south, in the river valleys, and along the coast. Domesticated varieties of plants and

large gardens demanded a substantial commitment of time and energy beyond what was required by the less formal wild gardens of the past.

The need for more work and a decrease in leisure time seems to be a universal experience among neolithic cultures worldwide. Some traditional, non-horticultural societies, such as the Hadza who live near Lake Eyasi in Tanzania where there is an abundance of game and wild plant foods, have rejected the horticultural ways of neighboring cultures altogether. The Hadza are able to meet their needs as hunter-gatherers by working an average of merely two hours each day.[7] One early encounter with a hunter-gatherer band of Micmacs—a close cultural relation of the Alnôbak who live to the northeast in the Maritimes—inspired the observation that they were always relaxed, never seemed to hurry or worry and that ". . . their days are all nothing but pastime."[8] It is likely that the Alnôbak had to work longer and harder as they came to rely upon agriculture for their survival.

If you could travel around Gedakina during the second millennium, traversing both time and distance along the way, you would discover that broad, flat floodplains made of sandy loam, especially those located where the growing season was 140 days or longer, sprouted villages along with the first gardens.

Imagine you are hiking in the land of the *goasak,* the "little white pines," among the intervales of the upper Connecticut River valley. On this humid summer day, you walk up the east bank of the river near Woodsville, New Hampshire. A soothing call of brief notes, "COO . . . COO . . . COO . . . COO," drifts from amid the tall trees; the lugubrious mating song of *belaz,* the passenger pigeon. *Gasko,* the great blue heron, starts as you approach, beats its wings laboriously, and rises from the marsh at river's edge as it croaks, "vraahnk, vraahnk." You come to the inside of an oxbow and decide to climb over the land rather than circumvent the snaking riverbend. Scrambling upslope through oak and pine forest, you crest the rise and a world opens before you.

Broad, flat fields enfold both banks, continuing like serpentine green ribbons along the contours of the river beyond the next bend. People of all ages, families, dot the verdant swath as they tend their expansive gardens. Every so often the plink of stone against stone rings out as someone's hoe strikes a rock hidden in the soil. Small bark structures are scattered throughout the fields. You watch as someone emerges from one of the structures and rushes toward a flock of crows that has landed in the garden. As the boy approaches the crows he waves his arms and cries out, *"Spigwihla, nanabihla!,"* "Fly up, go, quick!" The crows rise in a raucous chorus of protest and make for the edge of the forest where they perch on the uppermost branches of some old, dead trees.

Your gaze sweeps down from where the crows have landed and you notice a village in the distance on a flat terrace well above the fields. The village is made up of a number of long wigwams, *Alnigamigol,* each with an arched roof and several smokeholes. A few smaller, dome-shaped *Alnigamigol* are set off to the edge of the forest by a stream. Numerous small, conical lodges are scattered along the edges of the fields where people are working. Smoke from cooking fires wafts up through the smokeholes of these lodges, which appear to be made from bark. Some lodges are of a light shade like that of the canoe birch and others are dark like the bark of an elm. A few people near these lodges are hunched over and intent on some kind of work, but most are laboring in the gardens.

Down in the fields, the sound of women and children singing draws your ear and you notice that one group has started to plant, hoe, and weed in unison to the rhythm of the song. You watch this spontaneous dance of the planters, entranced as if lost in a dream, unaware of the passing of time.

Many generations among those who live *Goasek,* "where the white pines are," planted their vast gardens of corn, squash, and beans along those riverbanks. Travelling upriver between the future sites of Littleton and Lancaster, you pass some fields that snake along the Connecticut for over five miles. Whenever you encounter fields that have been left fallow

for a few years, you see thousands of seedlings rooted in the soil of what will one day be a county called Coos, a place of small pines.

Villages and gardens, large and small, dapple the verdant valleys born of the rich sandy loams of floodplains throughout Gedakina. If you were to follow the ancient trail that leads east from the Goasek lands in the vicinity of Littleton along the path of *Ômanosek,* "fishing place," the Ammonoosuc River, you eventually come to its source at Ammonoosuc Lake in Crawford Notch. Continue east through the Notch where the looming hills seem to close in around you, then over the drainage divide to Saco Lake, and down the Saco River. When you at last come to the wide valley of Intervale, you discover a large village of more than one hundred lodges surrounded by a high palisade of logs.[9] The Pigwacket or *Bigwakik* dwell in the steep-sided valley of *Bigwaki*, "an echoing land." Here on the west side of the Saco River, enfolded by the grandeur of numerous small mountains, more than 100 acres of gardens are being tended on the fertile plains. Other villages and gardens are scattered along the floodplains where the Saco River flows east through Conway and the broad valley beyond.

Many villages, large and small, are found near the coast, along the Piscataqua River and its tributaries, and at Odiornes Point. Here as well as at the confluence of the Taylor and Hampton Rivers farther south are several villages of the Winichanat, those who live *Wiwnijoanek,* "where the water flows around it." Their extensive gardens of maize, beans, and squash, including pumpkins, produce large winter stores.

Moving back to the west, deep into the interior, is the roiling water of a river named *Bemijijoasek,* "where the side entering current is," the Pemigewasset. Upstream along the Pemigewasset for some distance, hard by its fertile banks at Livermore Falls, is a small agricultural village that is one of the northernmost to be found in the valleys of the White Mountains. Farther to the south, where the Winnipesaukee River comes together with the Pemigewasset, a village that dates back thousands of years, to the age of stone and bone, is now the site of a significant garden. Centuries from now, in what will one day be known as Willow Hill in the town of Franklin, settlers from distant lands will find a mortar-like depression worn into the surface of a glacial erratic in which corn was ground using a large pestle of stone or hardwood suspended from an overhanging branch.[10]

Your journey through the past continues from this place. If you canoe south down the Merrimack River passed Sugar Ball Bluff and other villages scattered amid the Penacook's expansive fields, you could paddle your canoe over to the western bank and hike in to Turee Pond about one mile southwest of Bow Mills. The summer village northeast of the pond is well known as a place to gather and prepare great quantities of dried blueberries, *bakwsataizatal,* for winter provisions. Return to the canoe and continue paddling south to where *Senikok,* "to the stones," the Suncook River flows in from the east. The Suncooks have planted large gardens in the intervales on both banks of the Merrimack River in Bow and Pembroke. Pull the canoe up and hide it along the eastern shore, then travel by foot along the trail that follows the Suncook River upstream. Soon you pass a favorite place of fishing for salmon and shad near where the Main Street bridge will one day pass over the river. Continue on your journey and you enter deeply into the land of the Suncook, up into Chichester, Pittsfield, Barnstead, and Gilmanton Iron Works.

Make your way back to the canoe and travel downstream to where the town of Merrimack will one day bear the namesake of the river "deep water," *Molôdemak.* Here, below what is now called Wildcat Falls, a tributary widens and the water slows as it enters the main branch from the west. This is the "watching and waiting place," *Skawôhigan.* Some of the Souhegan who inhabit this watershed and share a name with this river are tending crops in the rich sandy loam alongshore.

Hundreds of years from now, the gardens of the *Skawôhigan,* and others throughout Gedakina, will be buried beneath a thick layer of soil. Ancient corn will one day be discovered in Litchfield across the river from Merrimack.[11] Among the oldest vestiges of garden crops uncovered will be the charred remains of maize at the mouth of the Sugar River in Claremont.[12] And about 10 miles to the south, on the western shore of the Connecticut River at an old village site near the base of Skitchewaug Mountain, the aged, carbonized remains of corn, beans, and squash will become the oldest yet unearthed in northern New England. The remnants of these crops will have survived 900 years in grass-lined pits that were once used for storage and refuse.[13]

In a wonder of temporal juxtaposition, the venerable crops at Skitchewaug had been planted in soil atop the remains of life from a period of far greater antiquity; trapped in the underlying quartzite and quartz-pebble conglomerate that metamorphosed from the sand and rocks of a Paleozoic beach. Preserved in this bedrock are the 425 million-year-old fossils of marine animals that lived here when this was a shallow tropical sea, including corals, brachiopods, sea snails, and trilobites. Fossils from this paleobeach will also be found east of the Connecticut River in Montcalm and on both Croydon and Moose Mountains.

How were the early gardens of Gedakina created? Why was it possible for the People to sustain their crops year after year? Often the garden was begun during the time of *Benibagos,* the "Leaf Falling Moon." Stone axes were used to scarify the bark at the bottom of each tree and a ring of fire was lit around the base. After the fire had burned down, the charred wood was chopped away and another fire lit. As with the creation of dugout canoes, the cycle of burning and chopping continued until the tree was felled. Fire was used for clearing throughout much of Gedakina, from the village of the *Zokwakiiak* or Sokwakis, "the ones who broke away," in the southern Connecticut River valley near Hinsdale, to the *Bigwakik,* the Pigwacket along the Saco River.[14] Larger trees were removed, then brush was burned along with the branches of fallen trees. Occasionally, in small gardens, trees were only girdled and they stopped leafing out in a year or two when the tree exhausted its store of food. But this practice was labor intensive and dangerous; whenever the wind blew or heavy rains soaked the dead wood, branches broke off and fell onto the gardeners below.

Soil was prepared by breaking up the roots of ferns, shrubs, and wildflowers with axes and hoes. Sharp-edged materials, including axe-shaped stones, the shoulder blades of moose and deer and, along the coast, large clam shells, were attached to wooden handles to make hoes. Tired soil was occasionally sweetened with crushed shells and sometimes, after the same soil had been planted for a few years and fertility needed to be replenished, a shad or alewife was placed in each seed hill for fertilizer.[15] But the common, long-term management practice was to move a village every ten or twelve years when the fertility of the soil became depleted.[16]

Traditionally, seeds were planted when the danger of frost was past, or when the tender, young, emerald-green leaves of the white oak were as large as a mouse's ear.[17] Men and boys helped around the garden but women and girls did much of the work. Horticulturalists throughout the region grew many of the same crops. The *Zokwakiiak,* whose village was along the Connecticut River at the mouth of the Ashuelot, as well as people from another village of the interior who lived *nansawi,* "between," the Nashua and Merrimack Rivers, planted corn, beans, squash, pumpkins, and gourds.[18] Grown together, corn, beans, and squash form a simple, elegant garden ecosystem. Corn stalks provide supports for the beans to climb, while the roots of beans, which are legumes, enrich the soil with nitrogen that fertilizes the corn. In between the corn, the broad leaves of both squash and beans shade the soil and help to control weeds. One variety called *bebonki skamon* or "north corn," which was grown by the *Zokwakiiak,* produced ears that matured in only 90 days.

Each family grew and harvested 30 to 40 bushels of corn and other crops. A delicacy that was much-anticipated in late summer, when the corn was sweet but had not gone by to the starchy stage, was a juicy ear

Bean vines climb corn stalks and insects feed in the Alnôbak garden. *Photo by Michael J. Caduto.*

of roasted fresh or "green" corn. Corn that was not harvested green was allowed to mature until later in the season. After the harvest, corn and beans were dried. The mandible of a white-tailed deer was commonly used to shell corn from the cob. Squash and pumpkins were cut into strips and also dried for storage. Crops were stored in pits lined with grass or bark. Great quantities of dried corn were ground into meal using a stone mortar and a pestle made from either hardwood or stone. Mortars were also fashioned from a piece of log several feet long with the center hollowed out down to within a few inches of the bottom.

Meals were simple but delicious. In addition to being roasted, green corn was sometimes boiled in the kernel to create a kind of corn mush or *samp*. Dried kernels of corn were pounded and coarsely ground in a mortar, then boiled to create a kind of hominy. Succotash, which was made by boiling an equal amount of corn with beans, was often embellished, as were other dishes, by adding dried squash or pumpkin that had been boiled or steamed. When eaten together, the amino acids contained in corn and beans complement one another to provide a source of protein as high in quality as venison.

From elderberry blossom to squash flower, acorn to corn, and butternut to bean, as time passed the People expanded their horizon of edible and useful plants along the continuum from the wild to the domesticated. Winter stores were plentiful with chestnuts, beechnuts, butternuts, walnuts, hickory nuts, hazelnuts, and acorns. Once they had been boiled several times to draw off the tannins, acorns were dried, parched, ground, and often mixed with cornmeal. Many plants were encouraged in the wild and seeds were often propagated: rose, dock, choke cherry, grape, chenopodium, wild beans, false buckwheat, hog peanut, hawthorn, false Solomon's seal, dropseed, bramble, bedstraw, and grass.

Gathering and preparing food consumed much of the time invested in survival. Hard work brought rewards to extended families whose lives were increasingly focused on one particular region, who moved seasonally between summer and winter villages that lasted a decade or more. But there was ample time for sharing and visiting among relatives, friends, and between neighboring villages. Moments passed, frozen in time, when life breathed in the songs of birds near the garden, in the squeals of children shooting the rapids that effervesced past the village shores, in a languid summer day imbibing the sweet scents of blueberry juice on fingers warm with the sun and dancing amid the twiglets of green.

With every meal, each gift from *Ki,* Earth and *Gici Niwaskw,* "Great Spirit," thanks was given. The first cup of water was poured back into the stream to return the gift; the first ear of corn harvested was placed back at the foot of the Corn Mother in gratitude; a gift of seeds was left in each patch of wild and medicinal plants in atonement for the sacrifice of others. Songs, dances, and ceremonies grew to celebrate the harvests of wild strawberries and blueberries, and to mark the seasons of Sun, *Gizos,* and of Moon, *Nanibôsad,* the "all night walker." Gedakina flourished. It was a land of plenty in a time when change was imperceptible—a leaf following *Gizos* across the day of an azure sky.

# 8. Circles of Giving, Flesh, and Spirit

Their religious teachings permitted no wasteful or arbitrary
destruction of life in any form. In taking animals for food or
for skins, the survivors, as breeding resources, were
constantly considered . . . Ages of harmonious co-living
with the life of the forests, swamps and ravines of the
Eastern woodland, left them the sense to accord to all
forms of life the right to live, to propagate and fulfill their
own destinies, as man himself claims it.

—Frank G. Speck,
*Aboriginal Conservators*, 1938

ॐ☉   ॐ☉   ॐ☉   ॐ☉

*A* group of hunters wait patiently along the edge of a mature beech
forest that borders a beaver pond where a steep hill sweeps down to the
south and dips beneath the reflective waters. One of the hunters places the
narrow end of a birch bark horn to his mouth and, holding the wide
opening upward, blows a call that will attract any moose in rut that hears:
ugh-ugh, oo-oo-OO-OO-OO-OO.

They squat together, well hidden in the brush, waiting for a moose to
appear beneath the golden face of the rising Corn Moon, Skamonkas. Each
hunter carries a longbow and has a quiver of arrows hanging by a strap
along his back. His knife is sheathed and hangs from a cord around his
neck. In the deepening darkness, one hunter notices the cold, pale light of
ghost wood, jibaasakw, glowing from atop an old rotting log.

Their simple garments are meant to keep them warm and dry as they
wait, motionless, while the cool air of the late summer night sinks into the
valley. Each hunter has donned a brain-tanned deerskin breechclout and a
belt tied with several wraps, the fringed ends dangling. Moose-hide
moccasins with a "rabbit-nose" toe, which are virtually waterproof, are
worn over soft foot coverings made of rabbit fur. They will wear moosehock moccasin overshoes later when the deep winter snows arrive.
Moccasins are attached to deerskin leggings that reach up to the thigh and

*in turn are tied to a belt and gartered below the knees. Woven shirts are covered with a long-sleeved, moose-hide coat that can be fastened when the cold sets in. A long deerskin shirt hangs beyond the tops of leggings and half-way down the thighs.*

*The youngest men, who are not yet married, wear their hair long and loose. A few have it tied down with a headband. Married men use a leather thong to tie their hair up into coiled top-knots. On this evening, several of the hunters wear hats made from the furred skin of a young buck with the antlers still attached. Others wear hats made from the skin of a moose's shoulder adorned with a crest fashioned from the long white fur of the animal's hump.*

*Patiently they wait. No one speaks. The hunters have fasted for many days in preparation for this hunt. They have asked Gici Niwaskw, the Great Spirit, for help in finding food and they requested permission of moz, the moose, to provide what they and their families need to survive. They reminded moz that they have always been thankful, have never wasted the meat or skin that he has given to them; that they always return the bones to where moz was found. The married men have not been with their wives for a half-cycle of the moon. And so they wait. Wait in hope that the Spirit has heard their prayers.*

*Reverently, they sit and watch the stars appear in the dusky sky. A lone wolf cries out from the slopes above. No moose comes.*

*Something stirs. At first it is merely a presage; a deeper silence that pushes aside the crepuscular voices; comes a harbinger, a single leaf stirs, then another. A breeze moves the branches amid a growing, rushing sound like distant rapids flowing across the evening sky.*

*"Belazak are coming!" cries one of the hunters.*

*A warm, living gale rushes across the treetops, blowing the leaves toward the south and swaying the branches. The dim light drains instantly from the sky as countless beating wings occlude Skamonkas and the stars beyond.*

*Then a din, a deafening roar fills the world as tens of thousands of powerful wings back-paddle against the cool, damp air; millions of primary feathers clacking as the front of the flock alights. Belazak, passenger pigeons, wash over their world, breaking wave by wave upon the sea of beeches.*

*"KEE . . . KEE . . . KEE . . . KEE," come the calls of each bird, but they are lost in the cacophonous roar that throbs in the hunters' ears. One of the young hunters turns to his companion and shouts, but his mouth seems to utter silent words that cannot surmount the din.*

*"Ayeee!" someone cries as they leap to their feet and begin to fire arrows aloft. Branches give way and startled birds try to take flight before crashing*

*to the ground. Hunters strike at the fallen. With each downdraft, the*
*pungent, stinging scent of guano wafts over them. Skamonkas is at the top*
*of the sky before the avian tide begins to ebb. One of the hunters lights a fire*
*by which they can see to prepare their prey for the journey home.*

*Hunting continues and fallen birds are tied together by their feet; prey*
*caught while angling the skies. Finally, when the strings of these ample birds*
*are as long and heavy as the hunters can carry, they prepare to struggle back*
*to camp with their loads. Before he leaves, each hunter takes the first bird*
*that he killed and places it on that spot, giving thanks to belaz and to Gici*
*Niwaskw.*

*Then, with some carrying their prey in pack baskets and others in hide*
*packs suspended from their foreheads by a tumpline, they labor through the*
*long shadows cast by the Corn Moon. Nearby, hearing the two-footed*
*hunters approaching, others who have also partaken of the bounty of belaz*
*slip into the night on wings and padded feet:* megezo *the eagle,* wôkwses *the*
*fox,* môlsem *the wolf,* awasos *the bear,* azeban *the raccoon,* gokokhas *the*
*barred owl,* apanakes *the marten, and, unseen to all,* wigwedi, *"have no*
*tail," the lynx. Overhead, bats,* madagenihlasak, *are circling, veering, and*
*dipping as they feed on the hoards of insects that plague the flocks of*
*belazak.*

*"Beboniwi—In winter" says one of the hunters, "we will be able to slide*
*our food back to the village on hunters' sleds,* nadialowi kawzowadigan.*"*

*Stopping often to rest, the hunters make their way toward the camp they*
*have pitched near a sheltered, south-facing ledge in the next valley. Belazak*
*are still audible in their distant wake one valley away; a feathered waterfall*
*crashing incessantly upon the forest. When they finally arrive at the lean-tos,*
*the hunters carefully place the packs bearing the gifts of food upon the*
*hemlock boughs that cover the ground inside. Then, with the first hint of*
*morning light peeking through the doorways, they lie on the bearskin*
*bedding and slip into the world of dreams.*

—The southern downslope of Kenyon Hill,
just east of Gwenitegok, "Long River,"
Lyme, New Hampshire,
600 years ago

In the eyes of dying passenger pigeons, *belazak,* in the face of a mother giving birth, in the patience of a teacher sharing a lifetime's knowledge of healing plants with his apprentice, a step is taken along the journey of the Great Circle. With words and acts that are meant "to give back," *li bedegimaga,* the People touch the lives of all around them; human beings as well as the plant and animal people. The core of this fundamental relationship is a receiving borne with gratitude, humility, and respect that slides along the continuum with a generosity of spirit that does not distinguish the gift from the giving. Interconnection is the essence of maintaining balance and living in right relationship, of assuring the dignity of body, mind, and spirit in the midst of the daily acts necessary for survival.

The gifting tradition of the Alnôbak resonates with indigenous peoples throughout the world.[1] Among the Maori in New Zealand, a people of Polynesian descent, the spirit of Hau resides in both the giver and recipient. *Hau* is the force that moves the receiver to reciprocate, and creates the power that the giver holds over the one to whom a gift has been bestowed.[2] The spirit Hau lives in nature, amid the forest and the game animals; it dwells in the hearts of human beings, connects us to others and compels us toward recompense. Whenever a Maori hunter hunts birds in the forest, the Hau can only be satisfied and balance restored by giving some of the food to the priests, the *Tohunga.* The priests have placed the *mauri* in the forest—the power that ensures the game birds will be plentiful. By giving food to the priests, the *mauri* is satisfied and the forest will teem with game birds who return the gift to the hunter.[3] The circle is completed. Other forms of reciprocity are found in Polynesia, Micronesia, and among the Hindu in India with their gifts of cattle.

One form of giving in North America is the potlatch of the Salish and certain other cultures in the Pacific Northwest. Whenever a Nootka chief obtains an abundance of food or material goods, he holds a "giving-away" ceremony and offers his bounty to others as a *patshall,* a gift. The communities of many North American peoples are based on sharing in order to maintain positive relationships, to avoid envy and resentment, to keep peace and, at times, to build ties of obligation. Reciprocity is the foundation for leadership among many Native peoples of the Plains—a generous sharing of shelter, horses, meat, and other goods to the most needy, especially to those who are poor or have been widowed.[4] This is true among the Osage, Plains Cree, Siksika (Blackfoot), the Shoshoni of the Great Basin, and many others. Among these traditional peoples, it is a source of honor, pride, and popularity for a chief to be one of the poorest in the tribe. Poverty is the mark of a leader's wisdom and selflessness.

In harsh environments, sharing is crucial for survival and as a way to foster interdependence within the community. The Inuit of the Arctic share easily of their shelter and of the big game they hunt. Greatness grows from generosity; miserliness is the root of failure and personal disgrace. Far away in the temperate climate of the Southeast, each family among the Muskogee (Creek) contributes a share of their harvest freely to a common store of food—community property that is available for anyone in need.

Moving within the Circle upon which the lives of countless indigenous peoples turn, and evolving from the early practices established by their ancient forebears, the People who have lived in Gedakina throughout the past millennium and before adopted their own rituals of reciprocity and reconciliation in gratitude for the gifts from the Creator and from each other. These general practices are expressed in the specific rituals for each plant and animal that is picked or hunted.

*A hunter sets a snare or a deadfall trap near a tree,* alnakwam. *"Grandfather," he says, "I ask permission to seek this gift of food for my family. Demakwa, 'Tree Cutter,' see my clear heart. I know the sacrifice you will make to help us live."*

*The next day, when the hunter returns and finds a beaver in his trap, he says, "Thank you, demakwa, for this gift. I will soon come back to bring you home, to help you walk the Star Trail." On the way back to his village, the hunter springs his empty traps. It has been a good season and this beaver is all that they need for now; it would be disrespectful to take more.*

*Arriving back at the village, he carefully skins the beaver, scrapes the hide, and stretches the pelt tightly inside a drying rack. One tooth is saved so it can be set in a handle to form a small, curved knife. The other tooth will be used to etch designs into pottery and to sculpt a clean edge along the rim of the fresh pots. That evening, before any of the meat is cooked and eaten, a bit of the fat and some tobacco are burned on the coals as offerings to Dabaldak. Every part of the animal is eaten or used in some way— nothing is wasted.*

*At dawn, the hunter places the bones of demakwa in a skin bag that he hangs around his neck. As he moves through the forest to reset his traps, he stops at the pond of the Tree Cutter.*

*Taking the bones from the bag and placing them into the water where demakwa was caught, he says, "Thank you, my friend, for your generosity. May your journey to the spirit world be an easy one and may you see your family and friends once again. I return this gift, that your relations might see many children and remember us when we are in need."*

ℰↄⓈ   ℰↄⓈ   ℰↄⓈ   ℰↄⓈ

Every living thing has its own particular power, including the plant and animal people. The People themselves have their own personal power. Even the air and water, the rocks, soil, and wind are alive with the spirit of the Creator—rivers and streams, mountains, springs, and burial grounds. Earth, *Niona Nigô,* "Our Grandmother," is herself a source and force of life. Dabaldak cares for all living things, especially the animals and medicinal plants.

As long as the hunter and his family follow the spirit of the Circle and keep the Gift moving, the animals will present themselves and offer food when it is needed. If, however, they should be wasteful, disrespectful, or ungrateful, if they should kill the young of birds or other animals, if they should hunt a pregnant doe, then bad fortune will befall the hunter's family. The game animals will disappear and a time of scarcity will come to the village.

Some say that the Little People, the *Manôgemasak,* even though they are shy and do not like to be seen, are always watching. They often travel in small stone canoes or sometimes they paddle *mazalôpskwolagwsizal,* "little clay canoes." The hunter searching for *nagwibagw sibs,* the "under leaf bird," the woodcock, amid the brushy shore of an oxbow marsh, the families fishing along a riverbank, may happen to look in the direction of the Manôgemasak. But the Little People do not want to be seen so they dive beneath the surface and disappear. There they enter the realm of the denizens of the deep, the *Alômbagwinnosizak,* "Little Underwater

People." These Little Peoples are aware of how the plants and animals, the little things in nature are being treated, and they know how to use their powers.

When there is a break in the Circle, an imbalance caused by human beings, some part of nature is always watching. Some are so greatly feared, the underwater serpent and lizard, that they are only mentioned in winter when they are trapped under ice so thick that they cannot hear and will not be tempted to do harm to those who venture out on the waters. If the swamp spirit is angered, it may lure children to the wet places, never to be heard from again. *Bemola,* "he who goes flying"—the great soaring creature that is part human and part bird—wields immense powers; a hunter out of balance faces his wrath. One who treats the animals well, however, will be aided if Bemola chooses to wield his tremendous strength and influence over the elements in the hunter's favor.

Like all living things, the Alnôbak need to kill in order to live. The impacts of their existence are sometimes beneficial to the natural world, and sometimes not. Their relationship to the land is not one of perfection, but of living in balance. Principles and practices by which to live grow from the stories that express deeply held beliefs in the sacredness of plants, animals, and all of Creation. These spiritual ideals and tenets exist at one end of a continuum and the day-to-day reality of a need to survive lies at the other extreme. Somewhere in between, the sacred and the practical lies the true heart of the People.

ભ૭   ભ૭   ભ૭   ભ૭

Long ago the thin needles of pines and hemlocks were the only leaves that grew. There were no leaves of maples and oaks to turn colors when the cold nights of the Corn Moon, *Skamonkas,* arrived. Not a single flower petal or blade of grass could be found. It was a cold, barren world where the animals could find shelter only in caves and crevices amid the rocks and in the hollows of decaying trees. Winter, *bebon,* stretched to "the end of the world," *matkamigapoda.*

Gici Niwaskw saw the starkness of the land. He felt compassion for the animals as he thought of what a hard, harsh life they must live.

"I must help soften the edges of the world," he thought. "The *awaasak,* the wild animals, deserve a warm and pleasing home to live in. They need food to eat."

And so he sent *Niwaskw Zigwan,* the Spirit of Spring, to visit Earth. She ran across the land with feet that tread as lightly as the brush of a mouse's ear. Whenever her eyes fell upon a tree, its branches sprouted leaves with the greens of youth. Grass and all manner of flowers unfurled at her glance. Infinite colors sparkled and sweet scents filled the air. Her soft breezes flowed as a river of warmth through the hills and valleys of the land, renewing Earth with abundant life.

Within each footprint, wherever Niwaskw Zigwan touched Earth in any way—be it a finger, a hand, a knee or even her nose—plants bearing nuts, berries, roots and other kinds of wild foods began to grow. Every time part of Niwaskw Zigwan met the soil, a different kind of plant sprouted, each with a life of its own. From those early days the food plants brought by Niwaskw Zigwan helped the children of Gici Niwaskw to survive and keep joy in their hearts.[5]

*Photo by Michael J. Caduto.*

A view through the eyes of their nomenclature is a clear window on how the Alnôbak see and understand their surroundings with a relationship both familiar and immediate; with names that reach across thousands of years and speak to anyone who has an intimate relationship with the plants and animals who dwell in Gedakina. Hummingbird, *nanatasiz*, the "little mute one" sips the nectar of flowers, *peskwatawa*, "they are open." Gray squirrels, *msanigok*, "big squirrels" store the seeds of the black walnut, *bedegômenozi*, the "round nut tree," while the fruit of the choke cherry, *adebîmenákwàm*, the "woody plant with dry mouth fruit," and those of *mozmezí*, the "moose bush" or mountain ash, are a favorite food of the cedar waxwing, which is known as *Magwasiz*, the "Little Mohawk" because the crest on its head resembles the cut of a Mohawk warrior's locks.

Rain birds, *zogelônihlak.*

By day, swallows, the "rain birds," *zogelônihlak,* dip the surface of the ponds while drinking and, perhaps, to pick off a morsel of insect food in the form of a water strider, *demakwasiz,* the "little beaver." The nuthatches who circle around the branches and walk up and down the bark of trees are *cigôlôdawasizak,* "little upside down climbers." They may flit past a "pounder" or "knocker," *lôbatahigas*—a woodpecker chiseling for a meal beneath the bark. But when *Gizos* sinks below the horizon, bat, the "leather bird," *madagenihlas,* cruises the night air in quest of its food of bugs, *awahôdosak,* "little spirit ones," or "little devils."

Two out of every three bird names given by the Alnôbak are descriptive: the namesakes of the remaining birds are based on the sounds they make.[6] A warm summer night descends and a whip-poor-will repeats its name incessantly from the bush, *"papoles, papoles, papoles, papoles."* In the north woods, the deep, sonorous call of a barred owl, *gokokhas,* rings out from the dense greens of one of its favorite nocturnal roosts, a balsam fir, *kokokhôakw.*

As the growing season comes to an end, leaves fall from *senômozi,* "rock woody plant," the sugar maple. Soon the Alnôbak will be tending trap lines in the snow, perched atop the delicate forms of footgear fashioned with frames from the snowshoe wood, *ôgemakw,* the white ash;

tending traps tied down with rope made from the basswood, *wigebi-mezi*, the "fibrous bark woody plant" or "bast tree." Up in the winter trees, sparkling the clear, crisp light with its vibrancy, a chickadee, *"kejegigihlasiz,"* the "little kejegigi bird," calls out its name, *"kejegigigi, kejegigigi, kejegigigi."*

Now imagine that you are in the north country, the home of *mkazawi-ossagakw,* "black poplar," the member of the aspen family whose leaves emanate the strong scent of the balsam fir, *kokokhôakw.* The land of the red spruce, *mskask,* and black spruce, *mskak,* where the growing season is short and the traditions of hunting and gathering are still the primary means of subsistence, is also the home of *keskejagwa,* the "moose bird," who will one day be known as the gray jay, whiskey jack, or Canada jay.

From the shores "at clear lake," *Wôbagok,* Lake Umbagog in the northeast, to the headwaters of *Gwenitegok,* Long River, to the north-west, and lacing the slopes, valleys, and gaps of the White Mountains, *Wôbiwajoak,* the People have created trails for hunting, trading, travel-ling, and for access to fine sources of knapping stone. If you accompany a party of sojourners into the *Wôbiwajoak* during the first days of the Planting Moon, *Kikas,* your long journey will start amid the white pines and oaks of the sandy soils near the village in the lowlands. Working your way up a river valley, you occasionally muck through swamps of balsam fir, red maple, and white pines.

You skirt the margin of a bog that has formed along the edge of a poorly drained glacial kettle pond. Walking out beyond the drier edge where young stands of white cedar and tamarack are growing, you notice that the ground begins to quake under your weight. You reach an open mat of peat dappled with islands of stunted black spruce trees: venerable centenarians whose crowns barely reach to your shoulder. These small trees are rocking gently as the bog mat undulates with the waves you create. From shrubby clumps of leatherleaf along the edge of the open water that lies ahead, swamp sparrows are singing their melodious, repet-itive mating call. At about the place that you notice a bog turtle slip from the shore along the center of open water, you decide to stop, for the float-ing, quaking mat of *Sphagnum* moss that barely supports your weight is slowly sinking. As you watch the water rising above your ankles, your eye is drawn to the dewy-ended hairs of a tiny plant near your feet. Peering closer, you see that the hairs have bent over against a delicate, spatulate leaf, entrapping a black fly like those that are swarming around your eyes and ears. On the way out of the bog, you notice where the tube of an in-sectivorous, water-filled plant has been crushed beneath the cloven hoof of a moose that passed earlier that morning. Among the People who live in the north country, moose are the most important source of meat; they take the place that white-tailed deer hold in the diet of the Alnôbak who live in the valleys, toward the coast, and in regions farther south. You gesture and ask the name of this strange, tubular plant that has been trodden. Someone points and replies, *ahamoakezen,* "hen's moccasin."

Trace your path back to dry land and the trail begins to climb up a steep ravine. For every 1,000 feet you will climb this day, the climate and the natural communities of plants and animals that you encounter will be like those that you would pass if you journeyed 300 miles farther north.

Your companions stop to examine the remains of one of last season's trap lines; a *gelahigan,* a deadfall trap or culheag. Two long, heavy logs have been laid lengthwise, one atop the other, and lashed together on one end to form a hinge of bast.

"How does it work?" you ask. One of the men lifts the log while the other takes two smaller sticks in hand. He lays one stick across and perpendicular to the top of the lower log and a bit more than the length of two hands in from the open end. He then sets the other stick upright with one end resting on the round edge of the lower stick while the top end props the upper log.

"*Nihlôjiwi galahamawa tekwigwsanigan*" he explains while pointing to the trigger mechanism, "It holds back the heavy log of the deadfall trap." A small piece of bait is tied to the lower stick and it is backed by a small, circular enclosure woven from hemlock branchlets. When the animal—perhaps a bear, fisher, fox, marten, lynx, or wolf—sticks its head into the enclosure and tugs at the bait, the lower stick rolls out from under the support stick causing the upper log to crash down and instantly crush the animal's skull against the lower log. It is a sudden, violent, and efficient method of killing.

You hike about one quarter mile along the old trapline before you come to another *gelahigan.* These traplines, you are told, are normally tended daily during the moons of the Moose Hunter, *Mozokas,* of late winter, and *Bebonkas,* the Winter Maker, at about the time of winter solstice. Scent trails and bait are used to lure animals in the direction of the traps.

A short distance up the trail, someone calls the group over to the site of an old snare. A hunter had forgotten to spring one of his snares during the last run at the time of *Bebonkas.* Amazingly, a snowshoe hare, *bebonkiimadegwas,* has been caught in the snare that very morning. You reach out and run your fingers through its soft, thick, white fur, feeling the warm, limp body. One of the travellers bends down and removes the hare's head from the noose and thanks the animal for its sacrifice. He pulls his stone knife from where it is hanging around his neck, opens the belly of the hare and stuffs snow inside the body cavity to help preserve

Setting a *gelahigan,* a deadfall trap.

the meat during the journey. Then he ties a piece of deerskin around the animal and places it into his game bag.

Now you wend up through ravines of red and sugar maple, white and yellow birch and beech, darkened where the deep greens of hemlock boughs drape the north faces. Upward, well above 2,000 feet in elevation, you finally emerge into beautiful open forests of birch, beech, maple, and red spruce. The clear light of mid-morning is brilliant as you enter a stand of ancient canoe birches, *maskwamoziak,* light that reflects from the pure white bark marked only with thin horizontal lines. Someone takes one of your hands and guides a finger along one of these lines and says "*Yoda alnakwam ligen nasawan.*" "This tree, it is breathing."

Lines of snow still cling to the course of the trail of this north-facing valley. In a short while, it becomes necessary to take the snowshoes, *ôgemak,* from where they are slung over your shoulders and lace them onto your moccasins. While cinching the moose-skin bindings, you are struck by the simple elegance of the frames that are bent and fashioned from white ash, *ôgemakw*. Within the tear-drop space created by the frame is a cross-piece on which the balls of your feet swivel as the toes dip with each step. The interior of the frame is hung using a close-meshed hexagonal webbing, much finer than anything you have ever seen on a snowshoe. Most of those around you are wearing these graceful snowshoes, but some are fastening webbed snowshoes that are oval and others don those of a simpler design still—not much more than pieces of bark with toeholes cut into them. In some distant past, the *Ojiaak Bebonki,* "People of the North Country," taught the Alnôbak how to fashion the webbed *ôgemak*.

"*Majkômgwad. Psôngwata,*" says someone in your group as he begins to walk through the heavy, wet snow. "It is hard snowshoeing. The snow is deep."

Trudging along, you discover sets of fresh, paired animal tracks pressed into the soft surface of the wet snow. Alerted, the group begins to move slowly and quietly. Moments later, the first man in line stops, motions with his hand and whispers, "*Sagwasiz.*" Farther along, in the direction he is pointing, you spy an ermine, a short-tailed weasel, with its fur a patchwork quilt in transition between the white of winter and the brown of summer. A white-footed mouse dangles lifeless from its mouth. The ermine sits alert atop a small, snow-covered stump and nervously sniffs the air. Catching the scent of your group, it dives into a hole in the snow and is gone.

At last you reach your destination; a small hollow suggestive of a cave at the base of a rocky precipice. It would be impossible to journey higher; your guides knew that this particular cave would just be attainable at this point in the season. Hunting had been good that winter but an unusually large number of arrows had been lost. The fine, even-grained quartz from this cave would provide more than enough raw material for fashioning new points, as well as some raw stone to trade with the villages to the east, where the dark fire-rock lies everywhere—the finest flint stone that there is.[7]

Without wasting time, some of the men start pushing away the snow and picking up palm-sized stones wherever they lie about. Others take large hammerstones from their packs and begin to crack pieces of quartz from the rich vein along the cave wall. By mid-afternoon, the packs are filled with as much weight as the men can heft and carry back to camp. As you are leaving, you notice a number of men standing near the mouth of the cave and talking beneath their breath. Each of them takes something from a small pouch tied to his waist and leaves an offering of tobacco—a gift of gratitude in return for that of the stone.

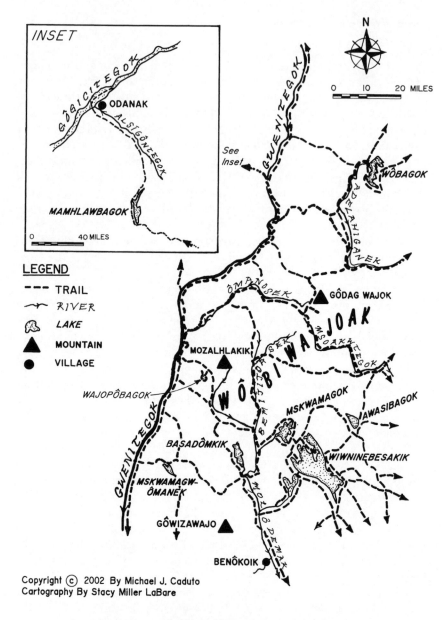

N

INSET

GÔGICITEGOK

● ODANAK

ALSIGÔNTEGOK

MAMHLAWBAGOK

0    40 MILES

0    10    20 MILES

GWENITEGOK

See Inset

WÔBAGOK

ADELAHIGANEK

ÔMANOSEK

GÔDAG WAJOK

WÔBIWAJOAK

MSOAKWEGOK

MOZALHLAKIK

WAJOPÔBAGOK

BEMIJIJOKSEK

MSKWAMAGOK

AWASIBAGOK

BASADÔMKIK

WIWNINEBESAKIK

GWENITEGOK

MSKWAMAGW-ÔMANEK

MOLÔDEMAK

GÔWIZAWAJO

BENÔKOIK ●

### LEGEND

- - -   TRAIL

~~   RIVER

  LAKE

▲   MOUNTAIN

●   VILLAGE

# SOME ANCIENT TRAILS
# OF WÔBIWAJOAK
## (The White Mountains)
# AND BEYOND

On the way back down the trail, the group moves silently and swiftly; feet finding the same places along the trail that they followed as young men who, adventure in their hearts, followed their fathers to this revered place for the first time. Their young strides had stretched to find the footsteps of their fathers in the snow, who as youths themselves had traced the tracks of their fathers, and down through the generations who walked a trail through this *pasadenak,* this "pass between the mountains" that would one day be called Jefferson Notch.

An ancient network of trails laces through hills, valleys, passes, and notches of *Wôbiwajoak,* the White Mountains: trails to places of good stone and fertile hunting grounds, trails that connect distant villages and relatives, trails that are the roots and branches of a flourishing system of trade in the north country, and trails that bring the Alnôbak close to the powerful spirits who dwell in the *Ginadenak,* the "very high mountains" amid the *Gitadenak,* the "great mountains." These trails cross Gedakina in a harsh era of deep winter snows that linger long; a period of time that started about 600 years ago and will last for 400 years; a time when the climate is much colder than it had been and later will be.[8]

Moccasin footsteps move along these time-worn trails; they trace the faults and fractures, the rifts and rills of a quilted landscape of alien terranes, knit together by heat and time, riding upon Earth's deep, molten currents. The lay of the land, its diverse network of interconnected rivers and valleys, made it accessible to the Alnôbak through time.

Knowledge of these trails is one of the most important legacies to each new generation. But trees grow and change in appearance, they are blown down in windstorms and burned in fires. Floods and the runoff from heavy rains can wash trails away and make them unrecognizable. At places along the trail that can be confusing or are prone to sudden changes, arrows cut into blaze trees, *cilakwtahôzi,* are often used to point the way. Carvings are sometimes created as signposts that communicate more detail. A canoe with two men paddling is carved into the side of a pine tree along the shore of *Wiwninebesakik* to represent a route of portage.

Several major trails converge in Bristol. A trail from the north that runs up along the *Bemijijoasek,* the Pemigewasset River, meets with the trail named after the lake known for its sandbars or "land rising under water," *Basadômki,* Newfound Lake. Both meet with another trail that comes east from the water known for "salmon fishing," *Mskwamagwômanek,* Mascoma Lake, and follows what is now called the Smith River, passing through Danbury. Somewhat to the north, the trail along the river of the *Mskwamagw Keloskamagwônek,* the "salmon fish eggs," which will one day be known as the Baker River, joins the *Bemijijoasek* from the northwest. This trail continues to the northwest through the Oliverian Notch, passes a seasonal home of the Alnôbak along the shores of Wachipauka Pond, *Wajopôbagok*, "a mountain pond," and resolves itself in the valley of the "Long River," *Gwenitegok*, the Connecticut. Back at the valley of the *Bemijijoasek*, and farther still to the north, the trail is joined by the Kancamagus Trail in the present-day town of Woodstock.

Trails that range from the *Wôbiwajoak* are used by some of the eastern cultures, including the *Msoakwtegw* (Saco), *Bigwaki* (Pigwacket), *Adelahigan* (Androscoggin or Amarascoggin) and the *Ginebagw* or *Ginebaga* (Kennebec), those who live near "large lakes" or by the river where "the water is high." In time, a trail will trace a tortuous route from "fish trap place," *Adelahiganek*, the Androscoggin River, and north to a community that will be known as *Odanak*, the "village," at the confluence of the *Alsigôntegok*, "empty cabin river," the Saint Francis, and the *Gôgicitegok*, "very great river," the Saint Lawrence.[9] From Berlin Falls, the route begins with a paddle north up the Dead River, through Dead River Pond, and below a high bluff on the western flank of Mount Jasper—the site of a cave located well above the pond that cuts 14 feet into the rock from which rhyolite is obtained for making projectile points. The trail continues past Head Pond and follows the North Branch of the *Ômanosek*, the Ammonoosuc River to West Milan. From here, the trail turns west via the Upper Ammonoosuc to *Gwenitegok*, the Connecticut, in Northumberland, then 15 miles up *Gwenitegok* to North Stratford. Here the trail follows the Nulhegan River to Island Pond, then over the height of land to the Clyde River, then northeast until it reaches and crosses "an expansive lake," *Mamhlawbagok*, Lake Memphramagog. Finally, the trail meets the St. Francis River and follows this to the Saint Lawrence. Another branch of this trail splits off in West Milan, travels overland to Robbin's Brook, follows along to the Androscoggin River, and upstream until it reaches the shore of *Wôbagok*, Lake Umbagog. Less than 15 miles northwest of *Wôbagok*, just north of Dixville Notch, is a geographic couple—a lake and a 2,780-foot mountain that today are both named "Abenaki," after a common name for the Alnôbak.

Many trails cut high up into the mountain passes and beyond, where seasonal sojourners and the seekers of stone, game, and spirit among the Alnôbak leave indelible traces of their passing. An ancient bowl is left high up on the slopes of *Mozalhlakik*, the "cow moose land," Mount Moosilauke, and a number of ancient sites are located near campgrounds that will one day be used by the Appalachian Mountain Club in the upper elevations of *Wôbiwajoak*. At least 12 percent of the ponds located in the White Mountains are reached by trails and used by the Alnôbak.[10] A sketchy tale of life at these sites will one day be read by students who de-

Clouds form near the summit of *Gôdag Wajo*, Hidden Mountain, the tallest peak in the Wôbiwajoak, White Mountains. *Photo by Michael J. Caduto.*

cipher the ancient clues found in arrowheads, spearpoints, and other implements fashioned of quartz taken from the nearby slopes. One day, the "Edmands Path" will traverse the general vicinity of a trail that now follows Abenaki Brook and climbs Abenaki Ravine on the northwest slope of 4,761-foot Mount Eisenhower.

Here, where the mists swirl and the constant churning of a bad spirit, *maji niwasku*, roils the whitewater weather that washes over these mountains, the majestic head of *Gôdag Wajo*, "hidden mountain," rends the windy currents that loop and eddy down its leeward slopes. It is said of *Gôdag Wajo* and of many other powerful beings that *bamadenainak*, "they live at the mountains." Some say that atop the peak we now call Mount Katahdin lives a powerful creature of flight known as *Bemola* or *Bmola*. With the body of an enormous eagle that is covered with mottled feathers, and a gigantic head that resembles a man, Bemola flies vast distances to the north and south and is so powerful that he can sweep up a full-grown moose in his claws. From atop *Gôdag Wajok*, his voice carries throughout most of Gedakina, yet, in the midst of flight above a village, he can hear someone whispering his name. At this, when his wrath boils, Bemola throws bolts of lightning and creates heat so intense that it causes the trees and lodges to burst into flame. Some say Bemola is a great storm-bird who uses his expansive wings to whip the winds into squalls of fury that generate powerful swirling banks of dark, angry clouds that pelt the land with rain and snow. When his heart is moved with compassion, however, he comes to the aid of a traveller, especially a hunter in need of help.

Climbing the high peaks on which Bemola comes to rest, a person can see much of the portion of Gedakina that will one day be New Hampshire: from the heights of *Gôdag Wajok* and east to the dramatic peak of Mount Chocorua, then south to the top of *Gôwizawajok*, Mount Kearsarge. Viewed from these great heights, this wide and varied land appears as a boundless wilderness. Over the span of the 2,000 years or so leading up to the middle of the second millennium, thousands of people in hundreds of villages live here, tucked away amid this expansive space. Near the end of this time, the population is roughly 25,000.[11] This is more than ten times the number of people the land could support before the arrival of horticulture; a time when ancient peoples subsisted on hunting and gathering.

In the Upper Valley of the landscape drained by *Gwenitegw*—including the Indian Stream and the rivers named Israel, Ammonoosuc, Mascoma, Sugar, Cold, and Ashuelot—at least 130 villages, family sites, and encampments exist at various periods during this same span of time.[12] Among the areas that the People live on the eastern shore of *Gwenitegw* are places that will one day be known as Lancaster, Haverhill, Orford, Lyme, Dorchester, Hanover, Lebanon, Enfield, Canaan, Plainfield, Claremont, Sunapee, New London, Charlestown, Walpole, Stoddard, Westmoreland, Spofford, Chesterfield, Swanzey, Hinsdale, and Winchester.[13]

The largest numbers of people are denizens of the hundreds of sites that are occupied at different times within the watershed of "deep water," *Molôdemak*, the Merrimack River, its tributaries, and their interconnected lakes, including the "land around lakes," *Wiwninebesaki*. Among the tributary rivers in this region are the Pemigewasset, Beebe, Baker, Smith, Winnipesaukee, Blackwater, Contoocook, Soucook, Suncook, Piscataquog, Souhegan, Nashua, and Little. With the exception of Lake Sunapee in the west and Lake Umbagog in the northeast, all of the largest lakes in today's New Hampshire eventually drain into *Molôdemak*: Lake Winnipesaukee; Newfound Lake; Squam or "Salmon" Lake, *Mskwamagok*; Winnisquam Lake, *Wiwnimskwamagok*, "salmon fishing all around"; and *Msinebesek*, "great lake," the Massabesic.

Across this great interior—in year-round villages, seasonal homesites, and places where travellers camp for a time—the People leave behind signs of their daily lives. One day in the distant future, these sites will reveal themselves to strangers who will live throughout the countryside of this region, in cities, villages, and rural places bearing the names of Plymouth, Newfound Lake, Bristol, Winnipesaukee, Governor's Island and many other islands in Lake Winnipesaukee, Moultonborough, Melvin, Wolfeboro Falls, Alton Bay, Weirs Beach, Laconia, Lochmere, Clark's Island in Silver Lake, Sanbornton, Tilton, Franklin, Belmont, Sutton, Boscawen, Penacook, Loudon, Concord, Allenstown, Suncook, Hooksett, Amoskeag Falls, Manchester, Goff's Falls, Merrimack, Litchfield, Nashua, Salem, and along the Little River in Kingston and Plaistow.

One of several village sites on the shores of Massabesic Lake just east of Manchester is known throughout the region as a magnificent roost for *belazak,* passenger pigeons, where thousands of birds congregate. *Belazak* feast on a variety of berries and fruits, insects, worms, snails, seeds of the pine, hemlock, maple, and elm, as well as acorns, chestnuts or *wôbimenal,* "white berries," and mast produced by the beech, *wajoimizi,* the "mountain tree," which is also their favorite nest tree. Countless pigeons flock on the mudflats of Great Bay near Durham during low tide and many nest in the oak woods in Exeter. Once *belazak* begin the nesting season, they are not hunted until the young birds have fledged.

Each year in late spring, shad, some of the larger alewives, and the "red fish," *mkwamagw,* the salmon, begin arriving in the rivers that drain the *Wiwninebesakik* and in the headwaters of the *Bemijijoasek,* the Pemigewasset. Shad continue upstream to complete their life cycle in the warmer waters of the lakes but salmon do not stop to spawn until they reach the cold, rocky, whitewater streams and rivers. By late May, multitudes of leaping salmon and masses of writhing shad that often weigh 10 pounds or more are caught, scooped into dip nets, and stuck with spears. Others encounter weirs made of interwoven brush that is anchored with lines of poles supported by piles of rocks built along and part-way across the river bottoms. The hapless fish bump along the weir as they search for a route to get around it. When they reach the end of the mesh of brush, they swim into baffled nets from which few escape. The People smoke, dry, and store these fish for the winter in pits lined with bark or grass.

In late August and early September, when the eels are running down to the ocean where they will swim south and spawn in the Sargasso Sea, eel weirs are built in many rivers in such places as Franklin, Tilton, and Lakeport. Each trap consists of two short lines of piled rocks built on an angle to meet at a point directed downstream. A space is left where the two rows of rock meet and an eel pot is placed there; a round basket with a hole for the eels to enter. Whenever the young, 3- to 4-inch shad inadvertently get caught in the eel pots on their way down to the ocean at the end of *Demezôwas,* the Harvesting Moon, they are released and allowed to

Salmon leaping the falls are a sign of spring in many rivers around Gedakina.

continue their journey. It is here, in the prolific *Wiwninebesakik,* that many people come to spend the coldest moons of the year in some of the largest winter villages of the interior.

Downstream, in the valley of *Molôdemak,* there are many villages of the *Benôkoiak,* "falling hill people," the Penacook. Some of the smaller villages are found on the shores of ponds throughout their homeland, including Long Pond, Shellcamp, Loon, Turkey, Turee, Turtletown, and

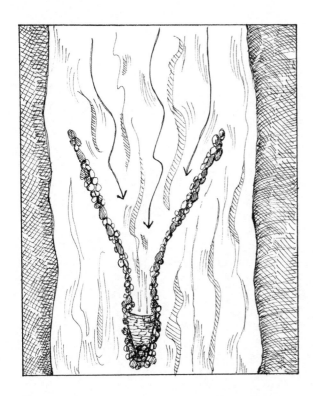

An eel pot placed in the run of a stream during their migration to the sea near the end of *Demezôwas,* the Harvesting Moon.

Rocky Ponds. Other *Benôkoiak* villages line the shores of the Contoo-cook River and its tributaries, the Warner and Blackwater rivers. Each village is situated where there is fertile land for the gardens, a good source of water, and easy access to the seasonal fishing grounds and to water-ways on which to travel. The *Benôkoiak* travel far to collect the fine clay along the shores of Bow Brook to create pots that turn gray, ruddy, or even black when fired.

The hard work that is necessary to create elegant pottery is well re-warded. Peoples of many different beliefs, languages, and adornment come from as far west as the Great Lakes, *Msinebesal,* to trade goods at the main settlement at Sugar Ball Bluff on the eastern shore of *Molôdemak.* Here the visitors often sit on soft deerskins atop bark-covered floors inside conical bark wigwams, *Alnigamigol.* Each *Alniga-migw* is made of eight to ten poles with their ends dug into the ground to form a circle of about 12 to 15 feet across and the tops tied together at a center post. At the base of the center pole is a large, flat stone stood on end. In front of this stone is a hole ringed with hand-sized stones in which a cooking fire is burning. Resting nearby on a smaller prostrate stone are a

mortar and pestle made of granite and a spoon and ladle carved from bison horns that were brought by traders past. Stew is cooking in a large clay pot hung from a pin driven into the center pole just above the fire; the earthy scent of the food fills the *Alnigamigw*. The young woman stirring the pot has several bone needles hanging from her waistband. On a clear day, the piece of bark that shields the smokehole is pushed aside and the bearskin flap that covers the door is rolled up to allow the air to blow through.

Leaning against the walls, hanging from lodgepoles, and stored on shelves of branches and strong woven mats are the tools and utensils of daily life: bows and arrows, flint knives, spears, and clubs for hunting; a stone axe for peeling bark and chopping wood; a stone hoe; a wedge for splitting; a stone hammer and gouge for carving; and a large stone maul for pounding ash logs to create strips of wood for basket making. Grooves are carved around the granite and slate headstones of the axes and hoes, around which the split ends of the handles are fitted and securely lashed. Strings of dried fish are hanging along the sides of the *Alnigamigw*— strings of the alewives that were caught with dip nets; strings of the shad and salmon ensnared and speared while shooting the roily, rocky waters on their way to spawn in the lakes and headwaters that feed *Molôdemak*.

When the families who live in the *Alnigamigol* and the visiting traders have finished bartering, they often walk into the heart of the village to join other families in the central chamber of one of the large, rectangular longhouses. Every family that lives in the longhouse has its own room, cooking fire, and smokehole. Scattered among the families gathered in the large meeting space are amulets and other symbols of common emblem animals painted on clothing, including turtle, bear, wolf, muskrat, beaver, hummingbird, otter, raccoon, and grouse. Certain animals are adopted as guides in the natural world because a particular family associates with that animal's character or because it is one of the most important sources of food and materials for that family. Families that have adopted the same animal emblem often join together to form a family band and share a hunting territory.

After the great fish runs of springtime have subsided, the peoples of the *Molôdemak* region, and even the *Zokwakiiak* of the *Gwenitegw* valley near the mouth of the Ashuelot River, often make long journeys to the seacoast to catch fish and shellfish. Many travel into the drainage basin of the Piscataqua and its tributary rivers of the Branch, Little, and Cocheco. Other rivers that drain into the Great Bay and Little Bay before they in turn empty into the Piscataqua are the Bellamy, Oyster, Piscassic, Lamprey, Squamscott, and the Exeter. The names of the native peoples of this region reflect the nature of the waters and their surroundings: the Piscataqua or *Beskategwa*, "a branch river"; the Cocheco or *Bamijoak*, "where the swift current passes"; the Newichwannock or *Nôwijoanek*, "at the long rapids"; the Squamscott or *Mekwapskok*, "at the red rocks"; and the Agawam, who take their name from either *Waodagwômek*, "canoe landing place," or *Sagwidema*, "deep tidal waters." These last two peoples tend the southeastern door of the Alnôbak, which opens upon the land of the Massachusett, *Msiwajok*, "at the big mountain."

Denizens of this countryside between the land and the sea and others who visit this environment experience a beauty and abundance that contrasts with elemental extremes. Villages are scattered throughout valleys braided with flowing waters and amid the numerous hidden bays and inlets in places like the Seabrook Marsh. Inhabitants of one village at Adam's Point in the Great Bay near Durham journey out beyond the calm

Plying the coastal waters in large dugout canoes, the Alnôbak used harpoons to fish for cod, swordfish, and tuna, and to hunt porpoises, seals, and small whales.

waters and into the often angry seas in large, ocean-going canoes to fish for cod and to hunt for porpoises, seals, and small whales. Their weapons include harpoons bearing lance-like tips of bone that are notched on one side with a series of barbs.[14] Once the harpoon penetrates the skin, the tip gradually works its way deeper into the blubber and flesh as the prey struggles to escape. Great volumes of dried meat and cod are put up for the winter by coastal families and brought back by visitors to their homes in the interior.

Bones of the white-tailed deer are fashioned into a tool used for opening clams, quahaugs, and other shellfish and for etching designs into pottery. After the shellfish have been eaten, the shells of scallops and others are used to imprint designs into fresh clay. Large, sturdy shells are fashioned into bowls or attached to wooden handles and used as blades for hoeing the garden. Small shells are worked with care to form intricate jewelry. Mother-of-pearl is made into beads, strung, and used for "small white trade beads," *wôbôbial* or wampum.

Inland and farther to the north, in the heart of the Saco valley, the *Bigwakik* live at the eastern door of Gedakina, the land of the People, and are strongly influenced by the culture and language of the *Benapskak*, the Penobscot, a people dwelling "at the down sloping rock." Several seasonal encampments and gatherings of family dwellings are found along the banks of the Saco River where it flows through Crawford Notch. There are significant villages in Bartlett and Intervale, between

North Conway and Conway, and in Fryeburg. Smaller seasonal encampments and family sites are found along the banks of some of the Saco's tributary streams such as Mill Brook in Conway, and, most likely, along significant tributaries such as the Sawyer, Ellis, and Swift rivers as well as Pequawket Brook. Feeding into the Saco from the west are the Ossipee River and its headwaters and tributaries, the rivers Chocorua, Bearcamp, Lovell, Beech, Pine, and South. A number of villages are found on the shores of Ossipee Lake, inhabited by those who live in the land *Awasibagok,* "beyond the water."

In the farthest northeastern reaches of the future New Hampshire, in the watershed near *Wôbagok,* are the villages of the Androscoggins or Amarascoggins. These Alnôbak families live southwest of one of the eastern peoples, the Norridgewock—those who live *Molôjoak,* "at the deep current." Rivers that are the source and tributaries of the Androscoggin include the Magalloway, Swift, Diamond, Dead, Moose, Peabody, Rattle, and Wild.

This place of long winters, turbulent rivers, and expansive lakes flush with crystal waters is the northeastern gate of the Alnôbak, where many a long-legged moose grazes the edge of a bog, where snowshoe hares flee from the cats of wild, and where sinuous northern pike stalk the emerald depths in quest of hapless prey. An eagle circles and veers overhead, buffeted by a swift-moving chill wind that scuds the mountain peaks thick with evergreen forests, which reach out with coarse, dark fingers to embrace the distant horizon.

# 9. Cycles of Seasons

꩜   ꩜   ꩜   ꩜

Akwôbakka, *"this time last year,"* when the full orb of Kikas, *the Planter,* had just set behind the early morning trees, the boy Ceskwadadas *dove into an icy pool along the banks of* Bagôntegok, *Butternut River. He swam underwater toward the shallow ripples where the fish struggled to swim upstream. As he surfaced, Ceskwadadas let out a "Whoop!" and proudly held aloft the season's first catch of the red fish,* mkwamagw. *That is how he came to be called Kingfisher.*

On this day, as he finishes an early morning meal of corn stew, butternuts, and acorn bread, Ceskwadadas sits and nervously fidgets with the roots of the black spruce that lash the inner layer of bark onto the arched lodgepoles of his family's niben Alnigamigw, *their summer wigwam.* It seems like his family is taking all day to prepare to go fishing for mkwamagw.

Ceskwadadas's mother and grandmother are well known throughout the region for harvesting and preserving great volumes of butternuts, bagônal. They share this largess so generously with others that bagôn has become the family's emblem—the only emblem in the village that honors a tree.

Finally, Ceskwadadas's mother picks up two baskets. She gives one made from birchbark to his sister and then hands Ceskwadadas a fine basket woven of ash splints.

"Come, Ceskwadadas," says his mother in jest, "It's time to go. Hurry up, we have all been waiting for you!"

Trying to ignore his mother's teasing, Ceskwadadas holds the rim of the basket up to his nose and sniffs the rich scent of the braided sweetgrass that is woven into the rim. One of his favorite smells, it always transports him to the hot, late summer canoe trips into the marsh where the sweetgrass, mskikoizal, grows. The pattern in which the mskikoizal is woven reminds Ceskwadadas of the design that his family imprints onto the outside of their pottery using a cord woven of the fibers from the stems of milkweed, azibizak. Other geometric and floral patterns, made from paints or woven from porcupine quills and moosehair, are seen throughout the village on everything from moccasins and canoes to belts, pouches, cups, pipes, garters, and containers fashioned of skin and bark.

"Oliwni gia," says Ceskwadadas as he stands, "Thank you." His mother looks at him with pride. Ceskwadadas has long hair that drapes loosely over his shoulders. Someday, when he is married, he will wear his hair coiled in a knot. He has exchanged his winter leggings and his favorite bear-skin jacket that has a porcupine-quill design woven into it for an early summer breech-clout that is tied around his waist. Ceskwadadas's family's winter clothes will hang near their bearskin beds inside the Alnigamigw until the cold weather returns, including the beaver-skin blankets that they wrap around their heads to stay warm when the bitter winds blow.

Just before Ceskwadadas leaves the Alnigamigw, he grabs a conical hat with two turkey feathers sticking out of the top and puts it on to keep the mkazawigejosizak, the blackflies, from getting into his hair and biting his scalp. When his mother, grandmother, and sisters see Ceskwadadas emerge from the Alnigamigw wearing moccasins, a breechclout, and the hat, they point to him and fall into fits of raucous laughter.

"Gikina Ceskwadadas, Look at Ceskwadadas," says his sister who is called Nighthawk, Beskw, because she never seems to sleep and loves to gaze at the night sky. "Madegwôgwezo, He looks like a rabbit!"

Red-faced, Ceskwadadas takes the hat off and brings it back into the Alnigamigw. "It is just as well," he thinks to himself. "I know this is father's ceremonial hat and he would have been angry if he found out I was wearing it."

Ceskwadadas comes out of the Alnigamigw and looks over at Beskw, intending to yell at her. When their eyes meet, however, he can only smile. He recalls all of the tricks he's played on her in the past and knows that he'll think of a good joke to repay her for mocking him. Besides, Ceskwadadas can see that his younger sister is in that fragile stage when young girls are sensitive about everything he says to them.

Beskw is wearing a fine pair of beaded moccasins, a painted skirt the length of her knees, and a porcupine quill–embroidered blouse that reaches half-way down to her thighs. Unlike her mother's hair that is held back with a headband, and her grandmother's that is tied in a loose coil atop her head and adorned with flowers, Beskw's hair is made up neatly into two braids that reach almost down to her waist, each of which is tied at the end with a deerskin thong.

Ceskwadadas recalls the work that he and his father did to prepare and soften that deerskin, how they mixed some of the brain with the soft, white marrow and soaked the skin in that foul-smelling blend. After they cured the skin in the smoke of a slow-burning fire, his mother rubbed and stretched it until it was completely dry. Then she scraped it with the rounded blade of a flint knife, worked it with her teeth until it was extremely soft, and died it purple with the juice of blackberries.

*As he stands and recalls the pleasing aroma of boiled blackberries,
Ceskwadadas's revery is broken by the voice of his mother from where she
and the others are disappearing over a rise in the direction of the river.
"Ceskwadadas," she calls, "Dokimezi ni naowihla! Wake up and come
here!"*

*Ceskwadadas starts from his daydream and runs along after his family.
His mother and grandmother look at one another and shake their heads,
laughing.*

*"He has much to learn," says Ceskwadadas's grandmother, "but he is
thoughtful and has a good heart." One day, when he has become a man,
Ceskwadadas may walk the same trail as his father and be chosen as
zôgemô, the village chief.*

—*Along the shores of Bagôntegok, "Butternut River,"
Contoocook, New Hampshire,
500 years ago*

    ❧    ❧    ❧    ❧

When Ceskwadadas enters his family's long bark house, he passes an emblem painted inside that symbolizes a bear—a group from which many
healers come. The knowledge and wisdom that he acquires from his elders
will show Ceskwadadas how to maintain a positive relationship with the
guiding animal spirits and how to enlist the benevolent side of their nature
to assist his family band and village. In addition to this relationship with
the land that provides the subsistence needs of his village, Ceskwadadas
will have to communicate with the land of the ancestors, to seek their in-
sight and wisdom. Most of all, he will need to live a life in balance; to
embody a spirit of generosity and loyalty in relationship to the People that
is continuous with the circle of giving and receiving that he maintains with
the beings in the natural world—plants and animals, the rocks and
water—all of which are *bemôwzi*, alive. If he becomes a well-loved and respected *zôgemô* or chief, Ceskwadadas will welcome visitors to the village
and he will facilitate many celebrations among the Alnôbak; feasting,
singing, and dancing at the seasonal festivals of maple sugaring, the strawberry harvest, the picking of first corn, and the mid-winter ceremony.

Ceskwadadas will not make decisions on his own, however. Like his
father, who is out on this day trying to resolve a disagreement between
two families over the boundary of their hunting territories, Ceskwadadas
will learn how to listen to others in the circle of elders and heads of families and to offer solutions to problems that arise—to use his powers of per-
suasion to facilitate a consensus and to foster a vision among the people.

His grandmother and the other elder women will have a particularly strong say in the direction of these decisions. At times, Ceskwadadas and the village council will advise joining with neighboring families, villages, and even the peoples of distant regions within *Wôbanaki*, "Dawnland," when a threat arises that is too great for the families to surmount alone.

Whenever it is decided that war, *aodowôgan*, is necessary to ensure the survival of the village, a special war chief will be chosen to lead the others. At times, Ceskwadadas and his people hear of a highly organized group of five nations who live far to the west on the other side of *Bitaw-bagok*, the "Lake Between," a body of water that will one day be known as Lake Champlain. But the ones that Ceskwadadas's people refer to as *Magwak*, and who call themselves *Haudenosaunee*, "People of the Longhouse," live so far to the west that they have always been regarded as a distant threat. Still, each grown man keeps a *baskhôdebahigan*, a war club or "head breaker" hanging in the family's *Alnigamigw* just in case it is needed. Each man fashions his *baskhôdebahigan* from the root ball of a young hardwood tree, using the trunk as a handle and sharpening each of the smaller roots to form an array of ominous spikes.

The deadly *baskhôdebahigan* or "head breaker" was used as a war club.
*Photo by Jeffrey Nintzel, courtesy Hood Museum of Art, Dartmouth College.*

Travelling back in time to visit the homeland of Ceskwadadas and Beskw near the banks of the *Bagôntegok*, you would find a people with a remarkable knowledge of the natural world and how to use it to survive. As the Alnôbak are molded by the land they inherit from the elders, they, too, sculpt, carve, sew, cook, gouge, chop, and chisel everything they need from the basic elements around them: stone, bone, skin, sinew, flesh, fur, bark, wood, and clay. You would find, nearly five centuries ago, that the People were so successfully adapted to living in their environment that their numbers range from twenty-five to thirty thousand and as high as forty thousand throughout the land that would be New Hampshire.[1]

Resources around the larger villages provide for up to four or five hundred people. Some families live within a central village that is often protected by a high wall of upright logs. Smaller villages of individual extended families are arrayed around the main settlement. Families move seasonally within large, permanent homelands that encompass the riverside places for fishing in the spring, the croplands for summer gardens, the hunting grounds of fall and winter, and the winter village. Within this home range, land is divided into family hunting territories; depending on the tradition within each family, hunting rights pass down through either the men or the women. Villages move every ten years or so when garden soil near the village needs to rest to replenish itself and when weeds have multiplied to the point where they are numerous and hard to control. Periodic migration within the home range is also necessary because, in time, firewood becomes hard to find in the vicinity of the village and game animals become scarce, requiring time for their populations to recover. Refuse pits eventually fill up and multiply, attracting raccoons, skunks, and other animals that can be a nuisance.[2]

Within each journey of Sun, *Gizos*, and the passing of the moons, the survival of the People melds a combination of sustainable horticultural practices with the ancient traditions of fishing, hunting, and gathering. It is true that Ceskwadadas's village and others of warmer, fertile valleys rely more on horticulture for their food when compared to villages in the colder uplands and northern regions where hunting, fishing, and gathering are still the most important means of survival. There is, however, a strong similarity in how Ceskwadadas's village, and others throughout Gedakina, survive during the yearly cycle of the moons and seasons.

As a witness to the yearly activities of the Alnôbak, you would discover a people who live a hard-working, yet varied and interesting life. Their seasonal movements to natural environments of richness and abundance are exquisite beads in a land of beauty, beads that string a necklace of thirteen moons—moons that are symbolized by an equal measure of large scales that adorn the back of every turtle's shell.

Every year in the heavy snows of late winter, during the moon of *Zogalikas*, the "Sugarmaker," maple sap, *zogalinebi*, is gathered in birchbark buckets from the groves of sugar maples. Sap is also gathered from *winsak*, the "sweet birches" of yellow and black. A diagonal slash is made in the bark of each tree, down through the inner bark, and a hollowed-out elderberry twig is forced into the lower end of the gash. Sap flows down the twig and collects in a birchbark bucket. Some of the clear, cool sap is dipped up with a birchbark cup and drunk as a refreshing, mildly sweet treat of the early season. Sap is then boiled in a clay pot or a birchbark bucket until it reaches the consistency of maple syrup, *zogalosôbôn*. Some

Pulling on the lives of the Alnôbak, *Nanibôsad,* "the all night walker," marks the progression of the seasons. *Photo courtesy UCO/Lick Observatory.*

of the sap is boiled beyond this point to create maple sugar, a rich source of energy when the People journey distant trails. Birch sap is boiled into a less-concentrated sweet drink with a strong essence of wintergreen.

When *Kikas,* "The Planter," arches across the skies of spring, women and children spend much of their time gathering early greens, ground-nuts, and other edible roots. Many families move to temporary lodges on terraces above the rivers and lakes where they can witness and partake of the countless fish and migrating birds that swarm the skies, sag the branches of trees, and froth the roiling waters in a drama that bears testimony to the generosity of the Great Spirit, *Gici Niwaskw.* The spring diet is virtually all fish and migrating birds. Passenger pigeons, ducks, geese, cormorants, brants, and other migrants are hunted with bows and ar-

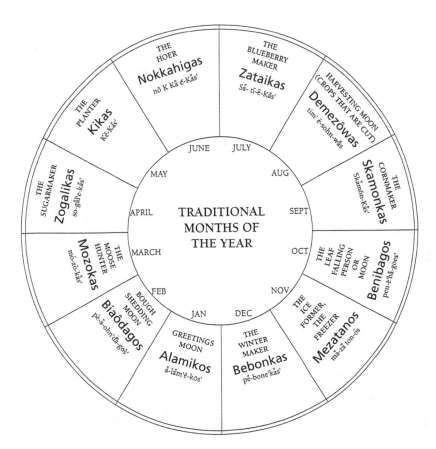

Traditional Moons of the Alnôbak. *Courtesy Jeanne A. Brink.*

rows, nets and bolas. Families are fishing with spears, seine nets, hooks, hand lines, weirs and, after sunset, from canoes bearing seductive torches lashed to the prows, drifting ghostly through the mists. In the lakes and slow bends of the larger rivers, they catch bass, northern pike, perch, catfish, and sunfish. Dace and other minnows are often used for bait. Swift waters bring a bounty of suckers, alewives of about a pound, shad of from 4 to 6 pounds or more, and individual adult salmon that range upwards of 20 to 30 pounds. All the while, alongshore, a mix of aromas tells of fish being gutted and cleaned, filleted into strips, and cured by smoking on racks near the fires and drying in the sun.

Summer villages are often located along rivers not far from the fishing grounds. The larger villages of about four hundred people must plant 80

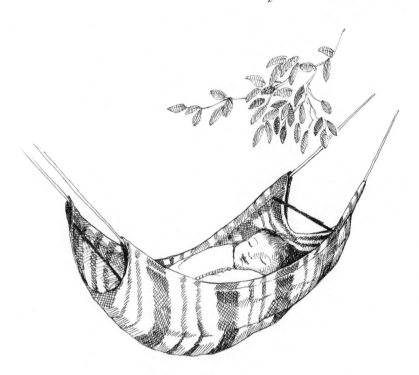

to 100 acres of crops every springtime.[3] Mounds of eight-row flint corn and another variety that matures even sooner are ringed with three or four seeds of mostly red kidney beans that are pushed into the side of each hill of corn. In between the mounds are planted the seeds of pumpkins, bush scallop squash, summer crookneck squash, gourds, and Jerusalem artichoke. Off to one side in the garden is a small plot of ceremonial tobacco that is usually grown and tended by the men. Close to where the families are working, babies sway from blanket hammocks hung just above the ground from a sturdy but supple overhanging branch that is rocked gently by the hand of each early summer breeze. Other, very young children are carried around the garden swaddled in a soft, deerskin wrap and tied to a cradleboard.

Summer advances with the coming of the Hoeing Moon, *Nokkahigas*, and the garden demands long days of weeding, hoeing, and mounding soil around the base of the corn to encourage prop roots and to stabilize the stalks. A second crop of corn is later planted to create a staggered harvest and to extend the season for eating ears in the sweet or "green" stage. Fishing tails off as the spawning runs subside.

In early summer, the fragrance of the first ripe fruits and berries wafts over anyone who goes picking in the forest, along the riverbanks, and in the overgrown fields that were once cropland. The berry season begins with the first whiff of the floral sweetness of ripe wild strawberries, *mski-koiminsak*, "little grass berries." Soon Solomon's seal is ready to pick with its dangling seeds that taste like tender, young peas. Elderberries, blueberries, wild currants, blackberries, and raspberries are each harvested when their time arrives. Some are eaten fresh, and some are squeezed into juice or dried and stored for winter use. Blueberries, in particular, are preserved in great quantities and their ripening comes when *Zataikas*, the "Blueberry Making Moon" arches across the night sky.

Over the course of the growing season, when the black flies, *mkazaw-igejosizak*, and later the mosquitoes, *begwes*, become unbearable, families head down to the riverbank, lakefront, or seashore and swim or canoe out from shore onto the waters and into the breezes to escape the incessant appetites of these "blood-sucking insects," *wikwadigasak*. For these occasions and when there is a need to travel, birchbark canoes and *amasolal*, "dugout canoes," are always waiting at the waters' edge. Occasionally a *pkwahaol* or "peeled boat" is seen among them; a canoe fashioned from the bark of elm or spruce.

After the garden is well underway, the parents and older children of many villages leave the crops to be tended by elders, who also remain behind to care for the youngest children. It is believed that the two ages have the most in common and that elders have much wisdom to share with the young because they are closest to each other on the circle of life: infants are just beginning and the elders are nearing the completion of their journey. Although they will be missed, it is natural for the rest of the family to leave them, to don their pack baskets and blanket packs, to paddle and portage the birchbark canoes as they head south or east to summer camps along the seashore. Here they are glad to visit again with their summer friends on the coast and to share stories of the time that has passed.

But the summer is short and the People make efficient use of time gathering clams, mussels, quahaugs, and oysters. They spear lobster in the shallows, trap smelts in their seine nets, and venture out onto the deeper waters for cod. When enough flesh from the shellfish, fish, and lobsters has been cleaned and dried to fill their packs as heavy as they can carry, the family begins the arduous trip home with this important seashore supplement for their stores of winter food. At any time during this journey or whenever they can be caught, quail, turkey, grouse, and a number of other small animals are hunted for a fresh meal.

As late summer and early autumn approach, eels are caught in traps set in the spawning streams that lead from the larger lakes. Ash splints, spruce roots, and the barks from birch and basswood are gathered for making baskets during the long winter months ahead. With the coming of the Harvesting Moon, *Demezôwas,* many of the medicinal plants are now ready to be gathered and dried or otherwise prepared for later use, such as yellow birch bark for diarrhea and rheumatism, sweetfern leaves and jewelweed sap for poison ivy, basswood bark and slippery elm bark for infected wounds, the bark of striped maple for creating a poultice to reduce swollen limbs, milkweed sap for treating warts, sumac berries for making a tea to soothe a sore throat, and willow bark tea for colds and muscle aches.

It is imperative to be especially careful and respectful when picking and gathering medicinal plants. Permission is asked of the plant and of Gici Niwaskw. Only a small amount is taken from any patch of plants, merely thinning out the growth and leaving many of the plants behind to continue the next generation. Never is the tallest "Grandmother" plant picked from any growth of medicinal plants: She, who is the progenitor of all others in that place, is left behind out of respect and to assure the fecundity of her kind. Finally, a prayer of thanks is offered to the four directions and a gift of seeds from that plant is left to propagate more of them, or in its place, a symbolic gift of tobacco to complete the circle and restore the balance.

With every chop of the hoe, with each pluck of a weed, the garden grows closer to the moon of *Skamonkas,* the "Corn Maker." During a good year in the cornfields, *skamonikikônal,* the corn stalks reach 5 to 6 feet tall and yield enough ripe ears to produce a harvest of about forty bushels of corn per acre. The first ear of ripe, green corn—one that is "in the milk"—is picked and placed back in the garden with a prayer to the Corn Mother thanking her for this gift of life. After the songs and dances of the Green Corn Festival, the first ears of the harvest are eaten boiled and roasted on the cob as *kakikwsôzo.* Green corn kernels are removed from the cob and boiled to create samp, or they are boiled and steamed together with fresh squash.

Most of the corn is left to mature beyond the green and into a starchy ripeness. This corn is harvested, then the husks are pulled back and braided together to form long strings of dangling ears that are hung from the lodgepoles and dried for the duration of a moon or more. Dried seed corn that will be planted the following spring is left attached to the cob, but dried corn that is meant for eating is shelled by using the jaw bones of white-tailed deer, as well as thin, palm-sized scraping stones to remove the kernels from the cob. Beans and slices of squash are also dried and stored with the corn in baskets that are placed in winter storage pits lined with bark and grass.

As the season progresses, a variety of additional foods will be prepared and stored, such as nuts and dried fish, meat, and berries, including large

Corn hanging inside the lodge to dry.

volumes of dried blueberries, *bakwsataizatal*. Chestnuts and butternuts are the most important fruits of the wild harvest that are put up as part of the winter provisions, along with white oak acorns, hazelnuts, beechnuts, walnuts, and sumac berries. Great quantities of chestnuts or "white berries," *wôbimenal*, are stored in southern and central villages so they can be prepared for eating during the winter months by boiling, roasting, and grinding into meal. Oil that rises to the surface when acorns are boiled to remove the tannins is sometimes skimmed off, preserved, and used as a flavoring for meat and as an anointing oil for sanctification. As they prepare the winter stores, everyone hopes for *Alnôbainiben*, a "Person's summer," the especially warm, sunny days that come in the midst of the autumn chill.

One of the blessings sought at this time of year is the gift of a successful hunt. When *Benibagos*, the "Leaf Falling Moon" rises and the trees are ablaze with fall colors, hunters retreat for a period of fasting and to seek a right relationship with the animals. When a hunter reaches this place of spiritual balance, the animals will offer to sacrifice their lives so that the hunter's family may live.

Hunting groups now leave the summer lodges near the gardens and journey to the uplands and to the northern parts of the home range, where they live in seasonal hunting lodges. Each group, which is chosen by a mature hunter, consists of his sons and brothers and their family members. A hunting group may also be composed of the hunter's daughter and her husband.

Among the necessities that hunters pack as they prepare to depart from the seasonal home base is a blanket hammock and a length of rope braided from the inner bark of the "bast tree," *wigebimezi*. These and other essentials are often carried in pack baskets that are also made from strips of basswood bark. Using their intimate knowledge of the areas rich in deer and other game, the hunters bait their trap lines and string them out for several miles. In addition to traps, the basic weapons of the hunt are the knife, bow and arrow, spear, snare, pitfall trap, and the *gelahigan* or deadfall trap.

Every hunting group catches the game that is most prevalent in their territory. Overall, however, the most important game animals that feed a typical village are fairly consistent in their order of importance in the diet: deer, bear, moose, beaver, raccoon, bobcat, woodchuck, porcupine, gray and red fox, skunk, rabbit, red and gray squirrel, muskrat, chipmunk, mouse, and shrew.[4] Deer, bear, and moose are the three greatest sources of winter protein among the Alnôbak. Moose and beaver are even more significant in the catch of hunters in northern regions. Although dogs are well-loved and respected, during times of scarcity when survival is threatened, they become one of the top three or four providers of meat. Other wild prey are taken when they can be found, including elk, turkey, otter, wolf, marten, lynx, partridge or ruffed grouse, spruce grouse, snapping turtle, and migrating birds such as the passenger pigeon, Canada goose, hooded and common mergansers, and a variety of ducks. Meat is cut into strips, dried, and smoked by hanging on the lodgepoles and by draping over racks placed by the fires.

In the northern and middle regions of Gedakina, deer are most commonly stalked individually by a few hunters and their dogs, especially when the first snows come and tracking is easy. During the moon of *Mezatanos*, "the Ice Former," hunters in the southern parts of Gedakina sometimes light a fire, *skweda*, and use it to herd deer into enclosed areas. Drive-lines of brush are ignited, which frighten the deer toward funnel-shaped enclosures. Deer are snared or shot with arrows when they come through the restricted space.[5]

The four most important game animals among the Alnôbak
*(top to bottom, left side first):* white-tailed deer, black bear,
moose, and beaver.

Late autumn is a time of the much-anticipated harvest festival. Singing, dancing, storytelling, and feasting go on for several days and the
main meals are not complete without the meat of bear. After the festival
has passed and the long nights of winter settle over Gedakina, families remain in the hunting grounds until late December, the end of the moon
known as *Bebonkas*, the "Winter Maker." Then they return to the main
village in time for the mid-winter ceremony.

During the months ahead, after the appearance of the "Greetings
Moon," *Alamikos*, come the long days of fishing through holes chopped
in the ice. Women spend much of their time cleaning skins with stone
scrapers, preparing and tanning hides, making clothing with awls and
bone needles, decorating clothing with porcupine quills and moosehair
paints, weaving ash baskets, and creating bark buckets using birchbark,
spruce roots, and pitch. Men use the time when they are not out hunting
and fishing to make tools and to fashion dugouts and birchbark canoes.
They can accomplish almost anything they need to in the winter village
using the basic tools of an awl, hand axe, gouge, adze, and crooked knife.

Winter months are not simply times of working hard and waiting out
the cold moons. Everyone looks forward to sunset when it is time to
*adelôgwadeboka*, "cook the evening meal," to once again imbibe the rich,
earthy scents that waft from the hearth. In the clay pots that hang over
cooking fires and in the wooden troughs where hot rocks simmer enough

stew for a large family, the simple ingredients from gardens both cultivated and wild are deftly combined and stirred with spoons and ladles of
horn and crafted gourds. Delicious and varied meals and drinks are
served in dishes and cups of wood and birch bark, then eaten with the fingers or by using a spoon carved from shell or horn. Food is usually served
family style in large wooden bowls. While the Alnôbak diet includes hundreds of domesticated and wild ingredients, the most important staples
are moose and deer, fish, corn, beaver, and bear.

Dried kernels of corn are worked with a stone mortar and a pestle of
stone or hardwood until they form *pezedamôn,* ground corn. Hulled corn
kernels are boiled in lye made from the ashes of a hardwood fire to create
*belagikwtal,* which is sometimes used in soups or boiled until tender to
make hominy, *kakikwtal.* Parched kernels are pounded into corn meal,
*skamonnoktahigan,* and combined with a bit of water to form a dough
that is molded into small cakes that are baked on a flat stone in front of
the fire. Cornmeal dough is also shaped into small loaves, wrapped in
corn husks, *kwalaskoniganal,* and baked slowly in the ashes at the edge
of the fire to make corn bread, *skamonabôn.* Many meals are accompa-
nied by a drink made from parched corn meal and warm water that is
sweetened with maple sugar. This rich beverage is drunk from cups fashioned of birchbark or gourds.

Corn is often combined with other ingredients and *môwigisoak,* "they
are cooked together." Succotash, a traditional dish of corn and beans, is
high in protein. Some soups and stews are made from a base of corn or
corn meal or they are thickened with hominy. Rich, hearty soups often
contain fish and fishheads, meat, beans, squash, pumpkins, roots, or
groundnuts. Moose lips and tongues and even beavertails are occasionally
added as delicacies in soups and stews. Certain tender species of gourds
are also eaten as *kwôlaskw wasawa,* "gourd-squash."

The hard work of the growing season is constantly rewarded with a
bounty of wild winter food stores. Acorn meal is added to soup as a
thickener. It is also wrapped in green leaves and baked in the ashes to
form acorn cakes. Chestnuts and butternuts are boiled, roasted, and
ground into meal. Hickory nuts are shelled and roasted. Dried blueberries are used in soups and in many other dishes. As the winter goes on, the
storage pits empty of their corn, beans, dried blueberries, and other foods
and they are filled with refuse.

Meat is eaten raw, broiled on coals, or roasted on a forked stick.
Breasts of *belaz,* the passenger pigeon, which have been preserved by
smoking and drying, are often cooked in squab oil. Whenever the hunters
go out to *belazoka,* to "hunt pigeons," this flavorful oil is saved in such
large quantities that it is not unusual for each family to use 5 or 6 gallons

in one winter. Often, when visitors are being entertained and during festivals and feasts, large holes are dug in the ground and lined with hot rocks. Meat and beans are wrapped in leaves or bark and placed in this hole, then a fire is built on top and the food is left to bake.

Often, after the evening meal, families gather in one of the large meeting places in the center of a longhouse. Most nights, during the winter, these large openings become a "storytelling place," *talôdokazwôgan*. Often, a child turns to an aunt, grandfather, uncle, or parent who is a good storyteller, *nodôtlokad*, and asks, *"Liolaldamana lôdoka niona ôtlokôgan?"* "Please tell us a story?" Several tales are told during the course of the evening; tales of great deeds, of how things came to be in the world, of frightening monsters, and, perhaps, of the humorous adventures of *Azeban* the Raccoon Trickster. The final story before the children drift off to sleep is always a gentle or humorous tale with a good heart— a tale that sows the seeds of good dreams.

A storyteller, *nodôtlokad,* weaves a tale by the fireglow.

One evening, Beskw, the young girl named "Nighthawk," asks, "*Nigô,* 'Grandmother,' where did people come from?"

"Long ago," comes the reply, "Dabaldak created the first man and woman from a piece of stone. He breathed life into them."

"But we're not made out of stone!" Beskw exclaims, laughing.

"*Nda awôsiz,* No child. Those first people had cold, hard hearts. They did not care about anything or anyone. They pulled up the trees and stepped on the animals. They were destroying everything."

"What did Dabaldak do, Nigô?"

"One night, as the stone people slept, he inhaled the life back from them and they never awoke. You can still see their shapes lying down in the tops of the hills against the sky."

"But Nigô, then there were no people left alive."

"So Dabaldak carved the shapes of many people into the side of a big *ôgemakw,* an ash tree. Then he stepped back and shot each person with an arrow of life. As the arrows entered, they disappeared and those people stepped out of that tree, alive. They were the first Alnôbak."

"Did they destroy the world, too, Nigô?"

"*Nda awôsiz,* their hearts grew from a living tree. They cared for the plants and the animals, and for each other. They are your *negônzosak,* your ancestors from long, long ago."

"But who creates the people now?"

"There is an old one, *Kiigawes,* our Earth Mother. Whenever *Gizos,* Sun, is warm and bright, she creates all living things that are born into the world."[6]

ᥱᥣᥰ    ᥱᥣᥰ    ᥱᥣᥰ    ᥱᥣᥰ

As the winter progresses, the time of heavy snows arrives with the "Bough Shedding Moon," *Biaôdagos.* Sometimes there is little to do but stay close to the village and tend to the daily chores of life. Hearty souls venture out into the forest for deep winter travels by snowshoe and to-boggan. Hunting trips follow the routes along traplines carefully laid within clearly defined winter hunting territories in the northern part of each family's home range. Occasionally, during a hard winter, black bears are taken as they sleep in their dens. During the moon of the "Moose Hunter," *Mozokas,* the largest members of the deer family, whose shoulders stand taller than the height of an adult, are more easily stalked in the soft, deep snows that restrict their ability to get around.

With the return of *Zogalikas,* the "Sugarmaker," the yearly cycle of life among the Alnôbak begins anew. The running of sap through the trees signals more than the start of the sugaring season. As the inner bark flows with sap coming down from the treetops, the growing cells just inside of this layer swell with the water and nutrients needed for new growth. At this time, when the growth cells and inner bark become soft, it is easy to cut and slip the outer bark off the *maskwamozi,* the canoe birch, in large unbroken sheets. Late winter is the traditional time for building and repairing the family's birchbark canoe.

First, a canoe birch must be found that is at least 2 feet in diameter. A prayer of incense smoke is then offered to Gici Niwaskw and the tree is asked for permission to use its bark to make a canoe. Then the tree's bark is studied to decipher where to cut and create a piece that is as blemish-free as possible. A bed of hemlock, spruce, or pine boughs is laid down in the location that the tree will fall to cushion its landing and protect the bark. As the base of the tree is alternately being chopped with a stone axe and burned, it is spoken to with gratitude using kind, respectful words.

Once the tree has been felled, the upper end of the log is separated from the crown by chopping and burning. Now, two smaller logs are laid down, a bit over 20 feet apart, with each lying across an end of the place where the tree will lie as it is being worked on. Long poles are used to roll the birch trunk up and astride these end logs. A lengthwise incision of about 18 feet is made through the bark along the top of the suspended trunk, then each end of this piece of bark is cut completely around its girth. A low fire is lit underneath the birch in order to keep the bark pliable as the edges of the long seam in the bark are gradually pried up using a tempered hardwood chisel. Eventually the entire piece of bark is separated from the tree, creating a canoe shell of about 6 feet wide and 18 feet long called a *wigwas,* "piece of bark suitable for one canoe." This bark is rich in oils that will enable it to withstand prolonged exposure to water without decaying.

Every measurement is made as the craftsman has been taught, using the age-old tradition of hands, fingers, knuckle joints, arms, and, where a length is too long to be measured with a part of the body, strips of ash basket splint. Finer cutting and splitting are done using a crooked knife consisting of a curved wooden handle onto which is fitted and lashed a sharp blade fashioned from a beaver's incisors. Larger-scale carving is accomplished with a stone adze and a hammer, while drilling is done using stone drills or by spinning a projectile point or the tip of a knife.

Rocks are now placed along the bottom of the canoe to weigh it down. The outside of the bark is then bent and held up on each side with stakes that outline the spindle pattern of how the canoe will be shaped when it is finished. The birchbark is cut and sewn as necessary while it is being fashioned into a shell that tapers on each end. Each cut, seam, and knothole is plugged with pitch from either a pitch pine or white pine, then the entire inside of the bark is given a generous coat of pitch. The rails are fashioned from birch or spruce, drilled with notches where they will receive the ribs, lashed to the long upper edge of the birchbark shell and tied together on each end using roots from the black spruce. Several hundred feet of these flexible roots will go into the canoe, each of which had to be dug up and split with a knife into sections about 6 feet long. Cross-pieces of maple, ash, or larch are fitted in between and across the rails as thwarts and as handles to use when carrying the canoe upside-down over a long portage.[7]

Now it is time for *abonskan,* "putting in the ribs of the canoe." Within the bark casing, a frame of nearly four dozen ribs is constructed, each of which is about 2 inches wide, ⅜ inch thick, and tapers to about 1 inch where it fits into the joints drilled into the rails. These ribs are made from freshly cut green ash or oak that can be bent without splitting. After each rib is fitted and completed, it is held on an angle, pushed up into the notches that await it in the rails, gently tapped into place against the inside of the bark, and allowed to dry. Once all of the ribs have dried, the craftsman removes and puts them aside, being careful to store them in the same order that they were arranged in the canoe.

Now, thin overlapping pieces of northern white cedar are laid lengthwise for sheathing within the birchbark shell. These cedar strips line the inside of the bark in a pattern that fans together at each end where the canoe narrows. Once the sheathing is complete, the ribs are tapped into place for good, firmly anchoring the sheathing between the ribs and the bark shell. The bottom of the canoe is now broad and nearly flat. All joints and seams are plugged with spruce gum applied to the outside. Finally, the canoe is fitted with paddles made from spruce, maple, or ash and with a long rod for poling through shallow water. Any leaks that arise will be plugged using the spruce gum or pitch that is stored on board in a small birchbark bucket.

About three to four weeks after it was begun, the *maskwaolagw,* "birchbark canoe," is finished. It measures about 16 feet long, nearly 3 feet across at the widest point of the beam, and about 14 inches deep. Each end sweeps up to a high, graceful point and is decorated with a series of alternating triangles and half circles on the upper part of the outside edge for a few feet back from each tip. It weighs less than 100 pounds and can safely carry people and equipment weighing more than five times its own weight—adequate for a journey that includes three or four people and their gear.

Both men and women will ply the waters using the elegantly tapered paddles that will propel the canoe during the ten years or so that it will last if it is well cared for. These lightweight bark craft are so versatile that they can be guided slowly through the deep waters of a wide river or paddled swiftly to ascend rocky streams, taking advantage of the shallow draft. Family and friends gather around to offer a prayer of thanks as the canoe-makers gently and ceremoniously slip the prow into the water, step inside, and paddle away for the first time.

Building canoes and wigwams, *Alnigamigol,* growing the gardens, hunting, and other daily and seasonal subsistence activities place a heavy demand on resources. Whenever a village moves to a new environment within its larger home range, the tired land that is left behind needs to remain fallow for twenty-five to fifty years before it is replanted so the soil can replenish and become fertile enough to produce the eight bushels of corn needed for each person in the village every year. A larger village of around four hundred people needs roughly 330 to 580 acres of cropland within the home range to allow for enough land to be continuously cultivated while other cropland is lying fallow and resting.[8]

Everyone works together to make the *Alnigamigol* at the new village site. During the interim, when the voices of the workers in the gardens fall silent and the cries of children no longer echo through the treetops, the old village grows up to grasses and wildflowers, then blackberries, young pines, and aspens. These old settlements, with habitats in varying stages of regrowth, provide an abundance of plant foods and a diversity of habitat for animals that thrive in the new growth and are an important part of the Alnôbak diet, including rabbits, white-tailed deer, bear, moose, and woodcock. Here, where children once ran amid acres of open field, the nasal mating call of *nagwibagw sibs,* the "under leaf bird," now rises from beneath the thick brush before its stout, mottled body is carried aloft on whistling wings into a salmon sky.

PART III

In the Balance

# 10. Life, Death, and Medicine

୧୬  ୧୬  ୧୬  ୧୬

*The boy Ceskwadadas now stands on the threshold of manhood.
During the sweat, ôpsazi, his spirit teacher, niwaskw agakigamwinno,
guides him on a journey to the four directions. After entering the yellow
door of dawn in the East, wôbanek, he travels to the south, nibenakik, the
place of things new and growing and green, and then to the west, the place
of those things yet to come in the red of sunset, nakihlôd, which leads to
life in the next world. He moves along the Circle to the whiteness of the
north, bebonki, the place of fasting, quiet, and clarity, of healing and
peace.*

*"Four directions," his* niwaskw agakigamwinno *tells him, "one for every
season and one for each journey in the Circle of your life."*

*Ceskwadadas emerges from the eastern door of the* adalômpsazimeg, *the
dome-shaped sweat lodge covered with bearskins, through the Door of Life.
Now he leaves the comfort of the familiar faces in his village and travels to
the secluded place where he will stay for the four or more days of his fasting
time,* manosakôdin. *Ceskwadadas leaves with only a few possessions tied to
his belt: a wooden cup, a stone knife, and a small skin bag containing his
fire-making tools, a pipe, some tobacco, and several wooden carvings of his
namesake, the kingfisher. Only his teacher will accompany him on this
journey, but even he will fall back as Ceskwadadas walks the final distance*

to his secret place. His teacher remains nearby to watch the boundaries and protect Ceskwadadas during this vulnerable time.

Ceskwadadas lights a fire and begins a fast that will last for at least four days. During this time, he avoids sleeping and subsists on nothing more than the clear water of a spring that emerges from an outcropping near his place of seclusion: a cave at the base of a cliff that reaches up near the top of a small mountain. Ceskwadadas sings, plays songs on his flute, and offers prayers of incense from his pipe. He seeks a vision for his true life and the power to move along that journey.

After a few days, Ceskwadadas enters a trancelike state of hunger and his visions begin to focus. They are filled with the sights and sounds, the smell and feel of wigwedi, "have no tail," the lynx. Ceskwadadas picks up some charcoal from the fire and begins to draw these images on the face of the rock in the cave. Ceskwadadas has found an ally to lend its power, protection, and guidance.

Through these new eyes, the young man stalks and consumes a snowshoe hare. He climbs a steep, jagged cliff and leaps among the outcroppings until he reaches a broad, flat, sun-drenched rock at the rim of a steep declivity. Wigwedi's mate and cubs tumble from the mouth of a cave set just back from the edge of the precipice. They rub up against him in greeting as the air fills with their smells and the sounds of contented purring. Now Wigwedi curls up with his family in the warm rays of Gizos and guards his lair.

The young man sees a clear path ahead of him for the first time. It is a season in life for raising a family, of hunting for their food, and of fighting to protect them. During the last night that he will spend in seclusion, he digs up a young birch tree that has a root ball with several branching rootlets. After washing off the dirt, he dries the wood by his fire and begins to carve.

By morning his handwork is complete and, despite the days of fasting and sleeplessness, his heart beats hard and fast with excitement. He stands at the mouth of his cave, holds the wooden likeness of his namesake aloft, and speaks to Gici Niwaskw, the Great Spirit. In a clear, reverent voice, he says, "Oliwni gia Gicinemahômek, *Thank you Grandfather.* Nia wizwôgan ligen *Wigwedi! My name is Lynx!*"

ею    ею    ею    ею

At the age of thirteen, soon after reaching puberty, Wigwedi's experience of passage has given him an ally or helper, a guardian spirit, and has increased his sense of personal power, his medicine. When his younger sister Beskw, "Nighthawk," reaches the beginning of menstruation, she too will undergo a time of transition from childhood, from which she will come forth as a young woman. Her mother, grandmother, and aunts will build a small Moon Lodge that is set apart from the village but is not too distant. Here, the elder women will keep a close watch as Beskw, in her visions, will seek a guardian spirit of her own to teach and help her through the coming years of marriage, of giving birth, and of raising a family. Beskw will be kept in seclusion at this time because women in this stage of life possess a power that is dangerous for men to be near.

Similar to Wigwedi, thousands of young adults among the Alnôbak, including Wigwedi's ancestors and his descendants, experienced their vision quests throughout the hills and valleys of Gedakina. Some left signs of their journeys painted and carved in caves, *dawapskaal,* places "down inside rock," and in rocky places, *bamapskakal.* Medicine persons who were communicating with animal helpers during spirit journeys also created many paintings and petroglyphs. Paintings of people, game animals, a reptile, and birdlike creatures are found along the shores of one lake in southwestern Maine that lies just over the border from New Hampshire.

Well to the south and west, along the south bank of the West River and a short distance upstream from *Gwenitegok* in Brattleboro, a rock is carved with an array of petroglyphs that include six birds, two figures that could be snakes or eels, and one that is a dog, wolf, or fox. Twenty

Petroglyphs along the banks of the West River.

The petroglyphs at Bellows Falls. *Photo by Michael J. Caduto.*

miles upstream from these symbols, carved into bedrock on the west bank of the Connecticut River below Bellows Falls, a number of petroglyphs depict faces, including several with antennae. These may represent beings who watch over the animals in the water and on land. They also bear a remarkable resemblance to rock carvings that portray Kokopilau among the Pueblo peoples of the southwest, such as those that were carved at a site that will one day be called the Indian Petroglyph State Park northwest of Albuquerque, New Mexico. Kokopilau was a grasshopper person who played his flute and spread the seeds of good plants from a hump on his back as he led the people on their migrations to the four directions. Carvings of Kokopilau are found on rocks throughout the range of his travels, from South America, throughout the southwest, and up into Canada. It is possible that Kokopilau's flute was heard this far to the east.

As children of the Alnôbak, Ceskwadadas's and Beskw's rites of passage into adulthood come after a warm, loving upbringing during which they spent much time with their grandparents. Beskw was also taught many things by her paternal aunt and Ceskwadadas's paternal uncle was like a second father. Both children watched, listened, and practiced until they gained mastery of each skill. In this way, they learned the traditional songs, how to decorate clothing and build canoes, how to knap stone to make arrowheads, how to weave, cook, sew, and hunt, and how to sing the canoeing song in unison when paddling down the river in a group.

Oftentimes, what at first seemed to be a single new undertaking became a lesson in every aspect of traditional life and interconnection with the natural world. When learning how to build a canoe, the children had to recognize the distinctive markings of the canoe birch and the correct time of year to fell a tree and slip its bark. They needed to identify the black spruce and had to know how to dig and prepare the roots for lashing. White spruce roots would not do because they were too brittle. It was essential to know which tree to cut for wood to make the sheathing, thwarts, rails, and ribs as well as all aspects of woodworking and the artistic designs and materials used to decorate the birchbark. Most importantly, the children absorbed the practical and spiritual customs associated with gathering respectfully from the wild.

Although she did more work around the *Alnigamigw* than Ceskwadadas, Beskw was not the only one who did household chores as a young child. As young as five or six years old, the children were expected to do their share in taking care of their siblings and the cousins who were younger than they were. This is the same age that Ceskwadadas's uncle taught him how to fashion and shoot a bow and arrow. He had to wait until he was ten, though, before his father and uncle felt he was responsible enough to accompany them on his first hunting trip.[1]

The siblings did their share of work but the adults made sure that Ceskwadadas and Beskw had plenty of time in which to play. When they were young, they spent endless hours tossing a ring made from a bent willow twig over an upright pin stuck into the middle of a slice from a pine tree. As he matured, Ceskwadadas became one of the most accomplished young archers in the village. His prowess during the stalking games—the tests of stealth that helped the village youth to hone their hunting skills—was legend. Beskw was so fast in the running games that she could best many of the boys. She also had a large collection of dolls that she had fashioned from corn husks. Older children sometimes joined in when it was time to play lacrosse or handball, an early form of baseball that was usually played by adults.

When the winter snows flew, the children slid and wove their way down narrow, winding trails through the forest while standing on a long piece of wood with an upturned end. Younger children sat upon wider, sled-like versions of this design, squealing as they coasted downhill. Snowsnake was one of the favorite games played by both children and adults. Long, smooth sticks of hardwood—sometimes engraved with elaborate designs—were carved so that the leading end turned up slightly. These were slid downhill along well-packed tracks in the snow that were sprinkled with water to create an icy glide. The snowsnake that traveled the farthest won the game.

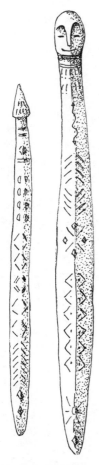

Snow snakes like these are slid along icy tracks in the snow to see whose travels the farthest.

Whenever Beskw or Ceskwadadas did something that was disrespectful or hurtful to another person or a being in nature, the adults refrained from using physical punishment. To do so, they believe, breaks the child's spirit and teaches violence as a means of getting one's way and solving problems. Instead, the misbehaving child is taken aside and confronted with stern admonitions about the consequences of bad behavior. Other children also show their disapproval when someone misbehaves, and the desire to be accepted creates a powerful force for positive social interactions. When a child is repeatedly difficult to reason with, that child is subjected to an extreme form of social stigma during which his or her face is blackened with a bit of bear grease mixed with powdered charcoal. This only happened once to Ceskwadadas, when he was being absent-minded and wasteful of the deer meat during a period of scarcity. Rarely, in extreme cases, a child is put outside and not allowed into the wigwam for a period of time.

Now that he has become a young man, Ceskwadadas is already looking at the young women of neighboring villages in a different way. He met someone last year during the midwinter ceremony to whom he is very attracted. She is called "Song Sparrow," *Kaskaljas,* because of her beautiful voice. Ceskwadadas spoke to her for some time and they seemed to have an easy way of being together. In time, upon completing his own rite of passage and after Kaskaljas had come of age, Ceskwadadas made his intentions known by sitting outside her *Alnigamigw* after dark and playing a song on his flute, a song that he wrote to express his feelings for her. But Ceskwadadas knows that much has to happen if he is to marry Kaskaljas.

First, his parents have to pay a formal visit and make a request of Kaskaljas's parents for her hand in marriage to Ceskwadadas. If the girl's parents agree, Ceskwadadas will have to go hunting for an impressive prey, such as a deer, bear, or moose, to show that he can feed a family well. He might give Kaskaljas a bundle of furs instead. Ceskwadadas's mother will have to present the gift to Kaskaljas's mother or aunt, who will then offer it to the girl as a formal proposal of marriage from Ceskwadadas. She might refuse the gift if she does not want to marry him. If she is willing, however, she will accept the proposal by placing an ear of corn inside Ceskwadadas's *Alnigamigw*.[2] Then he will go off and hunt again, giving the first game caught to Kaskaljas's mother and, perhaps, another impressive present for the bride-to-be.

The new couple will go to live with Kaskaljas's family. They will sleep side-by-side, but head-to-toe. If they fight often and elders agree that the match is not to be, the boy will lose his presents when the wedding is called off. If Ceskwadadas and Kaskaljas are deemed a good match—if the marriage seems right and everyone approves—an announcement will be made and the preparations for a wedding begun. All relatives, friends, and leaders in their two villages will be invited. Their life together as husband and wife will start with a wedding ceremony during which they will receive a wedding basket, many practical gifts to help them begin their own household, and no small amount of good-natured teasing. Afterwards, a great celebration will be held with feasting and dancing.

When Kaskaljas and Ceskwadadas have children of their own, they will complete the circle by sharing the old traditional stories that carry morals and lessons, including stories of *Azeban* the trickster, the benevolent Seven Brothers called the *Thunderers*, and Bemola, the powerful bird person. Educational stories, secular stories, and family stories will be shared year-round. Oral histories, genealogies, and age-old cultural traditions will be passed down word-for-word to the next generation.

Sacred stories will only be told in winter when the ice is thick and the underwater monsters cannot hear the tales. When sacred stories are told out of season, the Little People, Manôgemasak, turn into bees, mosquitoes, or black flies and teach the storyteller a lesson. Stories are so powerful that everything stops to listen. Stories told out of season can confuse the world of nature in which everyone knows that sacred stories are meant for the long cold nights of winter; the season of the frost, *topoihla*, not for the growing season when there is much work to be done. When these stories are told at the wrong times, the leaves that hear them will change color and fall from the tree prematurely. Seeds planted in the garden, who think it is still winter, will remain dormant and the crops will fail. Mother birds will stop to listen as their young go hungry in the nest.

Sacred stories and dreams are bridges between the Ordinary World—the land of the Alnôbak—and the land of the spirits. These are a form of communication that reveals what a person needs to know to live in balance, to keep his or her medicine strong, to share a kind heart guided by a clear mind. Medicine, *nebizon*, is sacred, the source of one's strength, wisdom, and power in the cosmos. *Nebizon* encompasses all aspects of life that act on body, mind, and spirit, as well as one's attitude toward them. This includes all forms of knowledge such as the advice of elders, natural and cultural laws, and lessons that arise from stories and oral tradition. *Nebizon* is sought through the vision quest, ceremony, fasting, and by seeking both joy and satisfaction in life. Adults carry a medicine bag, *nebizoninoda,* in which they keep special stones and other natural objects that represent their helpers in nature and bear testimony to the power received through their life experiences, particularly during the rite of passage and in later vision quests. Corn and tobacco are also kept in the *nebizoninoda* for use when giving thanks and making offerings.

Among the Alnôbak, a person's medicine resides in both the body and in the life force. Vital and alive, the life force embodies emotion, energy, and health. The wellness of a person's spirit depends on the state of his or her mind and the strength of relationships with Earth and Sky. All life is connected by the healing "water," *nebi,* that flows through veins replenished and renewed by the *nebizon* of Gedakina.

Overhead, the night fires of stars flicker in the inky blackness and *Mozokas* glares cold and bright against the deep snows of late winter. Her reflected light illuminates *Moz,* a moose, that is mortally wounded; an arrow protruding from its side.

Moz drops to her knees and rolls against the ground. Moz tries to get close to the healing power of *Begwiigawes,* Mother Earth. Time and again Moz pushes the arrow through the snow and into Begwiigawes, with each thrust driving the arrow farther into her side. Crimson petals of blood bloom and glisten on the ruffled white flakes.

Struggling to her feet, Moz staggers forward for a distance, drops again, and rubbing, pushes the arrow hard against the medicine of Begwiigawes.

Moz hears *nadialowinno,* the hunter, trudging through the snow, *wazôli.* Moz is spent; can do nothing but wait, heaving, pulling at each breath.

She senses nadialowinno as he kneels and strokes her shoulder. The stranger speaks gently and breaths into her nostrils. Moz feels a sharp sting on her neck, then she begins to slide toward the silence of a night where no fires burn.[3]

ℰℒ℘    ℰℒ℘    ℰℒ℘    ℰℒ℘

Begwiigawes gives the air and water to the People, the food and plants that heal. She has the power to restore balance between the Alnôbak and the natural world, between a man and a woman, between a person's body, mind, and spirit. A healer is a person of power—a man, *medawlinno*, or a woman, *medawlinnoska*—who stands at the heart of this relationship and can intercede to help others maintain and restore this balance. This often means finding a way to cure an illness that is unknown or one that persists for a long time. Healing is often a legacy among the Alnôbak; many healers are descended from a long, venerable lineage steeped in the traditions that are used to bring a state of health, *zôgelamalsowôgan*, to others in the village.

Herbalism is an important aspect of healing. Apprenticing under a practicing healer is a discipline that takes several years. The student often learns how to treat a variety of diseases, illnesses, and injuries, and then specializes in specific, related groups of diseases and the plants associated with treating them. Roots, barks, extracts, and oils are used to create poultices, teas, and salves. Knowledge of each specific plant—what it can be used to treat and how to prepare the healing parts of that plant—can only be acquired through lengthy and intensive training. Roots need to be boiled and softened to make a poultice for dressing wounds; teas have to be extracted to treat stomach upsets, colds, and sore throats. Persistent fevers are helped by participating in the purification of the sweat lodge and jumping directly into cold water after emerging from the intense heat. General body aches are wrapped in heated sods that are then shrouded in mats. Alnôbak medicine is sophisticated and well advanced: On the average a person lives for thirty-seven years.[4] But if a person survives childhood diseases and the many dangers faced as an adult, he or she may live well into the eighties.

A *medawlinno* or *medawlinnoska* must also be able to bring the spirit into balance. He or she may counsel a dream quest and ask for help from the guardian spirit. The healer's namesake is the loon, the "magic bird," *medawihla*. A healer can see into the heart of a person, can locate the physical aspect of an ailment by touch, and, at times, can even see what is to come. By looking carefully at the cracks and patterns that form when the shoulder blade of a deer or moose is seared in the fire, a *medawlinno* can read the signs of where to find game. At times a healer asks the aid of one or more of its animal helpers—a bear, an eel, or perhaps a bird. This may be why the petroglyphs along the West River near Brattleboro were created. These allies go out into the world to help the healer in his or her tasks and they need have no fear from the healer who is strictly forbidden from eating any of their kind. The most powerful among them can possess an animal's life force or even change into a bird or other animal to escape danger.

Music is one of the *medawlinno*'s greatest helpers. In addition to its traditional role in attracting a woman, the notes from a flute fashioned of cedar can help to draw game into the hunting grounds during times of scarcity or to lure enemies into a trap. The healer's wooden hoop drum is a tight stretch of fresh deerskin across which two tautly strung bands of sinew sing and speak to the spirits and the forces of nature such as wind, thunder, and lightning. Tobacco is often used at the beginning and during the conclusion of a rite, to ask for help and to send prayers of thanks to Gici Niwaskw. The *medawlinno* also presides over weddings, funerals, and other ceremonial occasions in the village.

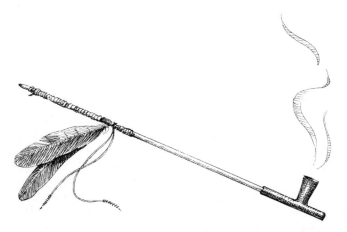

In death, as in life, the well-being of the Alnôbak is inextricably linked to the spirits and to the natural world. It is essential for the living to help each person who dies to complete the journey to the spirit world where they will live a life of contentment and be at peace. During the spring, summer, and autumn, burials take place as soon as possible. This is imperative because the spirit of the deceased lingers in this world in an unsettled state until that person is properly buried, sometimes causing illness and misfortune among the living. If someone dies when the ground is frozen, a scaffolding is erected to hold the body until the ground thaws. Red ochre is sometimes used to help protect the deceased from harmful spirits. Adults and young adults are dressed in their finest clothing and are given enough food to make the long journey to the place of the spirits up the path of the Milky Way.

Once they reach their new home, they will need all the things they used in life, so these are also interred: tools, utensils, weapons, and personal items such as a pipe and tobacco. Possessions of great value in Alnôbak society are often buried, such as pottery and implements made of copper that were obtained by trading with peoples far to the west. Sometimes when a chief dies, a *zôgemô,* an oval of tree seedlings is planted around the grave.

Men and women mourn for a year after their partners die. During this time, a widow may wear a hood, does not attend celebrations, and cannot remarry. If one of her children has died, she will cut her hair and blacken her face. When in mourning, widowers, too, do not attend festive occasions and they wear a mask of black mourning paint. Parents of a dead child are treated with special kindness and are given gifts of consolation. Later, when the mourning period is over, they will reciprocate the generosity and good-heartedness of others by holding a feast.

Virtually every village and seasonal settlement has a burial ground. Over the millenniums, the connection between the Alnôbak and Gedakina continually deepens as the bones of the ancestors become the land itself. The spirit and creation of Gici Niwaskw complete the circle in the soil that now nurtures the roots of plants and, in turn, every living thing that depends on plants to convert the life-giving force of *Gizos* into the essence and substance of survival. From the tallest mountain to the deepest valley, every site is a sacred expression of the Creator's spirit and every grain of soil is consecrated ground that speaks with the voices of the ancestors. As the old stories say, there is no greater desecration than to disturb the remains of a spirit at peace.

ℰℐ℗    ℰℐ℗    ℰℐ℗    ℰℐ℗

For four seasons the game animals had been scarce. A family with a young child journeyed for several moons before they were able to obtain enough food to last the winter. As the sun set on the last day's journey back to the village, they came across a small earthen lodge in the forest.

"I do not like the feel of this place," said the woman. "We should continue until we reach my father's lodge."

"No," said her husband, "I cannot walk another step. Let's sleep here in this old lodge and finish the journey in the morning."

Although it was against her best judgement, the woman agreed. After crawling inside the lodge, they lit a cooking fire, prepared a generous meal, and ate. As they lay down to sleep, the man crawled over to a ledge along the wall to place his pack there. He noticed that someone who had died was rolled in bark and resting on the ledge.

"We must go now!" the woman cried as she held tightly to their child.

"I am not worried," said her husband. "We will be safe for the night. Now go to sleep." With those words, he blew out the fire, lay down, and pulled his bearskin blanket around him.

His wife was too frightened to sleep. Sometime during the night, she began to hear a gnawing sound and thought that a raccoon or bear must be chewing on their provisions and stealing a meal. There she lay in the darkness, listening to the voices of *gokokhasak,* the barred owls, calling their names to each other across the valley.

When the woman rolled over to shake her husband and wake him, her hand touched something warm and wet. Her groping fingers slipped into a gaping hole that had been chewed in his chest.

Drawing back her bloody hand and screaming, she grabbed up her child and ran as quickly as she could through the darkness toward her father's lodge. When she began to near the lodge, she felt a presence behind her and turned to see a brilliant flame in pursuit. No matter how fast she ran, the flame kept getting closer and closer. With a final burst of speed, she reached her father's lodge and dove through the door just as the flame singed the nape of her neck.

"What is it?" cried her father as he was startled awake. The woman held her hand out in the orange glow of the coals left from his cooking fire and they both saw that is was red with blood. When she told her father what had occurred, he found it hard to believe.

"At daybreak," he said, "we will go and see what has happened."

The next morning, some of the people in the village who heard the woman's story thought she had killed her own husband. The woman left her child with a sister, then walked back through the forest with her father. Old though he was, he had a keen eye for tracking and helped the woman to trace her journey back to the earthen lodge in the forest. When she and her father entered the small doorway, they could see the body of her husband lying there in the dim light with a hole in his chest where his heart should have been.

"I must find out what has taken place here," said the woman's father. He crawled across the lodge and looked up at the body on the ledge. Slowly he peeled back the bark. When the head was uncovered, the father and daughter drew back in fear. The face and mouth of the body were drenched with fresh blood.[5]

୧୬  ୧୬  ୧୬  ୧୬

Alnôbak stories of life and death, tales of monsters and growling beasts, and of seeds quietly unfolding the first leaves of their kind from the warm spring soil of Gedakina—they all move along the circle of wisdom and are passed to each new generation. Through these stories, the world is created by Gici Niwaskw and folded into hills and valleys by *Ojihozo,* "he makes himself from something," as he drags his incomplete body across the landscape and creates his own being. *Bedegwajo,* "Round Mountain," a *medawlinno* from the days when Gedakina was still young, comes to control the whirlwinds and quell the fury of the Seven Brothers, the powerful yet benevolent Thunderers. Tales from ancient times tell of the great beasts called *bemosawôgan wajosizak,* "walking hills," the mastodons. In the eastern lands of Gedakina, a powerful being named *Gluskap* arrives from the sea with his grandmother, paddling a canoe made of stone. One tale is told of how Gluskap in his foolishness nearly kills the powerful Wind Eagle who blows winds of fury across a land stalked by the cannibalistic beast of the Forest Wanderer. Most frightful of all are the stories of peoples who dwell in the far north, whose minds have become afflicted by the dreaded Windigo spirit that causes them to crave human flesh.

But stories of a new whirlwind have begun to wash across the face of Gedakina. They tell of strangers who travelled here in large canoes that move without the need of paddles, who were blown across "the open ocean," *mamilizobagwa,* on the winds of the Wind Eagle. It is said that these people wear many clothes and moccasins as hard as the bark of a tree; that they cannot possibly feel Mother Earth, Begwiigawes, beneath their feet. In the north, they have come to trade for furs and other goods. They bring their own tales of creation and angle for the souls of the People, telling them that the old beliefs are untrue. Some say that the strangers moving up from the south have an appetite that knows no end, and that they consume the forest with their axes of metal teeth. *Wôbigijik naskapi* they have been called, "The Whites who eat endlessly without getting full." Like a swarm of beavers, *dademakwak,* they are chewing their way across Begwiigawes, and they are eating Gedakina.

# 11. Apcikozijik li Glôganek, Enemies at the Door

ℰℰ℘   ℰℰ℘   ℰℰ℘   ℰℰ℘

*H*e is known simply as Crow; he is as comfortable perched on a branch near the top of the tall white pine that overlooks the village of the Alnôbak as he is on the ground. An agile climber and swift afoot, he can move up and down through the trees and over the land faster than any other warrior in his camp. Because his dark eyes keep close watch on the whereabouts of the enemy and he is first to bring the news to others, and because his nose is narrow and pointed, he is Crow. Among the Mohawk, the Kanienkahageh, "People of the Land of Flint," his namesake possesses great power and is held in high regard.

Crow's head is shaved but for a thick band of hair that runs from his forehead, back over his crown, and down to the nape of his neck; hair made stiff by combing with bear grease. On this cold morning during the moon of the mid-winter ceremony, he is covered with a jacket and leggings of beaver skin worn with the fur on the inside. His feet are sheathed in two layers of close-fitting furs; an inner layer of snowshoe hare with the fur facing in and an outer layer of moosehock with the fur facing out to ward off snow and ice and to lend traction on the slippery winter ground. A necklace strung with the canine teeth from the wolf, his clan animal, dangles around his neck. True to his family's reputation, he is often among those who pick up a trail and lead the others in battle.

*In the faint light of morning, Crow watches a family near the center of the village. A young girl and a woman who looks like her mother emerge from a lodge to talk to one of the tall warriors Crow saw in the recent battle. Like many of the warriors from this village, this one is extremely tall, a height that is exaggerated as he stands next to these two women. Crow watches, straining his eyes, opening them wide to penetrate the dim light, shedding tears at the cold touch of the winter air, and wiping each eye with the back of his hand to clear his vision.*

*Crow is not fooled by the strong families he has seen among the enemies within the village. He knows that those ties only cause them to defend their homes and land with greater resistance and to fight with a vengeance. A large group of their warriors—with enough men for each day in the cycle of two moons—had already attacked members of his group and he had seen how well they fought. Although his people had killed half of them and captured a few, the others had escaped but not before killing two of his people for every one from the village. Among the dead had been his son. Crow had watched the life ebb from the depths of the young man's eyes and the pain of that moment burned in his chest.*

*"There," he says to himself, "the coward is going to join others near the village gate."*

*As swiftly, nimbly, and quietly as a squirrel, Crow scrambles down through the branches of the pine tree, leaps to the ground, and runs off in the direction of his war party. He knows that the others who have come to join the Kanienkahageh, the ones the English call the Seneca and Oneida, are awaiting his word to begin their attack as soon as the enemy steps outside the gate of the village. These two groups—the Seneca, Keepers of the Western Door, who call themselves the Nundawaono, "People of the Great Hill," and the Oneida or Onayatakono, "People of the Standing Stone"— have refused to negotiate with the enemy. As soon as Crow brings the word, the Kanienkahageh will join them as they take their positions and prepare to attack the group from the village.*

*Crow's heart races and his mouth is dry. At this moment, he has forgotten why the Kanienkahageh had first come to defeat this village. He sees only the image of his son's face, dying. Then, in Crow's mind twisted by grief, the face of his enemy takes the place of his son just as Crow's knife finds its mark.*

ᘒᕊ   ᘒᕊ   ᘒᕊ   ᘒᕊ

Meljasiz *feels the smooth shape and roundness of the* mazalôpskwisen *in her hand. She knows that this hard button of clay hanging around her neck holds special powers for the Alnôbak because it was made by the Little*

People, Manôgemasak. On many warm summer days while swimming in
the waters of Gwenitegok, she has spent hours looking upstream and
hoping to see the Manôgemasak come paddling toward her in their stone
canoes, hoping that she might glimpse the Little People before they see her
and dive beneath the surface.

Watching from shore one day, her grandmother had called out, "Come
back in. It is time to eat." After swimming up onto the rocks and shaking
herself off, she walked over to her nigô and sat down. "Some day," her
grandmother warned, "you are going to grow feathers and your toes will
join together like the feet of the Little Mitten." From that day forth, her
family had referred to her as Little Mitten, Meljasiz, the name of the small
water bird who has beautiful blue patches on its wings.

In her other hand Meljasiz holds an orange leaf from the tree senômozi
or "rock woody plant," the sugar maple. She had pressed it between two
pieces of bark from the canoe birch and dried it slowly so that it still shone
with bright color. Eight times in her short life Meljasiz has seen the leaves of
the trees burn the hills with a cold fire that slowly moves down into the
valleys. The leaf reminds her of a story her grandfather has told. Long ago,
on one of the last days of Skamonkas, the Corn Maker, her family's animal,
the Great Bear, fled a group of young hunters by climbing up into the stars.
The warriors followed as their arrows pierced the bear's thick hide, sending
spurts of blood down upon the hills. Every year at the same time, the
hunters again chase the bear and strike it with their arrows, turning the
leaves red with blood.

That thought of blood startles Meljasiz back into the present. During the
first days of the winter moon, Bebonkas, her father and uncle had gone out
with a group of about fifty warriors to fight the enemies. Her father was one
of only eighteen warriors from Meljasiz's village, the Zokwakiiak, who
returned, but her uncle was killed. The group had been surrounded by the
enemies who call themselves Kanienkahageh, the same people Meljasiz heard
her father refer to by saying Magoak, "they are cowards." Thinking of her
uncle, Meljasiz feels a sharp ache rising in her chest and tears welling up.

Sitting safely in her Alnigamigw, Meljasiz thinks that this pain must be
what her elders felt two generations ago when the silent enemy
maskihlôgan, smallpox, attacked their families and killed many; back when
her people lived in another village farther south along Gwenitegok. Meljasiz
was just old enough to remember their old village and imagined what it
looked like today, wondered if their old Alnigamigw was still standing.

But this was her home now; a place that she had grown to love, a home
surrounded by a land rich with beauty, oliginôgan. There were plenty of
warm days in which to grow the food in their vast gardens that sat high up
on the banks of the river. While she worked, Meljasiz could see far up and

*down the beautiful river valley. Some days when her brother was helping to*
*hunt for ducks in the marsh, Meljasiz did her part by fishing with a hook*
*and line.*

During the long heat of summer, the elders tended the gardens while
many of the families moved up to the headwaters of the rocky river that
flows past the mountain of which people often say "it is dark," Bezega, its
slopes both colored and shaded by many ancient pines. This is the same trip
the hunters take on their winter journeys from which they often return with
a moose, deer, or bear that is cleaned, cooked, and eaten safely inside the
high log walls of the village. Some families continued east to the edge of
mamilizobagwa for the summer, the big ocean, where they would catch fish,
namasak, shellfish, alsak, and lobsters, "the ones that grab,"
waodôpkenowadal.

"Meljasiz!" her brother calls as he lifts the bear skin that covers the door
and sticks his head inside. His familiar deep voice jolts Meljasiz out of her
revery. "Take care of your little brother while I am gone."

Meljasiz knows that her older brother is going out to negotiate with the
Magoak and the invisible Wôbigijik, "The Whites." She and her mother
stand, then they walk through the door and into the cold as her older
brother holds back the bearskin flap.

When she looks up into his eyes, she is gripped with feelings of dread for
his safety, feelings that are mixed with pride for the handsome young man
who stands before her. He is called Gwenakwezo Goa, "Tall White Pine,"
because his head reaches nearly to the top of the shoulder of a full-grown
moose. On this day, Gwenakwezo Goa is dressed as a formidable warrior.
He wears a collection of bear canines and moose incisors that have been
drilled and strung to form a necklace that leaves no question as to the
wearer's prowess, strength, and courage. He carries a weapon that is new to
the Zokwakiiak—a deadly baskhigan, "an exploding implement," for which
Gwenakwezo Goa traded nearly a year's catch of beaver pelts,
demakwaawak, to the Frenchmen, Blacmônak.

Gwenakwezo Goa girds himself for the difficult thing that he must do.
He knows that the Magoak are waiting for him and the others in his war
party, that they have been watching from the tall pines that grow a short
distance from the village. That very morning, in the first hint of light that
shone through the trees, Gwenakwezo Goa saw movement on a branch in a
pine that is high enough for someone to see over the log fence that
surrounds the lodges.

But the same logs that were put up to protect their families have now
become the walls of their prison. The Alnôbak must be able to move about
freely in their own homeland, and they have to hunt and fish to provide
winter food for their families, especially since the Magoak have already

stolen and destroyed most of the corn that was stored outside of the protected village. Gwenakwezo Goa and the others in the council have no choice but to try and negotiate with the Magoak, even if the words he speaks may spring forth with his final breath.

Meljasiz asks her mother, "Why must they leave the village and meet with the people who killed Dadaniz, Uncle?"

"These are things that you are too young to understand, Meljasiz," she replies, her breath steaming in the cold.

But Little Mitten knows some things. In the evening, after they think she has fallen asleep, Meljasiz lies still, with eyes closed, and listens to her elders talk about the fight over Begwiigawes. Meljasiz knows that her village is battling the Magoak warriors on this day. And she has heard that the real leader among the Magoak is a chief of Wôbigijik who leads them from far, far away; an Iglizmôn, "Englishman," who lives across mamilizobagwa, and whose moccasins have never even touched Gedakina. She also knows about the arrows tipped with the sharp, shiny points that her family obtained by trading furs to Wôbigijik, and that those arrows are now being used by her people to kill the allies of the same Wôbigijik.

Meljasiz shivers at these thoughts and holds tight to her necklace, hoping the mazalôpskwisen, the circle of clay made by the Little People, will protect her family. Praying while she says goodbye to Gwenakwezo Goa, tears sting her eyes and she hugs the waist of the brother who helped to raise her since she was an infant; praying that this will not be the last time she will ever feel his strength, smell his comforting scent, and gaze into his loving eyes.

—Near the mouth of the Ashuelot River,
Hinsdale, New Hampshire,
December 1663—
a winter of deep snows before the spring
when Meljasiz's village was abandoned.[1]

# Epilogue
## A Message from the Abenaki Nation

*T*his has been the story of a time before New Hampshire. But the Alnôbak did not suddenly disappear when that part of Ndakinna[1] now called the State of New Hampshire was etched on maps. While many fled for their families' safety to be with their refugee relatives in Canada and elsewhere, many returned. And there were those who never left; far more, I believe, than historians have been willing or able to acknowledge. It would have been very difficult for them to permanently leave their homeland, where countless generations of their ancestors' remains lay in the soil close by the riverbanks. It would be like a tree walking away from its roots; like the body walking away from the spirit. And we are still here in Ndakinna, having kept a low profile, usually concealing our identity for the social survival of the children within a dominant society that has often displayed a collective paranoia toward "Indians."

My uncle told me, "When we were children, we were told that we were not Indians, and we should never tell anyone that we were. One day, I looked at myself in the mirror and said, 'But I *am* an Indian.' So I went to Grandsir, which is what we called our grandfather, and asked, 'Grandsir, what tribe are we?' He looked very surprised that I had asked the question, and after a while he bent down and whispered in my ear, 'We're Abenaki.'"

People of Abenaki heritage are still coming out of their social closets, and we are banding together to form present-day tribal families, sharing family oral histories, learning our language and performing personal and community ceremonies. When we call ourselves native people we are assuming a set of responsibilities that we must not ignore. These include caring for the elders, nurturing the children properly, maintaining a respectful, caretaking attitude toward Mother Earth, being watchful that known and suspected burial places remain undisturbed, and assuming the proper reburial of those that have been exhumed.

If it is possible to describe our traditional spirituality in one word, I believe that word would be "respect." Our traditional senses of responsibility and respect have been well reflected in this volume. With these values, the embers of our ancestral fires are being carried forward to future generations of Alnôbak. The fire will not die.

—Charlie True, Member of the Tribal Council,
Abenaki Nation of New Hampshire

*Appendixes*

This map is painstakingly researched to convey a picture of the Alnôbak in this region around 1600, but we will never truly know which names the Alnôbak used when referring to their neighbors, near and far. The *Namaskik* (Amoskeag) and *Senikok* (Suncook) may have been local names for those who were part of the larger culture of the *Benôkoik* (Penacook). Cultural impacts and geographic shifts began soon after Europeans arrived. The name of *Bamijoak* (Cocheco) might have arisen somewhat later and referred to the combined remnants of the *Beskategwa* (Piscataqua) and *Nôwijoanek* (Newichwannock), those who survived the epidemic of either smallpox or bubonic plague that ravaged Native populations from Cape Cod to the Saco River from 1615 to 1617.

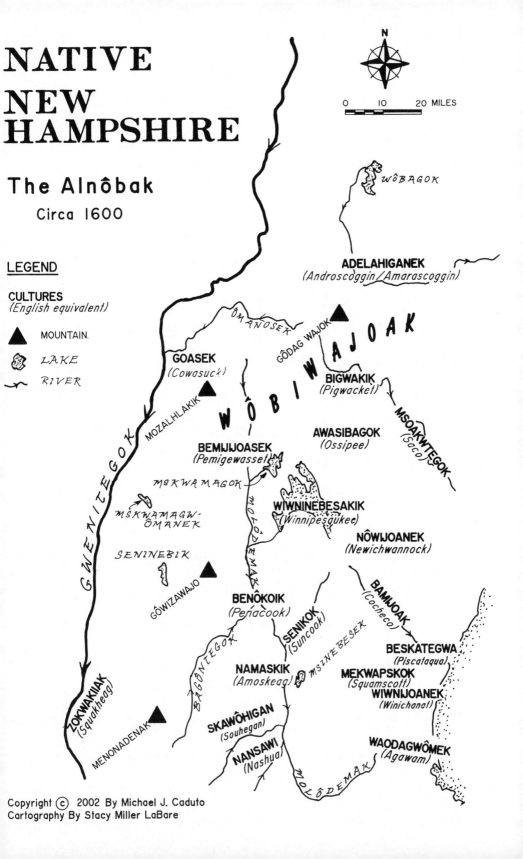

# NATIVE NEW HAMPSHIRE

## The Alnôbak

### Circa 1600

**LEGEND**

**CULTURES**
*(English equivalent)*

▲   MOUNTAIN.

🗺   LAKE

〰   RIVER

N

0   10   20 MILES

*WÔBAGOK*

**ADELAHIGANEK**
*(Androscoggin/Amarascoggin)*

*ÔMANOSEK*

*GÔDAG WAJOK*

**GOASEK**
*(Cowasuck)*

*MOZALHLAKIK*

**BIGWAKIK**
*(Pigwacket)*

*W Ô B I W A J O A K*

*MSOAKWTEGOK
(Saco)*

**AWASIBAGOK**
*(Ossipee)*

**BEMIJIJOASEK**
*(Pemigewasset)*

*MSKWAMAGOK*

*MSKWAMAGW-
ÔMANEK*

**WIWNINEBESAKIK**
*(Winnipesaukee)*

*MOLÔDEMAK*

**NÔWIJOANEK**
*(Newichwannock)*

*SENINEBIK*

*GÔWIZAWAJO*

*GWENITEGOK*

**BENÔKOIK**
*(Penacook)*

**SENIKOK**
*(Suncook)*

*BAMIJOAK
(Cocheco)*

*MSINEBESEK*

**BESKATEGWA**
*(Piscataqua)*

*BAGÔNTEGOK*

**NAMASKIK**
*(Amoskeag)*

**MEKWAPSKOK**
*(Squamscott)*

**WIWNIJOANEK**
*(Winichanat)*

**ZOKWAKIIAK**
*(Squakheag)*

*MENONADENAK*

**SKAWÔHIGAN**
*(Souhegan)*

**NANSAWI**
*(Nashua)*

*MOLÔDEMAK*

**WAODAGWÔMEK**
*(Agawam)*

# PRONUNCIATION GUIDE TO ALNÔBAK WORDS AND NAMES

Traditionally, Alnôbak is a spoken language only. Transcribing it into written form presents challenges that have been approached in different ways by Abenaki speakers, linguists, and students of the language. Throughout this book, the form used is that presented in the *Western Abenaki Dictionary* produced by Gordon M. Day and published by the Canadian Museum of Civilization as two volumes in 1994 and 1995. I have created the following pronunciation guide, with permission, by shortening and simplifying the longer, linguistic version presented in the beginning of both volumes of this dictionary: Abenaki–English and English–Abenaki.

## ACCENTS

The strongest accent falls on the last syllable of a word. Lesser accents fall on every other syllable counting back from the last syllable with the exception of syllables whose focus is the letter *e*. For example, *mòzagén*, "moose hide," and *mozàgeniyá*, "moose-hide material."

## LETTERS

The sounds of Western Abenaki words are represented by 23 alphabetized letters:

a b c C d e g h i j J k l m n o ô p s t w y z

*a* sounds like those in the English "mama," as in *Alnôbak* (Àhl-nohn-báhk), "The People" or "Ordinary People." When *a* appears before an *m* in the last syllable, it sounds like the *u* in *gum*, as in *Alnakwam* (Àhl-nah-kwúm), "an ordinary tree."

*b* is pronounced as the English *b* when it appears within a word, as in *azeban* (àh-zeh-báhn), "raccoon." Wherever *b* is the first or last letter in a word it sounds like the English *p*, as in *bebón* (peh-bóhn), "winter."

*c* is pronounced like the *ts* in the English *hats*, as in *Gôgicí* (Kohn-gee-tsée), "very great."

*C* is pronounced like the *ch* in "church."

*d* is pronounced like the English *d* when it appears within a word, as in *skweda* (skweh-dáh), "a fire." At the beginning and ending of a word, *d* sounds like the English *t*, as in *Debaldak* (Teh-bahl-dáhk), "the Owner."

*e* is pronounced as in "when."

*g* is pronounced as in "ago" when it appears within a word, such as in *nagwibagw sibs* (nah-gwèe-bah-gwúh síbs), "under leaf bird," the woodcock. When *g* appears at the beginning or end or a word, it sounds like the English *k*, as in *goa* (koh-áh), "white pine."

*h* is pronounced like the English *h* in "hunt," as in *menahan* (meh-nah-háhn), "island." When *h* appears in between vowels, it is sometimes dropped, so *lakahigan*, "hoe," becomes *lakaigan* (làh-kah-ee-gáhn [the second "h" is silent]). It is not dropped in some words like *awahôdosak* (àh-wah-hòhn-doh-sáhk), "little spirit ones" or "little devils" (bugs).

*i* is pronounced somewhere in between the English "bit" and "beat."

*j* is pronounced like the English *dz* when it appears mid-word, as in *nijôn* (nee-dzúhn), "child." At the beginning and end of a word, *j* sounds like the English *ts* in "lets." For example *jijiz* (tsee-dzéez), "baby."

*J* is pronounced like the *j* in "jump."

*k* is pronounced like the English *ck* in "pick," as in *Molôkak* (Mòh-luhn-káhk), "a deep place."

*l* sounds generally like the English *l*, but there is more tension in the tongue when it is pronounced. The sound of *l* is also influenced by the vowel that precedes it and follows it: *i* imparts a clear sound, as in *lintawôgan* (leent-tàh-wohn-gáhn), "a song." Double *ll* causes the *l* sound to be drawn out, as in *lla* (llah), "it is true."

*m* is pronounced as the English *m* in "mouse," as in *moz* (mohs), "moose."

*n* is pronounced as the English *n* in "night," as in *nolka* (nohl-káh), "the deer."

*o* is pronounced like the English *o* in "spoke," as in *wajo* (wah-dzóh), "mountain." In some words, the *o* is pronounced like the English *o* in "took" or "toot," as in *giona* (kee-oo-náh), "we."

*ô* is nasalized and generally sounds like the vowel in the French *pont* for "bridge," as in *Al-nôbak* (Àhl-nohn-báhk). When the *ô* is the last vowel in a word, or when it is followed by a *k*, it often sounds like the *u* in the English *bunt*, as in *Molôkak* (Mòh-luhn-káhk).

*p* is pronounced like the combined sounds of a *p* closing one word and the *p* beginning another, like so: "stop payment." For example, *apen* (ahp-pén), "groundnut."

*s* is pronounced like the English *s*, as in *mkasas* (`m-kah-sáhs), "crow."

*t* is pronounced like the combined sounds of a *t* closing one English word and the *t* beginning another, like so: "bent twig." For example, *nanatasiz* (nah-nàht-tah-sées), "hummingbird." A double t, *tt*, is extra long.

*w* is pronounced similar to an *o* when it appears before or after a vowel, as in *wasawa* (wàh-sah-wáh), "squash," and *wa* (wah), "this animate one." When *w* appears at the end of a word after a *k* or a *g* (which is pronounced like a *k* in this case), it is enunciated like a puff of air through rounded lips that relax as the letter is released, as in *asokw* (ahsóhkw), "cloud."

*y* is pronounced like *iy* but receives greater tongue tension when it appears before a vowel, as in *yaw* (eye-áh-w), "four."

*z* is pronounced like the English *z* when it appears mid-word, as in *môzmezi* (mòhnz-meh-zée), "moosestick" (mountain ash). When *z* appears at the beginning or ending of a word it is pronounced like an *s*, as in *zata* (saht-táh), "blueberry," and *moz* (mohs), "moose."

# PLACES AND RESOURCES TO VISIT

This list provides the names and addresses of each organization, as well as basic information on programs and exhibits. Telephone numbers are not provided because they are constantly changing. Please obtain the current telephone number and/or e-mail address of the organization you want to visit and inquire about the days and hours they are open for visits as well as directions to their location.

**Abenaki Indian Shop and Camp**
"Cathedral Woods"
Intervale, New Hampshire 03845

The camp was established by Chief Joseph Laurent in 1884 as a place of commerce for the trade in Abenaki baskets and other goods, and as a center for preserving Abenaki culture and language. These activities have been continued on-site by generations of the Laurent family. Today the camp preserves several centuries of Abenaki history and is listed on the National Register of Historic Places. The site includes an Abenaki gift shop and small museum, which offer an experience of living history, as well as five cabins, a wigwam, a totem pole, and a monument to Chief Joseph Laurent, author of the first Abenaki–English dictionary. As of this writing the camp is in transition and may reopen in the future.

**Amoskeag Fishways Learning and Visitor's Center**
6 Fletcher Street
Manchester, NH 03101

Programs focus on the history and current use of the river. The Fishways gives public tours of the fish ladder to see and study shad, river lamprey, American eels, and other migratory fishes. They also offer on-site school programs, camp visits, and programs on Native American history and fishing along the river. This center is owned by Public Service of New Hampshire and is run by the Audubon Society of New Hampshire in coordination with New Hampshire Department of Fish and Game and the United States Fish and Wildlife Service.

**The Libby Museum**
Box 629
Route 109 North
Wolfeboro, NH 03894

This museum offers an interpretive exhibit of Lakes Region archaeology. It also displays animal specimens, shells, minerals, fossils, artifacts from the Governor Wentworth summer residence, and clay tobacco pipes that were made in Wolfeboro by John Tabor. There is an exhibit that displays sculpture by Libby as well as a summer artists' gallery. Programs focus on natural history through school field trips and in-school programs, a summer day-camp for children in July and August, scheduled speakers, and occasional family walks.

## Manchester Historic Association
Millyard Museum
Old Amoskeag Mill #3
200 Bedford South (corner of Commercial and Pleasant)
Manchester, NH 03101

Research Library
129 Amherst St.
Manchester, NH 03101

This group collects Manchester history and makes it available to the public through exhibits and research collections. The Millyard Museum exhibit "Woven in History: 11,000 Years at Amoskeag Falls" includes Native American and colonial interpretive history. The museum offers on-site programs, school visits, and walking tours.

## Mount Kearsarge Indian Museum
Kearsarge Mountain Road
Warner, NH 03278

This extensive collection of Native American art and artifacts focuses on their meaning to Native American cultures, past and present. A special focus of the museum is the relationship of Native cultures to the land and of different cultures to each other. The museum offers public programs, workshops, crafts, performances, school visits, field trips, and pow-wows.

## Museum of New Hampshire History
The Hamel Center
6 Eagle Square
Concord, NH 03301

An excellent place to visit for an overview of New Hampshire history. The museum also offers rotating exhibits, public programs, and both on-site and travelling programs for schools. (See "New Hampshire Historical Society" below.)

## The New England Room at the Harvard Mineralogical Museum
24 Oxford Street
Cambridge, MA 02138

The museum has an array of precious stones from New Hampshire on display.

## New Hampshire Historical Society
30 Park Street
Concord, NH 03301-6384

The New Hampshire Historical Society is a nonprofit membership organization dedicated to preserving New Hampshire history through education, research, publications, exhibits, and the stewardship of historical archives and images at the Tuck Library (see below). The society publishes a periodical, *Historical New Hampshire,* and operates the Museum of New Hampshire History (see above).

## Phillips Anthropology Museum
Phillips Exeter Academy
Academy Building
Front Street
Exeter, NH 03833-2460

This exhibit about New Hampshire's original peoples, including a research library, is open to the general public for education and research. Displays include collections from the New Hampshire Archeological Society, the Phillips Exeter Academy, and local individuals. An array of ancient tools and other materials highlights the history of indigenous peoples from this region, with a focus on the coastal zone. The museum and library are open on most weekdays but, just to be sure, visitors are requested to contact the Anthropology Department at Phillips Exeter Academy before making the trip.

### Sandwich Historical Society Museum
4 Maple Street
Sandwich, NH 03227

The society and museum goals are to preserve the history of Sandwich. They have a library for the study of genealogy and history, a Junior Historical Society, and the 1850 Elisha Marston House that interprets colonial history and hosts rotating exhibits.

### Sargent Museum Center for Connecticut River Archaeological Research and Education
20 Central Street
Newport, NH 03773

The Sargent Museum has exhibits on archaeological sites in this region of the state. It also offers programs for children and the public to foster a better understanding of the past. (Note: The museum is also opening a main center at 88 Lowell St., Manchester, New Hampshire 03104, within a few years.)

### Tuck Library
30 Park Street
Concord, NH 03301

This is a phenomenal resource that offers historic documents, books, photographs, maps, and more. It is run by the New Hampshire Historical Society and is open to the public.

### The Woodman Institute
P.O. Box 146
182–192 Central Avenue
Dover, NH 03821-0146

The Woodman Institute has a fine collection of New Hampshire gemstones on display as well as other Native American, natural history, and science exhibits. Museums also have collections on seventeenth and eighteenth century furniture, local Dover artifacts and history, as well as on the American wars. Historic houses include the Woodman House, Hale House, and the Dame Garrison House that dates to 1675. Programs include speakers, school field trips, and occasional in-school visits.

# COMMON AND SCIENTIFIC NAMES
# OF ALL LIFE APPEARING IN THIS BOOK

**The names found in the text are featured here in bold print.**
The living things that appear in this book are arranged in general categories under each of the five Kingdoms: Animalia (Animals), Plantae (Plants), Fungi, Protista (Algae and their Allies), and Monera (including Bacteria). Generally, organisms are listed alphabetically within each category, according to common names. However, the names of fish, reptiles, invertebrates, and non-flowering plants are listed alphabetically within their various subgroups in order to better show those relationships. In a few cases, the Latin names alone are given for organisms that have no common name or are usually referred to using their Latin name.

## ANIMALS
## Vertebrates
(animals with a backbone) Chordata (phylum), Vertebrata (subphylum)

**Mammals,** Mammalia (class)

**anteaters,** Edentata (order), Myrmecophagidae (family)
**armadillos,** Edentata (order), Dasypodidae (family)
**bats,** Chiroptera (order)
**bear** (*see* bear, black)
**bear, black,** *Ursus americanus*
**bear, short-faced** (*see* bear, giant short-faced)
**bear, giant short-faced,** *Arctodus simus* (extinct)
**beaver,** *Castor canadensis*
**beaver, giant,** *Castoroides ohioensis* (extinct)
**bison,** *Bison bison*
***Bison antiquus*** (extinct)
**bison, steppe,** *Bison priscus* (extinct)
**bobcat,** *Lynx rufus*
**buffalo** (*see* bison)
***Camelops kansanus*** (extinct)
**camels,** Artiodactyla (order), Camelidae (family)
**capybara,** *Hydrochoerus holmesi* and *Neochoerus pinckneyi* (extinct)
**caribou** (of woodlands), *Rangifer tarandus caribou*
**caribou, barren ground,** *Rangifer tarandus*
**cat, scimitar,** *Homotherium serum* (extinct)
**cats,** Carnivora (order), Felidae (family)
**cattle,** Artiodactyla (order), Bovidae (family), Bovinae (subfamily)

cheetah (American), *Acinonyx trumani* (extinct)
chipmunk (eastern), *Tamias striatus*
cottontail (New England), *Silvilagus transitionalis*
deer, white-tailed, *Odocoileus virginianus*
dog, *Canis lupus*
elk or **Wapiti**, *Cervus elaphus*
elk, American (Wapiti), *Cervus elaphus*
elk, giant, *Megaloceros giganteus* (extinct)
elk, Irish, *Megaloceros giganteus* (extinct)
ermine (*see* weasel, short-tailed)
fisher, *Martes pennanti*
fox (*see* fox, gray, and fox, red)
fox, American (*see* fox, red)
fox, gray, *Urocyon cinereoargenteus*
fox, red, *Vulpes vulpes*
glyptodont, *Glyptotherium spp.* (extinct)
"grandmother porpoise that sings" (*see* whales)
hare, snowshoe, *Lepus americanus*
hippopotami, Artiodactyla (order), Hippopotamidae (family)
*Homo sapiens* (*see* primates)
horse, *Equus spp.*
horses (archaic), *Nannippus spp.* and many *Equus spp.* (extinct)
hyenas, Hyaenidae (family)
jaguar, *Panthera onca*
lemurs (*see* primates)
lion, American, *Panthera leo* (extinct)
lion, mountain (cougar or puma), *Felix concolor*
lynx, *Lynx canadensis*
mammoths, woolly, *Mammuthus primigenius* (extinct)
marsupials, Marsupialia (order)
     opossum, *Didelphis marsupialis*
marten, *Martes americana*
mastodon, *Mammut americanum* (extinct)
mink, *Mustela vison*
monkeys (*see* primates)
moose, *Alces alces*
moose, giant (moose-elk or broad-fronted moose), *Cervalces alaskensis* (Frick),
     *Alces latifrons* (Johnston) (extinct)
moose-elk (broad-fronted moose), *Cervalces alaskensis* (Frick), *Alces latifrons*
     (Johnston) (extinct)
mouse—general term for a number of small, native rodents in the families
     Cricetidae (mice, voles, and lemmings) and Zapodidae (jumping mice)
mouse, deer, *Peromyscus maniculatus*
mouse, white-footed, *Peromyscus leucopus*
musk ox, *Ovibos moschatus*
musk ox, woodland, *Symbos cavifrons* (extinct)
muskrat, *Ondatra zibethicus*
opossum (*see* marsupials)
otter (river), *Lutra canadensis*
pampathere, *Holmesina septentrionalis* (extinct)

**panther** (*see* lion, mountain)
**peccary,** *Platygonus spp.* (extinct)
**pigs,** Artiodactyla (order), Suidae (family)
**pine marten** (*see* marten)
**porcupine,** *Erethizon dorsatum*
**porpoises,** Cetacea (order), Odontoceti (suborder), delphinidae (family)
**primates** (order)
    *Homo sapiens,* Catarrhini (infraorder), Hominidae (family)
    **lemurs**—comprise three families among the Prosimians, including the
        Lemuridae, Cheirogaleidae, and Indriidae
    **monkeys**—New World monkeys: Platyrrhini, "flat noses" (infraorder); Old
        World monkeys: Catarrhini (infraorder), Cercopithecoidea (family)
**rabbits,** Lagomorpha (order), Leporidae (family)
**raccoon,** *Procyon lotor*
**rhinoceri,** Perissodactyla (order), Rhinocerotidae (family)
**rodents,** Rodentia (order)
**sabertooth,** *Smilodon fatalis* (extinct)
**seals,** Carnivora (order), Pinnipedia (suborder)
**sheep,** Artiodactyla (order), Bovidae (family), Caprinae (subfamily)
**shrew, masked,** *Sorex cinereus*
**shrews,** Insectivora (order), Soricidae (family)
**shrub oxen** or **shrub-ox,** *Euceratherium collinum* (extinct)
**skunk** (striped), *Mephitis mephitis*
**sloth, giant ground,** *Eremotherium rusconii* (extinct)
**sloth,** *Megalonyx spp.* and *Nothrotheriops shastensis* (shasta ground sloth) (extinct)
*Smilodon,* **the sabertooth cats** (extinct)
**squirrel, gray,** *Sciurus carolinensis*
**squirrel, ground,** *Spermophilus spp.*
**squirrel, red,** *Tamiasciurus hudsonicus*
**squirrels,** Rodentia (order), Sciuridae (family)
**stag-moose,** *Cervalces scotti* (extinct)
**tapir,** *Tapirus spp.*
**vole, meadow,** *Microtus pennsylvanicus*
**walrus,** *Odohenus rosmarus*
**Wapiti** (*see* elk)
**weasel, short-tailed,** *Mustela erminea*
**whale, right,** *Eubalaena glacialis*
**whales,** Cetacea (order), Odontoceti (toothed) and Mysticeti (baleen) (suborders)
**wolf** (*see* wolf, gray)
**wolf, dire,** *Canis dirus* (extinct)
**wolf, gray (timber),** *Canis lupus*
**wolf, red,** *Canis rufus*
**woodchuck** (groundhog), *Marmota monax*

**Birds,** Aves (class)

Hesperornithiformes (subclass)

    *Hesperornis* (extinct)

Neornithes (subclass)

    **auk, great,** *Pinguinus impennis* (extinct)

bobwhite, northern (quail), *Colinus virginianus*
brant, *Branta bernicla*
cardinal (northern), *Cardinalis cardinalis*
chickadee (black-capped), *Parus atricapillus*
condor, *Breagyps spp.* (extinct Pleistocene)
cormorants, Phalacrocoracidae (family)
cowbird (brown-headed), *Molothrus ater*
crow, common (American), *Corvus brachyrhynchos*
crows, Corvidae (family)
*Diatryma* or "Terror Bird," Diatrymiformes (order) (extinct)
dodo, *Raphus cucullatus* (extinct)
duck, wood, *Aix sponsa*
ducks, Anatidae (family)
eagle (bald), *Haliaeetus leucocephalus*
eagle, golden, *Aquila chrysaetos*
eagle, walking, *Wetmeregyps daggetti* (extinct)
eagles, Accipitridae (family), Buteoninae (subfamily)
geese, Anatidae (family), Anserinae (subfamily)
goldfinch (American), *Carduelis tristis*
goose, Canada, *Branta canadensis*
goose, snow, *Chen caerulescens*
grebes, Podicipedidae (family)
grosbeak, evening, *Coccothraustes vespertinus*
grouse, ruffed (partridge), *Bonasa umbellus*
grouse, spruce, *Dendragapus canadensis*
gulls, Laridae (family), Larinae (subfamily)
hawk, red-tailed, *Buteo jamaicensis*
heath hen, *Tympanuchus cupido* (extinct)
heron, great blue, *Ardea herodias*
herons, Ardeidae (family)
hummingbird, ruby-throated, *Archilochus colubris*
jay, blue, *Cyanocitta cristata*
jay, gray, Canada jay or whiskey jack, *Perisoreus canadensis*
jays, Corvidae (family)
junco (dark-eyed), *Junco hyemalis*
kingfisher (belted), *Ceryle alcyon*
Little Mitten, *Meljasiz* (*see* teal, blue-winged)
loons, Gaviidae (family)
mallard, *Anas platyrhynchos*
merganser, common, *Mergus merganser*
merganser, hooded, *Lophodytes cucullatus*
nighthawk (common), *Chordeiles minor*
nuthatches, Sittidae (family)
osprey, *Pandion haliaetus*
owl, barred, *Strix varia*
owl, snowy, *Nyctea scandiaca*
parakeet, Carolina, *Conuropsis carolinensis* (extinct)
partridge (*see* grouse, ruffed)
phoebe (eastern), *Sayornis phoebe*

pigeon, passenger, *Ectopistes migratorius* (extinct)
ptarmigan—rock ptarmigan, *Lagopus mutus,* and willow ptarmigan, *Lagopus lagopus*
quail (*see* bobwhite, northern)
rails, Rallidae (family)
rain birds, *zogelônihlak* (*see* swallows)
robin (American), *Turdus migratorius*
sapsucker (yellow-bellied), *Sphyrapicus varius*
shelduck, *Tadorna spp.* (extinct Pleistocene)
sparrow, song, *Melospiza melodia*
sparrow, swamp, *Melospiza georgiana*
sparrow, white-throated, *Zonotrichia albicollis*
squab—an unfledged passenger pigeon (*see* pigeon, passenger)
swallows, Hirundinidae (family)
teal, blue-winged, *Anas discors*
teratorn, *Teratornis incredibilis* (extinct)
terns, Laridae (family), Sterninae (subfamily)
turkey (*see* turkey, wild)
turkey, wild, *Meleagris gallopavo*
vulture, turkey, *Cathartes aura*
waxwing, cedar, *Bombycilla cedrorum*
whip-poor-will, *Caprimulgus vociferus*
woodcock (American), *Scolopax minor*
woodpeckers, Picidae (family)
wren, house, *Troglodytes aedon*

## Fish

Actinopterygii (class), ray-finned bony fish

alewife or alewives, *Alosa pseudoharengus*
bass—largemouth bass, *Micropterus salmoides;* smallmouth bass, *Micropterus dolomieui*
bullhead, brown, *Ameiurus nebulosus*
catfish (*see* bullhead, brown)
cod (Atlantic), *Gadus morhua*
dace, Cyprinidae (family)
eel (*see* eel, American)
eel, American, *Anguilla rostrata*
flatfish—winter flounder, *Pleuronectes americanus;* summer flounder, *Paralichthys dentatus*
minnows, Cyprinidae (family)
perch (yellow), *Perca flavescens*
pickerel—redfin pickerel, *Esox americanus;* chain pickerel, *Esox niger*
pike (*see* pike, northern)
pike, northern, *Esox lucius*
pout (*see* bullhead, brown)
salmon (Atlantic), *Salmo salar*
shad (American), *Alosa sapidissima*
smelt (rainbow), *Osmerus mordax*

**sturgeon**—Atlantic sturgeon, *Acipenser oxyrhynchus;* lake sturgeon, *Acipenser fulvescens*

**sucker** (white), *Catostomus commersoni*

**sunfish**—Centrarchidae (family), including the bluegill, *Lepomis macrochirus;* pumpkinseed, *Lepomis gibbosus;* redbreast sunfish, *Lepomis auritus;* and the black crappie, *Pomoxis nigromaculatus*

**swordfish**, *Xiphias gladius*

**trout**—brook trout, *Salvelinus fontinalis* (streams and rivers); lake trout, *Salvelinus namaycush*

**tuna** (bluefin), *Thunnus thynnus*

Agnathans, vertebrates "without jaws"

**conodonts**, Conodonta (class)—primitive, lamprey-like ancestors of chordates (extinct)

**lamprey** (sea), *Petromyzon marinus*

Chondrichthyes (class), "cartilaginous fish" whose skeletons do not contain true bone

**sharks**, Elasmobranchii (subclass)

**skates**, Elasmobranchii (subclass), Rajiformes (order)

**Reptiles**, Reptilia (class)

**Snakes**, Squamata (order), Serpentes (infraorder)

**rattlesnake**, *Crotalus horridus*

**snake, northern water**, *Nerodia sipedon*

**snake, water** (*see* snake, northern water)

**Turtles**, Testudines or Chelonia (orders)

**tortoise** (*see* turtle, common box)

**turtle, bog**, *Clemmys muhlenbergii*

**turtle, common box**, *Terrapene carolina*

**turtles, marsh**, *Clemmys spp.*

**turtle, painted**, *Chrysemys picta*

**turtle, snapping**, *Chelydra serpentina*

**turtle, spotted**, *Clemmys guttata*

*Dinosaurs* and other extinct groups and species

*Dimetrodon*

*Eubrontes giganteus,* "large true thunder"

*Grallator*

**mesosaurs**, *Mesosaurus*

*Otozoum,* "giant animal"

**plesiosaurs**

**prosauropod**

**Amphibians**, Lissamphibia (class)

**bullfrog**, *Rana catesbeiana*

**frog, green**, *Rana clamitans*

**labyrinthodont** (extinct)

**newt** (eastern), *Notophthalmus viridescens*

**spring peeper**, *Pseudacris crucifer*

**toad, American**, *Bufo americanus*

## Invertebrates
(animals without a backbone)

**Arthropods,** Arthropoda (phylum) (includes insects, crustaceans, spiders, mites, trilobites)

Chelicerata (subphylum)
  Xiphosura (class)
    **horseshoe crab,** *Limulus polyphemus*
  Arachnida (class)
    **spiders and mites**
crustaceans, Crustacea (subphylum)
  Malacostraca (class)
    Decapoda (order)
      **crabs** (true), Brachyura (infraorder)
        **crab, blue-shelled** (blue crab), *Callinectes sapidus*
      **lobsters,** Homaridae (family)
        **lobster,** *Homarus americanus*
      **shrimp**
  Maxillopoda (class)
    **barnacles,** Cirripedia (subclass)
    **ostracods,** Ostracoda (subclass)
    **seed shrimp**
insects, Insecta (subphylum)
  **beetles,** Coleoptera (order)
  **cockroaches,** Orthoptera (order), Blattidae (family)
  **dragonfly,** Odonata (order), Anisoptera (suborder)
  **fly, black,** Diptera (order), Simuliidae (family)
  **gnats** (biting) (*see* fly, black, and "no-see-um")
  **grasshoppers,** Orthoptera (order), Caelifera and Ensifera (suborders)
  **hemlock looper,** *Lambdina fiscellaria fiscellaria*
  **honeybee,** *Apis mellifera*
  **mosquitos,** Diptera (order), Culicidae (family)
  **"no-see-um"** (biting midge or punkie), Diptera (order), Ceratopogonidae (family)
  **water striders,** Gerridae and Veliidae (families)
Myriapoda (class)
  **centipedes,** Chilopoda (subclass)
**trilobites,** Trilobitomorpha (subphylum of extinct, ancestral arthropods)
  *Paradoxides*

**Brachiopods** (lamp shells), Brachiopoda (phylum)

**Bryozoans** (moss animals), Bryozoa (phylum)

**Corals,** Coelenterata or Cnidaria (phylum)

**Echinodermata** (phylum)

  **brittle stars,** Ophiuroidea (class)
  **sand dollars,** Echinoidea (class)
  **sea cucumbers,** Holothuroidea (class)
  **sea urchins,** Echinoidea (class)
  **seastars** (starfish), Asteroidea (class)

Pelmatozoa (subphylum)
    **crinoids,** Crinoidea (class)
      **sea lilies**
    Cystoidea (class)
      **pelmatozoan columnals** (extinct)

**Lamp Shells** (*see* Brachiopods)

**Molluscs,** Mollusca (phylum)(includes snails, clams, octopuses)

    **cephalopods,** Cephalopoda (class)
      ***Nautilus,*** Nautiloidea (subclass)
      **octopuses,** Coloidea (subclass)
    **clams,** Bivalvia or Pelecypoda (class)
      **mussels,** Mytilidae (family)
      **oyster,** Ostreidae (family)
      **quahaug,** *Mercenaria mercenaria,* Veneridae (family)
      **scallop,** Pectinidae (family)
    **gastropods,** Gastropoda (class)
      **sea snails**
      **snails** (terrestrial), Stylommatophora(order), such as *Succinea ovalis*

**Sponges,** Porifera (phylum)

**Worms** (all types), Protostomia (clade)

    **worms** (segmented), Annelida (phylum)

## PLANTS
### Flowering Plants (Angiosperms) and Cone-Bearing Plants (Conifers)

**Herbaceous Flowering Plants**

    ***ahamoakezen,*** "hen's moccasin" (pitcher plant), *Sarracenia purpurea*
    **artichoke, Jerusalem,** *Helianthus tuberosa*
    **barley,** *Hordeum vulgare*
    **bean, common,** *Phaseolus vulgaris*
    **bean, red kidney** (*see* bean, common)
    **bean, wild,** *Strophostyles helvola*
    ***bebonki skamon,*** "**north corn**" (*see* corn)
    **bedstraw,** *Galium spp.*
    **blueberry,** *Vaccinium spp.*
    **blueberry, swamp highbush,** *Vaccinium corymb*osum
    **buckwheat, false,** *Polygonum scandens*
    **bullrush,** *Scirpus spp.*
    **cattails,** *Typha spp.*
    **chenopod,** *Chenopodium spp.*
    **chenopodium,** *Chenopodium spp.*
    **corn,** *Zea mays*
    **corn, eight-row flint,** *Zea mays*
    **cottongrass,** *Eriophorum spp.*
    **crowberry,** *Empetrum nigrum* and *E. atropurpureum*
    **currant, wild** (black), *Ribes americanum*
    **daisy** (oxeye), *Chrysanthemum leucanthemum*
    **dandelion,** *Taraxacum officinale* and *T. erythrospermum*

dock, *Rumex spp.*
dropseed, *Sporobolus cryptandrus* and *S. heterolepis*
fireweed, *Epilobium angustifolium*
fordhooks (*see* squash, fordhooks)
gourd, bottle (hard-shelled), *Lagenaria siceraria*
gourd, ornamental, *Cucurbita pepo* ssp. *ovifera*
gourds, *Cucurbita pepo* (soft-shelled striped and warted gourds, ornamental
    gourds), *C. mixta* (silver-seeded gourds)
groundnut, *Apios americana (A. tuberosa)*
jewelweed, *Impatiens capensis* and *I. pallida*
leeks, wild, *Allium tricoccum*
maize (*see* corn)
marrows (squashes), *Cucurbita maxima* and *C. pepo*
marshelder, *Iva ciliata*
milkweed, *Asclepias spp.*
oats, *Avena sativa*
peanut, *Arachis hypogea*
peanut, hog, *Amphicarpa bracteata*
peas, *Pisum sativum*
peppers, *Capsicum spp.*
plantain, *Plantago spp.*
pumpkin—varieties of squash among *Cucurbita maxima, C. pepo* and *C. mixta*
rice, *Oryza sativa*
rose, *Rosa spp.*
rush, chairmaker's, *Scirpus americanus*
rye, *Secale cereale*
scallion, *Allium spp.*
snowberry (creeping), *Gaultheria hispidula*
Solomon's seal, false, *Smilacina racemosa*
Solomon's seal (great), *Polygonatum canaliculatum*
squash, *Cucurbita spp.*
squash, acorn, *Cucurbita pepo*
squash, bush scallop, *Cucurbita pepo*
squash, crookneck—most are *Cucurbita pepo*, a few are *C. mixta* and *C. moschata*
squash, fordhooks, *Cucurbita pepo*
squash, scallop, *Cucurbita pepo*
squash, summer, *Cucurbita pepo*, includes most commonly grown varieties (*see*
    squash, scallop, and squash, crookneck)
strawberry, wild, *Fragaria virginiana*
sumpweed (*see* marshelder)
sunflower (*see* sunflower, common)
sunflower, common, *Helianthus annuus*
sweetgrass, *Hierochloe odorata*
teosinte, *Zea mexicana*, also *Zea mays mexicana*
timothy (grass), *Phleum pratense*
tobacco, *Nicotiana rustica*
tomatoes, *Lycopersicon spp.*
water lily, white (fragrant), *Nymphaea odorata*
wheat, *Triticum aestivum*
wormwood, *Artemesia spp.*

**Trees and Shrubs** (the names of conifers are followed by a "c")

alders, *Alnus spp.*
apple, *Pyrus malus*
ash, *Fraxinus spp.*
ash, white, *Fraxinus americana*
aspen (poplar), *Populus spp.*
aspen, quaking, *Populus tremuloides*
basswood, *Tilia americana*
beech (American), *Fagus grandifolia*
birch, black, *Betula lenta*
birch, canoe (*see* birch, white)
birch, gray, *Betula populifolia*
birch, paper (*see* birch, white)
birch, sweet (*see* birch, black, and birch, yellow)
birch, white, *Betula papyrifera*
birch, yellow, *Betula lutea (alleghaniensis)*
birches, *Betula spp.*
birches, alpine—dwarf white birch, *Betula minor;* dwarf birch, *Betula glandulosa*
blackberries—common blackberry, *Rubus allegheniensis;* smooth blackberry, *R. canadensis*
bramble, *Rubus spp.*
butternut, *Juglans cinerea*
cedar, Atlantic white, *Chamaecyparis thyoides* (c)
cedar, northern white, *Thuja occidentalis* (c)
cherries, *Prunus spp.*
cherry, black, *Prunus serotina*
cherry, choke, *Prunus virginiana*
chestnut (American), *Castanea dentata*
conifers, Coniferophyta (phylum)—members of the pine and spruce families
elderberry—common elder, *Sambucus canadensis;* red-berried elder, *S. pubens*
elm (American), *Ulmus americana*
elm, slippery (red), *Ulmus rubra*
fir (*see* fir, balsam) (c)
fir, balsam, *Abies balsamea* (c)
grape—fox grape, *Vitis labrusca;* New England grape, *V. novae-angliae;* riverbank grape, *V. riparia;* summer grape, *V. aestivalis*
grass, grasses, Poaceae (Gramineae) (family)
gum, black (tupelo), *Nyssa sylvatica*
*gymnosperms,* "naked seeds" (*see* conifers; gymnosperms also include ginkgoes and cycads)
hawthorn, *Crataegus spp.*
hazelnut—American hazelnut, *Corylus americana;* beaked hazelnut, *Corylus cornuta*
hemlock (eastern), *Tsuga canadensis* (c)
hickory, *Carya spp.*
huckleberry, dwarf, *Gaylussacia dumosa*
ironwood, *Carpinus caroliniana*
ivy, poison, *Rhus radicans*
juniper, *Juniperus spp.* (c)
larch (tamarack), *Larix laricina* (c)

leatherleaf, *Chamaedaphne calyculata*
mangrove—black mangrove, *Avicennia germinans;* red mangrove, *Rhizophora mangle*
maple, *Acer spp.*
maple, red, *Acer rubrum*
maple, striped, *Acer pensylvanicum*
maple, sugar, *Acer saccharum*
mountain ash, *Pyrus americana*
oak, *Quercus spp.*
oak, black, *Quercus velutina*
"oak that has leaves with round fingers" (*see* oak, white)
oak, white, *Quercus alba*
pear, *Pyrus communis*
pine, *Pinus spp.* (c)
pine, jack, *Pinus banksiana* (c)
pine, pitch, *Pinus rigida* (c)
pine, red, *Pinus resinosa* (c)
pine, Scotch, *Pinus sylvestris* (c)
pine, white, *Pinus strobus* (c)
poplar (*see* aspen)
poplar, balsam, *Populus balsamifera*
poplar, black (*see* poplar, balsam)—poplar whose leaves emanate the strong scent of the balsam fir
raspberries—purple-flowering raspberry, *Rubus odoratus;* black raspberry, *R. occidentalis;* wild red raspberry, *R. idaeus;* dwarf raspberry, *R. pubescens*
sassafras, *Sassafras albidum*
sedge, Cyperaceae (family)
shadbush, *Amelanchier spp.*
spruce, *Picea spp.* (c)
spruce, black, *Picea mariana* (c)
spruce, red, *Picea rubens* (c)
spruce, white, *Picea glauca* (c)
sumac berries—red berries that can be boiled for making tea and that grow on staghorn sumac (*Rhus typhina*), smooth sumac (*R. glabra*), and shining sumac (*R. copallina*)—**not** *the highly toxic white berries found on poison sumac* (*R. vernix*)
sumac, staghorn, *Rhus typhina*
sweetfern, *Comptonia peregrina*
tamarack (*see* larch) (c)
walnut (*see* walnut, black)
walnut, black, *Juglans nigra*
willows, *Salix spp.*
winterberry, *Ilex verticillata*

## Non-flowering Plants

Clubmosses, Lycophyta (phylum), Lycopodiaceae (family)

> ground pines—the common name for several species of clubmoss that trail along the ground such as *Lycopodium obscurum* and *L. complanatum*

Ferns, Pterophyta (phylum)

**fiddleheads**—the edible spirals of spring growth of ostrich fern, *Matteuccia struthiopteris*

**Horsetails,** Sphenophyta (phylum), Equisetaceae (family)

**Liverworts,** Hepatophyta (phylum)

**Mosses,** Bryophyta (phylum)

moss, *Sphagnum, Sphagnum spp.*
peat—generally the fibrous, spongy organic remains of *Sphagnum* moss and other partially decomposed plants that accumulate in acid bogs (*see* moss, *Sphagnum*)

## FUNGI

**chestnut blight,** *Endothia parasitica*
**foxfire**—fungi that luminesce with a greenish-yellow or golden light, including the honey fungus, *Armillaria mellea;* Jack-my-lantern, *Clitocybe illudens;* the wood-destroying fungus, *Panus stypticus luminescens* and the *Pleurotus* fungi
**fungus**—a member of the kingdom Fungi that lives by breaking down dead organic matter
**ghost wood,** *jibaasakw* (*see* foxfire)
**lichens**—a complex interrelationship between fungi of the Ascomycota (phylum) and the Basidiomycota (phylum) and various species of algae. The fungi are the visible part of these fascinating organisms and the algae are enveloped within.
**mushrooms**—fungi of the Hymenocetes (class), within the Basidiomycota (phylum) that bear reproductive spores on conspicuous fruiting bodies. The fruiting bodies are themselves often called mushrooms, toadstools or brackets. The morels, truffles, and others among the Ascomycota (phylum) also produce "mushrooms."

## PROTISTA
## Algae and Their Allies

**diatoms,** Bacillariophyta (phylum)
**Foraminifera** (class)
**green algae,** Chlorophyta (phylum)
**seaweeds**—include the phyla Rhodophyta (red algae) and Phaeophyta (brown algae) as well as the family Ulvophyceae within the phylum Chlorophyta (green algae)
*Prototaxites southworthii,* Phaeophyta (phylum) (extinct)

## MONERA
### Bacteria

**blue-green algae,** Cyanophyta (phylum)
**Cyanobacteria** (phylum)—formerly known as "blue-green algae," Cyanophyta (phylum)

# NOTES

## CHAPTER 1. *THE PRIMORDIUM* (PAGES 7–14)

1. James Hutton, *Theory of the Earth: An Investigation of the Laws Observable in the Composition, Dissolution, and Restoration of Land Upon the Globe* (Edinburgh, Scotland: Royal Society of Edinburgh, 1785).
2. N. M. Ratcliffe, T. R. Armstrong, and J. N. Aleinikoff, "Stratigraphy, Geochronology, and Tectonic Evolution of the Basement and Cover Rocks of the Chester and Athens Domes," in *Guidebook for Field Trips in Vermont and Adjacent New Hampshire and New York,* ed. T. W. Grover, H. N. Mango, and E. J. Hasenohr (89th Annual Meeting of the New England Intercollegiate Geological Conference, Rutland, Vt., 1997), B6-1–55.
3. Thomas R. Armstrong, Ph.D., Research Geologist, United States Geological Survey, personal communication.
4. Jeremy Belknap, A.M., *The History of New Hampshire,* vol. 3 (Boston: Belknap and Young, 1792), 34.
5. Eugene L. Boudette, "The Geology of New Hampshire, The Granite State," *Rocks and Minerals* 65, no. 4 (July/August 1990): 306–12.
6. Ibid.

## CHAPTER 2. *THE CRUCIBLE AND THE CAULDRON* (PAGES 15–45)

1. Boudette, "The Geology of New Hampshire."
2. Wallace A. Bothner, and Herbert Tischler, "Fossils of New Hampshire: An Overview," *Rocks and Minerals* 65, no. 4 (July/August 1990): 314–20.
3. Bradford B. Van Diver, *Roadside Geology of Vermont and New Hampshire* (Missoula, Mont.: Mountain Press, 1987), 29.
4. T. R. Armstrong, R. J. Tracy, and W. E. Hames, "Contrasting Styles of Taconian, Eastern Acadian and Western Acadian Metamorphism, Central and Western New England," *Journal of Metamorphic Geology* 10 (1992): 415–26.
5. Bothner and Tischler, "Fossils of New Hampshire."
6. Boudette, "The Geology of New Hampshire."
7. Celia Thaxter, *Among the Isles of Shoals* (Boston: James R. Osgood & Co., 1873; reprint, Portsmouth, N.H.: Peter E. Randall Publisher, 1994), 17.
8. Luann Becker et al., "Permian-Triassic Extinctions?" *Science* 291, no. 5508 (23 February 2001): 1530–33.
9. Bruce Cornet, "Dicot-like Leaf and Flowers from the Late Triassic Tropical Newark Supergroup Rift Zone, U.S.A.," *Modern Geology* 19, no. 1 (August 1993): 81–99; Nicholas C. Fraser, "Cascade: A Triassic Treasure Trove," *Virginia Explorer* 9, no. 1 (Winter/Spring 1993): 15–18.
10. Van Diver, *Roadside Geology of Vermont and New Hampshire,* 186–87.

11. Chet Raymo and Maureen Raymo, *Written in Stone: A Geological History of the Northeastern United States* (Old Saybrook, Conn.: Globe Pequot Press, 1989), 116.

12. Michael Balter, "Fossil Tangles Roots of Human Family Tree," *Science* 291, no. 5512 (23 March 2001): 2289–91.

13. Donald C. Johanson and Maitland A. Edey, *Lucy: The Beginnings of Humankind* (New York: Simon and Schuster, 1981), 283–84.

14. Bothner and Tischler, "Fossils of New Hampshire."

15. Ronald B. Davis and George L. Jacobson, Jr., "Late Glacial and Early Holocene Landscapes in Northern New England and Adjacent Areas of Canada," *Quaternary Research* 23, no. 3 (May 1985): 341–68.

## CHAPTER 3. *OF WATER AND ICE* (PAGES 46–72)

1. Björn Kurtén and Elaine Anderson, *Pleistocene Mammals of North America* (New York: Columbia University Press, 1980), 236.

2. Although it is widely accepted that the tallest mountains in the Northeast were covered by the Wisconsinan glacier, there has been some recent debate about the subject. Dr. Eugene L. Boudette, who served as New Hampshire's State Geologist for many years, cites the presence of well-defined glacial striations as proof that the tops of New Hampshire's tallest peaks, including Mount Washington, were covered by the Wisconsinan ice sheet. Dr. P. Thompson Davis of the Department of Natural Sciences at Bentley College in Waltham, Massachusetts, and others have conducted research that they assert points to two possibilities, each of which indicates that the Wisconsinan ice sheet was not as thick as has been supposed: 1) parts of the top of Mount Washington were exposed much sooner than previously thought during the latter part of the Wisconsinan glaciation; or 2) glacial ice covered the peak but was so thin that the ice was frozen to the surface and did not cause much erosion. Personal communication with Dr. Eugene L. Boudette and Dr. P. Thompson Davis, 23 April 2001.

3. William MacLeish, *The Day Before America: Changing the Nature of a Continent* (New York: Houghton Mifflin, 1994), 36.

4. Van Diver, *Roadside Geology of Vermont and New Hampshire*, 71.

5. John C. Ridge et al., "Varve, Paleomagnetic, and ¹⁴C Chronologies for Late Pleistocene Events in New Hampshire and Vermont (U.S.A.)," 79–107; and Woodrow B. Thompson, Brian K. Fowler, and Christopher C. Dorion, "Deglaciation of the Northwestern White Mountains, New Hampshire," 59–77; both in *Late Quaternary History of the White Mountains, New Hampshire and Adjacent Southeastern Québec,* ed. Woodrow B. Thompson, Brian K. Fowler and P. Thompson Davis, a special issue of *Géographie Physique et Quaternaire* 53, no. 1 (1999).

6. Van Diver, *Roadside Geology of Vermont and New Hampshire*, 90.

7. Ridge et al., "Varve, Paleomagnetic, and ¹⁴C Chronologies."

8. Henry David Thoreau, *Cape Cod* (1865; reprint, New York: Penguin Books, 1987), 22.

9. James Walter Goldthwait, Lawrence Goldthwait, and Richard Parker Goldthwait, *The Geology of New Hampshire: Part 1—Surficial Geology* (Concord, N. H.: New Hampshire State Planning and Development Commission, 1951, 1958), 51.

10. C. Koteff and F. D. Larsen, "Postglacial Uplift in Western New England: Geologic Evidence for Delayed Rebound," in *Earthquakes at North-Atlantic Passive Margins: Neotectonics and Postglacial Rebound,* ed. Søren Gregersen and Peter W. Basham (Boston and Dordrecht, the Netherlands: Kluwer Academic Publishers, 1989), 105–23.

11. Carl Koteff, Ph.D., United States Geological Survey, personal communication.

12. David P. Stewart and Paul McClintock, *The Surficial Geology and Pleistocene History*

of *Vermont* (Montpelier, Vt.: Vermont Development Commission, Vermont Geological Survey Bulletin 31, 1969).

13. Davis and Jacobson, "Late Glacial and Early Holocene Landscapes"; Russell W. Graham, "Response of Mammalian Communities to Environmental Changes During the Late Quaternary," in *Community Ecology,* ed. Jared Diamond and Ted J. Case (New York: Harper & Row, 1986), 309.
14. Graham, "Response of Mammalian Communities," 309.
15. J. Alan Holman, *Pleistocene Amphibians and Reptiles in North America* (New York: Oxford University Press, 1995), 32, 42–43, 73.
16. MacLeish, *The Day Before America,* 53.
17. Graham, "Response of Mammalian Communities," 312.

## CHAPTER 4. *PEOPLE OF STONE AND BONE* (PAGES 75–93)

1. Dr. Richard A. Boisvert, New Hampshire Division of Historical Resources, Concord, New Hampshire, personal communication.
2. Edward F. Bouras and Paul M. Bock, "Recent Paleoindian Discovery: The First People in the White Mountain Region of New Hampshire," *New Hampshire Archeologist* 37, no. 1 (1997): 48–58; Richard A. Boisvert, "New Discoveries in Jefferson, New Hampshire," *American Archaeology* 5, no. 1 (Spring 2001): 44–45.
3. Peter A. Thomas, Ph.D., Department of Archaeology, University of Vermont, personal communication.
4. R. Dale Guthrie, *Frozen Fauna of the Mammoth Steppe* (Chicago: University of Chicago Press, 1990), 74.
5. Ibid., 210, 239–45.
6. George Peter Nicholas, II, "Late Pleistocene–Early Holocene Occupations of New Hampshire Glacial Lakes: Paleoindian Settlement, Subsistence, and Environment," *New Hampshire Archeologist* 21 (1980): 55–65.
7. Ibid.
8. Margaret Bryan Davis, "Climatic Instability, Time Lags, and Community Disequilibrium," in *Community Ecology,* 283.
9. Ibid., 271–73.
10. Margaret Bryan Davis, Ray W. Spear, and Linda C. K. Shane, "Holocene Climate of New England," *Quaternary Research* 14, no. 2 (September 1980): 240–50.
11. Davis and Jacobson, "Late Glacial and Early Holocene Landscapes."
12. MacLeish, *The Day Before America,* 76.
13. William A. Haviland and Marjory Power, *The Original Vermonters: Native Inhabitants Past and Present* (Hanover, N. H.: University Press of New England, 1994), 28.
14. Ibid., 31–34.
15. S. Boyd Eaton and Melvin Konner, "Paleolithic Nutrition: A Consideration of Its Nature and Current Implications," *New England Journal of Medicine* 312, no. 5 (31 January 1985): 283–89.
16. Ibid.
17. Shepard Krech III, *The Ecological Indian: Myth and History* (New York: W. W. Norton and Co., 1999), 31–32.
18. Eliot Marshall, "Pre-Clovis Sites Fight for Acceptance," *Science* 291, no. 5509 (2 March 2001): 1730–32.
19. Ibid.
20. N. Guidon and G. Delibrias, "Carbon-14 Dates Point to Man in the Americas 32,000 Years Ago," *Nature* 321, no. 6072 (19 June 1986): 769–71.

21. MacLeish, *The Day Before America,* 65–66.
22. Ibid., 66.
23. Bouras and Bock, "Recent Paleoindian Discovery"; Charles E. Bolian, "Weirs Beach: A Preliminary Report of the 1976 Excavations," *New Hampshire Archeologist* 19 (1976–1977): 47–55; Mary Lou Curran, "New Hampshire Paleo-Indian Research and the Whipple Site," *New Hampshire Archeologist* 33/34, no. 1 (1994): 29–52; Justine B Gengras, "Radiocarbon Dates for Archeological Sites in New Hampshire," *New Hampshire Archeologist* 36, no. 1 (1996): 8–15; Richard A. Boisvert, "Paleoindian Occupation of the White Mountains, New Hampshire," in *Late Quaternary History,* 159–74; Daniel F. Cassedy, *A Prehistoric Inventory of the Upper Connecticut River Valley* (Raleigh, N.C.: Garrow & Associates, Inc., 1991), 3, 30.
24. Rosalind D. Hanson, *America's First People* (Hopkinton, N.H.: New Hampshire Antiquarian Society, 1996), 56.
25. Gengras, "Radiocarbon Dates."
26. David W. Steadman and Paul S. Martin, "Extinction of Birds in the Late Pleistocene of North America," in *Quaternary Extinctions: A Prehistoric Revolution,* ed. Paul S. Martin and Richard G. Klein (Tucson: The University of Arizona Press, 1984), 466–77.
27. Haviland and Power, *The Original Vermonters,* 38.
28. Krech, *The Ecological Indian,* 33–34.
29. Ibid., 213.
30. MacLeish, *The Day Before America,* 88–97.
31. Krech, *The Ecological Indian,* 38.

## CHAPTER 5. *THE WARMING TIME* (PAGES 94–113)

1. Davis, Spear, and Shane, "Holocene Climate of New England."
2. Nicholas, "Late Pleistocene–Early Holocene Occupations of New Hampshire Glacial Lakes."
3. Davis, "Climatic Instability," 276.
4. Davis, Margaret Bryan, "Outbreaks of Forest Pathogens in Quaternary History," *Proceedings of the Fourth International Palynological Conference, Lucknow* 3 (1981): 216–28.
5. Colleen B. Duggan, "Dugout Canoes of New Hampshire," *New Hampshire Archeologist* 37, no. 1 (1997): 40–47.
6. Brian S. Robinson, "Seabrook Tidal Marsh Site: A Preliminary Report," *New Hampshire Archeologist* 19 (1976–1977): 1–7.
7. Victoria Bunker, "New Hampshire's Prehistoric Settlement and Chronology," *New Hampshire Archeologist* 33/34, no. 1 (1994): 20–28.
8. Steven L. Bayly, "Myth, History and Archeology in the White Mountains of New Hampshire," *New Hampshire Archeologist* 37, no. 1 (1997): 59–69.
9. Marshall Sahlins, *Stone Age Economics* (New York: Aldine Publishing Co., 1972), 14–17.
10. Peter A. Thomas, Ph.D., Department of Archaeology, University of Vermont, personal communication. Dr. Thomas tells of an anadromous fishing site discovered on the Connecticut River about 10 miles south of the New Hampshire border that dates back to at least 8,650 years ago. This site, at the present-day Turner's Falls, is about one and one-half times the distance up-river from the ocean as the fishing place at Amoskeag Falls along the Merrimack River.
11. Bunker, "New Hampshire's Prehistoric Settlement."
12. Sahlins, *Stone Age Economics,* 1.

13. Ibid., 19–21.
14. Ibid., 34.
15. Victoria B. Kenyon, "Prehistoric Site Location in the Merrimack Valley of New Hampshire," *New Hampshire Archeologist* 25, no. 1 (1984): 55–65.
16. Bolian, "Weirs Beach."
17. Justine B. Gengras, and Victoria Bunker, "Rescue Archeology at the Lodge Site, NH31-6-6," *New Hampshire Archeologist* 38, no. 1 (1998): 1–33.
18. Patricia W. Hume and Paul E. Holmes, "Two Sites on Little River: The Plaistow Dump Site (NH 46-34) and the BROX/Galloway Site (NH 46-35)," *New Hampshire Archeologist* 38, no. 1 (1998): 34–51.
19. Victoria B. Kenyon and Donald W. Foster, "The Smyth Site (NH 38-4): Research in Progress," *New Hampshire Archeologist* 21 (1980): 45–54.
20. Cassedy, *A Prehistoric Inventory*, 2.
21. George P. Nicholas II, "Meadow Pond (NH49-1): Changing Site-Landform Associations at a Multiple Component Site," *New Hampshire Archeologist* 25, no. 1 (1984): 31–54.
22. Cassedy, *A Prehistoric Inventory*, 13–14.
23. Ibid., 39.
24. Martha S. Brummer and W. Dennis Chesley, "Coastal Zone Survey of New Hampshire: Background Research and Testing Methodology," *New Hampshire Archeologist* 21 (1980): 35–44.
25. Laura Pope, "Wadleigh Falls Island NH 39-1: A Preliminary Site Report," *New Hampshire Archeologist* 22, no. 1 (1981): 8–15.
26. Robinson, "Seabrook Tidal Marsh Site."
27. Ibid.

## CHAPTER 6. *A LAND OF PLENTY* (PAGES 114–29)

1. Victoria Bunker and Jane Potter, "The Place Between: Archeology at the Mine Falls Park Site, Nashua, New Hampshire," *New Hampshire Archeologist* 36, no. 1 (1996): 38–64.
2. Nicholas, "Meadow Pond."
3. Solon B. Colby, *Colby's Indian History: Antiquities of the New Hampshire Indians and their Neighbors* (Center Conway, N.H.: Walkers Pond Press, 1975), 240.
4. Victoria Bunker Kenyon, "Prehistoric Pottery at the Smyth Site," *New Hampshire Archeologist* 22, no. 1 (1981): 31–48.
5. Victoria Bunker, "New Hampshire's Prehistoric Settlement and Chronology," *New Hampshire Archeologist* 33/34, no. 1 (1994): 20–28.
6. Jared Diamond and Ted J. Case, "Overview: Introductions, Extinctions, Exterminations, and Invasions," in *Community Ecology*, 65–79.
7. Duggan, "Dugout Canoes of New Hampshire."
8. N. Bazilchuk, C. Fastie, A. Heise, J. Kasmer, T. Naumann, R. Paul, D. Publicover, C. Savonen, S. Whidden, and K. Zimmerman, *The Physical Characteristics, Site of Discovery, and Method of Preservation of a Dugout Canoe Found at Shelburne Pond, Vermont*, report of the Natural Areas Program of the University of Vermont (Burlington, Vermont: UVM Department of Botany, 1985).
9. Duggan, "Dugout Canoes of New Hampshire."
10. Ibid.; Colby, *Colby's Indian History*, 247.
11. Belknap, *The History of New Hampshire*, vol. 3, 90.
12. Brian S. Robinson, "Seabrook Tidal Marsh Site: A Preliminary Report," *New Hampshire Archeologist* 19 (1976–1977): 1–7.
13. Genetic testing has raised a question: Which wolf was native to the New England

region—the gray (timber) wolf (*Canis lupus*) or the red wolf *(Canis rufus)?* DNA analysis conducted by Paul Wilson at Trent University in Ontario, and published in the *Canadian Journal of Zoology,* indicates that surviving specimens of the last wolves killed in the northeast are actually red wolves. See Wilson Ring, "Which Wolf? DNA Issue Clouds Debate," *Valley News,* 9 September 2001, p. B4.

14. Gordon M. Day, "The Indian as an Ecological Factor in the Northeastern Forest," in *In Search of New England's Native Past: Selected Essays by Gordon M. Day,* ed. Michael K. Foster and William Cowan (Amherst: University of Massachusetts Press, 1998), p. 36.

15. Tom Wessels, *Reading the Forested Landscape: A Natural History of New England* (Woodstock, Vt.: Countryman Press, 1997), 37.

16. Krech, *The Ecological Indian,* 103.

17. Stephen J. Pyne, "Indian Fires," *Natural History* 92, no. 2 (February 1983): 6–11.

18. Krech, *The Ecological Indian,* 108–109.

19. Day, "The Indian as an Ecological Factor," 36; Pyne, "Indian Fires."

20. Day, "The Indian as an Ecological Factor," 43.

21. Helenette Silver, *A History of New Hampshire Game and Furbearers* (Concord, N.H.: New Hampshire Fish and Game Department, Survey Report no. 6, 1957, 1974), 22. Silver cites Warren K. Moorehead, *A Report on the Archaeology of Maine* (Andover, Mass.: Phillips Academy, 1922).

22. Belknap, *The History of New Hampshire,* vol. 3, 92.

23. Silver, *A History of New Hampshire Game and Furbearers,* 21. Silver cites J. M. Cooper, "The Culture of the Northeastern Indian Hunters. Papers Robert S. Peabody Found," *Archaeology* 3 (1946).

## CHAPTER 7. *SEEDS OF CHANGE* (PAGES 130–46)

1. David Stewart-Smith, "The Pennacook: Lands and Relations, An Ethnography," *New Hampshire Archeologist* 33/34, no. 1 (1994): 66–80.

2. Colby, *Colby's Indian History,* 52.

3. L. Newsom, "Paleoethnobotanical Remains from a Waterlogged Archaic Period Site in Florida," paper presented at the annual meeting of the Society for American Archaeology, Phoenix, Arizona, 27 April to 1 May 1988.

4. Bruce D. Smith, "Origins of Agriculture in Eastern North America," *Science* 246, no. 4937 (22 December 1989): 1566–71.

5. Ibid.

6. My original version of this story draws on a number of sources, including Mrs. W. Wallace Brown, "The Legend of Indian Corn," *Journal of American Folklore* 3, no. 10 (July–September 1890): 214; "The Story of the First Mother," in *The Indians' Book,* ed. Natalie Curtis (New York: Harper and Brothers, 1907), 4–6; "The Origin of Corn" in Stith Thompson, *Tales of the North American Indians* (Cambridge: Harvard University Press, 1929; Mineola, N.Y.: Dover Publications, 2000), 51–52.

7. Sahlins, *Stone Age Economics,* 26–27.

8. Ibid., 29.

9. Colin G. Calloway, *Dawnland Encounters: Indians and Europeans in Northern New England* (Hanover, N.H.: University Press of New England, 1991), 148–49.

10. The Franklin Historical Society has moved this rock to a small park known locally as the Indian Mortar Park, which is located at the east end of town at the corner of Dearborn Street and Central Street (Route 3). The site is well marked with a historical plaque erected by the New Hampshire Division of Historical Resources. Another

boulder is located in this park on which, it is presumed, an Alnôbak fisherman carved a beautiful likeness of one of the countless shad that once ran up the Merrimack River and into the Winnipesaukee before the dams were built downstream.

11. Victoria Bunker, Ph.D., Alton, New Hampshire, personal communication.
12. Cassedy, *A Prehistoric Inventory,* 13; Andrea Ohl, "The Peopling of the Upper Connecticut River Valley," *New Hampshire Archeologist* 33/34, no. 1 (1994): 53–65.
13. Cassedy, *A Prehistoric Inventory,* 20.
14. Day, "The Indian as an Ecological Factor," 36–40.
15. Belknap, *The History of New Hampshire,* vol. 3, 93; Joseph B. Walker, "The Valley of the Merrimack," *Collections of the New Hampshire Historical Society* 7 (1860). Cited in Silver, *A History of New Hampshire Game and Furbearers,* 16; D. Hamilton Hurd, *History of Hillsborough County, New Hampshire* (Philadelphia: J. W. Lewis & Co., 1885), 142; Colby, *Colby's Indian History,* 245.
16. Krech, *The Ecological Indian,* 76.
17. Belknap, *The History of New Hampshire,* vol. 3, 93; Hurd, *History of Hillsborough County,* 142.
18. Colby, *Colby's Indian History,* 245; Hurd, *History of Hillsborough County,* 142.

## CHAPTER 8. *CIRCLES OF GIVING, FLESH, AND SPIRIT* (PAGES 147–71)

1. Lewis Hyde, "The Gift Must Always Move," *CoEvolution Quarterly* 35 (fall 1982): 10–31.
2. Sahlins, *Stone Age Economics,* 149–50.
3. Ibid., 158.
4. Ibid., 254.
5. This is an original version of this story, based on an old tale called "The Origin of Vegetation," from Helen Keith Frost, "Two Abenaki Legends," *Journal of American Folk-Lore* 25, no. 96 (April–June 1912): 188–90.
6. Frank G. Speck, *Bird-lore of the Northern Indians* (Philadelphia: Public Lectures of the University of Pennsylvania, vol. 7, 1921), 349–80.
7. Bayly, "Myth, History and Archeology."
8. Nicholas, "Meadow Pond."
9. Colby, *Colby's Indian History,* 273.
10. Bayly, "Myth, History and Archeology."
11. Stewart-Smith, "The Pennacook."
12. Ohl, "The Peopling of the Upper Connecticut River Valley."
13. Cassedy, *A Prehistoric Inventory,* 2–3.
14. Howard M. Hecker, "Jasper Flakes and Jack's Reef Points at Adams Point: Speculations on Interregional Exchange in Late Middle Woodland Times in Coastal New Hampshire," *New Hampshire Archeologist* 35, no. 1 (1995): 61–83.

## CHAPTER 9. *CYCLES OF SEASONS* (PAGES 172–91)

1. Stewart-Smith, "The Pennacook"; Silver, *A History of New Hampshire Game and Furbearers,* 7; John Moody, "Absolute Republick: The Abenaki Nation in 1791," *Vermont Bicentennial Newsletter* 3, no. 4 (Winter 1991): 6–7.
2. Peter Allen Thomas, *In the Maelstrom of Change: The Indian Trade and Cultural Process in the Middle Connecticut River Valley: 1635–1665* (Amherst, Mass.: University of Massachusetts Doctoral Thesis, 1979), 112; Day, "The Indian as an Ecological Factor," 45.

3. Thomas, *In the Maelstrom of Change,* 13.
4. Ibid., 352–56.
5. Hurd, *History of Hillsborough County,* 142; Silver, *A History of New Hampshire Game and Furbearers,* 17–18.
6. I have created an original telling of this story that I have heard told many times. Written versions of this story are found in the following: Charles G. Leland, *The Algonquin Legends of New England* (Boston & New York: Houghton Mifflin, 1898), 18–19; Kay Hill, *Glooscap and His Magic: Legends of the Wabanaki Indians* (New York: Dodd, Mead and Co., 1963); Joseph Bruchac, "Rooted Like the Ash Trees: Abenaki People and the Land," in *Rooted Like the Ash Trees: New England Indians and the Land,* ed. Richard C. Carlson (Naugatuck, Conn.: Eagle Wing Press, 1987), 2; Maine Indian Program, American Friends Service Committee, *The Wabanakis of Maine and the Maritimes: A Resource Book about Penobscot, Passamaquoddy, Maliseet, Micmac, and Abenaki Indians* (Bath: Maine Indian Program, 1989), C-2–C-3; Haviland and Power, *The Original Vermonters,* 194.
7. Edwin Tappan Adney and Howard I. Chapelle, *The Bark Canoes and Skin Boats of North America* (Washington, D.C.: Smithsonian Institution, Museum of History and Technology, 1964), 88–93.
8. Thomas, *In the Maelstrom of Change,* 112.

## CHAPTER 10. *LIFE, DEATH, AND MEDICINE* (PAGES 195–208)

1. Gordon M. Day, "Western Abenaki," in *Northeast,* ed. Bruce G. Trigger, vol. 15 of *Handbook of North American Indians,* series ed. William C. Sturtevant (Washington, D.C.: Smithsonian Institution, 1978), 148–59.
2. Ibid., 156.
3. There is an old tradition of animals seeking Mother Earth, *Begwiigawes,* to heal their wounds. I have often heard of the wounded moose and base this brief sequence on what I have learned. One written description of hunting and tracking the wounded moose is found in Natalie Curtis, *The Indians' Book* (New York: Harper and Brothers, 1907), 11.
4. Haviland and Power, *The Original Vermonters,* 185.
5. For my telling of this powerful story I drew from two versions that were recorded a century ago: Mrs. E. W. Deming, "Abenaki Witchcraft Story," *Journal of American Folklore* 15, no. 51 (January–March 1902): 62–63; and M. Raymond Harrington, "An Abenaki 'Witch-Story'," *Journal of American Folklore* 14, no. 54 (July–September 1901): 160.

## CHAPTER 11. *APCIKOZIJIK LI GLÔGANEK, ENEMIES AT THE DOOR* (PAGES 209–13)

1. Thomas, *In the Maelstrom of Change,* 251.

## EPILOGUE: *A MESSAGE FROM THE ABENAKI NATION* (PAGES 214–15)

1. *Ndakinna* is another form of *Gedakina,* "Our Land."

# FURTHER READING

## GEOLOGY AND EARTH HISTORY

Billings, Marland P. *The Geology of New Hampshire: Part II—Bedrock Geology*. Concord, N.H.: New Hampshire State Planning and Development Commission, 1956.

Jorgensen, Neil. *A Guide to New England's Landscape*. Chester, Conn.: Globe Pequot Press, 1977.

Meyers, T. R., and Glenn W. Stewart. *The Geology of New Hampshire: Part III—Minerals and Mines*. Concord, N.H.: New Hampshire State Planning and Development Commission, 1956.

Novotny, Robert F. *The Geology of the Seacoast Region of New Hampshire*. Concord, N.H.: New Hampshire Department of Resources and Economic Development, 1969.

Raymo, Chet. *The Crust of Our Earth: An Armchair Traveler's Guide to the New Geology*. Englewood Cliff, N.J.: Prentice-Hall, Inc., 1983.
This is a gentle introduction to geology for the novice.

Raymo, Chet, and Maureen Raymo. *Written in Stone: A Geological History of the Northeastern United States*. Old Saybrook, Conn.: Globe Pequot Press, 1989.

*Rocks and Minerals* 65, no 4 (July/August 1990), has a number of interesting articles including: Eugene L. Boudette, "The Geology of New Hampshire, The Granite State," 306–12; Wallace A. Bothner and Herbert Tischler, "Fossils of New Hampshire: An Overview," 314–20; John J. Bradshaw, "Gemstones of New Hampshire," 300–05; and Janet W. Cares, "Minerals of New Hampshire: A Checklist," 297–99.

Taffe, William J. *A Guide to the Physical Environment of New Hampshire*. Plymouth, N.H.: Plymouth State College Environmental Studies Center, 1977.

Van Diver, Bradford B. *Roadside Geology of Vermont and New Hampshire*. Missoula, Mont.: Mountain Press Publishing Co., 1987.
This is one of the best introductions to the physical environment of the region and it is full of suggestions for places to visit and see along the roadways.

Weishampel, David B., and Luther Young. *Dinosaurs of the East Coast*. Baltimore: The Johns Hopkins University Press, 1996.

## GLACIOLOGY AND GLACIAL ECOLOGY

Goldthwait, James Walter, Lawrence Goldthwait, and Richard Parker Goldthwait. *The Geology of New Hampshire: Part I—Surficial Geology*. Concord, N.H.: New Hampshire State Planning and Development Commission, 1951, 1958.

Guthrie, R. Dale. *Frozen Fauna of the Mammoth Steppe*. Chicago: University of Chicago Press, 1990.

Holman, J. Alan. *Pleistocene Amphibians and Reptiles in North America*. New York: Oxford University Press, 1995.

Kurtén, Björn, and Elaine Anderson. *Pleistocene Mammals of North America.* New York: Columbia University Press, 1980.

Martin, Paul S., and Richard G. Klein, eds. *Quaternary Extinctions: A Prehistoric Revolution.* Tucson: The University of Arizona Press, 1984.

## THE ALNÔBAK (WESTERN ABENAKI)

Bruchac, Joseph. *Long River, A Novel.* Golden, Col.: Fulcrum Publishing, 1995.

———. *The Faithful Hunter: Abenaki Stories.* Greenfield Center, N.Y.: Greenfield Review Press, 1988.

———. *The Waters Between: A Novel of the Dawn Land.* Hanover, N.H.: University Press of New England, 1998.

———. *The Wind Eagle and Other Abenaki Stories.* Greenfield Center, N.Y.: Bowman Books, 1985.

Bruchac's well-told versions of traditional Abenaki tales are among the most popular. His novels offer an intriguing, fictional glimpse into the world of the Abenaki's past, based on the lifelong insights of an accomplished author who is also a well-respected and knowledgeable member of the Abenaki Nation.

Calloway, Colin G. *The Abenaki.* New York: Chelsea House Publishers, 1989.

Part of the *Indians of North America* series, Frank W. Porter III, gen. ed. This book offers a clear, succinct, well-illustrated introduction to the Abenaki.

Colby, Solon B. *Colby's Indian History: Antiquities of the New Hampshire Indians and their Neighbors.* Center Conway, N.H.: Walkers Pond Press, 1975.

Colby's is an interesting and comprehensive book, albeit a bit dated.

Day, Gordon M. "Western Abenaki," in *Northeast,* ed. Bruce G. Trigger, 148–59. Vol. 15 of *Handbook of North American Indians,* series ed. William C. Sturtevant. Washington, D.C.: Smithsonian Institution, 1978.

Foster, Michael K., and William Cowan, eds. *In Search of New England's Native Past: Selected Essays by Gordon M. Day.* Amherst: University of Massachusetts Press, 1998.

Gordon Day's works offer one of the most comprehensive sources about Abenaki culture and language related to the broader context of New England.

Grumet, Robert S. *Northeastern Indian Lives, 1632–1816.* Amherst: University of Massachusetts Press, 1996.

See the chapter by Bunny Mcbride and Harold E. L. Prins called "Walking the Medicine Line: Molly Ockett, a Pigwacket Doctor," 321–47.

Hanson, Rosalind D. *America's First People.* Hopkinton, N.H.: New Hampshire Antiquarian Society, 1996.

Haviland, William A., and Marjory Power. *The Original Vermonters: Native Inhabitants Past and Present.* Hanover, N.H.: University Press of New England, 1994.

An enormously detailed history of Alnôbak culture in the western regions of Gedakina.

Maine Indian Program, New England Regional Office of the American Friends Service Committee. *The Wabanakis of Maine and the Maritimes: A Resource Book about Penobscot, Passamaquoddy, Maliseet, Micmac, and Abenaki Indians.* Bath, Maine: Maine Indian Program, 1989.

Noyes, Alice Daley. *Metallak, His Legacy.* Colebrook, N.H.: Liebl Printing Company, 1988.

Parker, Trudy Ann. *Aunt Sarah: Woman of the Dawnland.* Lancaster, N.H.: Dawnland Publications, 1994.

Price, Chester B. *Historic Indian Trails of New Hampshire.* Concord, N.H.: New Hampshire Archeological Society, 1989.

Price includes descriptions of trails, place names, and a map of the trails throughout
New Hampshire. It is well done and thorough, although some Abenaki words and place
names need to be updated.

Wiseman, Frederick Matthew. *The Voice of the Dawn: An Autohistory of the Abenaki Nation.* Hanover, N.H.: University Press of New England, 2001.

This thorough book presents the experience of the Abenaki through time as written
by a member of the Abenaki Nation. The last few chapters offer an in-depth look at recent events in the political and cultural growth of the People.

## NATIVE PEOPLES IN GENERAL

Braun, Esther, and David P. Braun. *The First Peoples of the Northeast.* Lincoln, Mass.: Lincoln Historical Society, 1994.

Crosby, Alfred W., Jr. *The Columbian Exchange: Biological and Cultural Consequences of
1492.* Westport, Conn.: Greenwood Press, 1972.

Josephy, Alvin M., Jr. *The Indian Heritage of America.* New York: Knopf, 1968.

Salisbury, Neal. *Manitou and Providence: Indians, Europeans, and the Making of New
England, 1500-1643.* New York: Oxford University Press, 1982.

Weatherford, Jack. *Indian Givers: How the Indians of the Americas Transformed the
World.* New York: Fawcett Columbine, 1988.

———. *Native Roots: How the Indians Enriched America.* New York: Crown Publishers,
Inc., 1991.

## LANGUAGE OF THE ALNÔBAK

Aubery, Father Joseph, and Stephen Laurent, transl. *Father Aubery's French Abenaki Dictionary.* Portland, Maine: Chisholm Brothers, Publishers, 1995.

This volume contains over 7,000 terms accessed by French-Abenaki, with English
crossreferencing and translation.

Day, Gordon M. *Western Abenaki Dictionary.* Hull, Quebec: Canadian Museum of Civilization. Volume 1: Abenaki-English (1994), and Volume 2: English–Abenaki
(1995).

Day compiled and organized this dictionary by drawing from thirty years of work
recording Alnôbak speakers of the language, 1956-1985.

Foster, Michael K., and William Cowan, eds. *In Search of New England's Native Past: Selected Essays by Gordon M. Day.* Amherst: University of Massachusetts Press, 1998.

This anthology has a number of excellent chapters dealing with Abenaki language,
including place names, dialect, tree nomenclature, and vocabulary.

Laurent, Joseph. *New and Familiar Abenakis and English Dialogues.* Quebec: Leger
Brousseau, 1884.

This dictionary, by Chief Joseph Laurent, was the first to chronicle the Abenaki language and usage in written form.

Masta, Henry Lorne. *Abenaki Indian Legends, Grammar and Place Names.* Victoriaville,
Quebec: La Voix des Bois-Francs, 1932.

This small book has an enormous amount of information about the language of the
Alnôbak, including stories that incorporate lessons in grammar, a brief primer on the
structure and use of the language, and a section on place names.

Speck, Frank G. "Aboriginal Conservators." *Bird Lore* (July–August 1938).

———. *Bird-lore of the Northern Indians.* Philadelphia: Public Lectures of the University of
Pennsylvania 7 (1921): 349–80.

## INDIGENOUS PEOPLES AND THE ENVIRONMENT

Adney, Edwin Tappan, and Howard I. Chapelle. *The Bark Canoes and Skin Boats of North America.* Washington, D.C.: Smithsonian Institution, Museum of History and Technology, 1964.
> See pages 88–93, "St. Francis."

Cronon, William. *Changes in the Land: Indians, Colonists, and the Ecology of New England.* New York: Hill and Wang, 1983.

Day, Gordon M. "The Indian as an Ecological Factor in the Northeastern Forest." In *In Search of New England's Native Past: Selected Essays by Gordon M. Day,* ed. Michael K. Foster and William Cowan, 27–53. Amherst: University of Massachusetts Press, 1998. This article was originally published in *Ecology* 34, no. 2 (1953): 329–46.

Krech, Shepard, III. *The Ecological Indian: Myth and History.* New York: W. W. Norton and Co., 1999.

Momaday, N. Scott. "A First American's View," in *National Geographic* 150, no. 1 (July 1976): 13–18.

Vecsey, Christopher, and Robert W. Venables. *American Indian Environments.* Syracuse: Syracuse University Press, 1980.

## HISTORY AFTER EUROPEAN CONTACT

Belknap, Jeremy, A. M. *The History of New Hampshire,* vol. 1. Boston: Reprinted for the author, 1784, 1792.

———. *The History of New Hampshire,* vol. 2. Boston: Isaiah Thomas and Ebenezer T. Andrews, 1791.

———. *The History of New Hampshire,* vol. 3. Boston: Belknap and Young, 1792.

Benes, Peter, ed. *Algonkians of New England: Past and Present.* Boston: Boston University, 1991.
> See the chapter by Gary W. Hume, "Joseph Laurent's Intervale Camp: Post-Colonial Abenaki Adaptation and Revitalization in New Hampshire," 101–13.

Calloway, Colin G. *The Western Abenakis of Vermont: 1600-1800.* Norman: University of Oklahoma Press, 1990.

———. *Dawnland Encounters: Indians and Europeans in Northern New England.* Hanover, N.H.: University Press of New England, 1991.

Daniell, Jere R. *Colonial New Hampshire: A History.* Millwood, N.Y.: KTO Press, 1981.
> Chapter 1 offers an indepth chronicle of the contact period. Other chapters cover the historical evolution of colonial New Hampshire's politics, people, and resources.

Grumet, Robert S. "Western Abenaki Country," 86–101, and "Pennacook-Pawtucket Country," 105–109. In *Historic Contact: Indian People and Colonists in Today's Northeastern United States in the Sixteenth through Eighteenth Centuries.* Norman: University of Oklahoma Press, 1995.

Silver, Helenette. *A History of New Hampshire Game and Furbearers.* Concord: New Hampshire Fish and Game Department, Survey Report no, 6, 1957, 1974.
> See chapters 1 and 2, "Primeval New Hampshire" and "The Colony," which cover the Alnôbak and their environment and the changes brought on by colonialism.

Thoreau, Henry David. *A Week on the Concord and Merrimack Rivers.* New York: Penguin Books, 1998.
> This book was originally published in 1849 and is full of period observations about the land and the People.

## OF GENERAL AND RELATED INTEREST

Johnson, Charles W. *The Nature of Vermont: Introduction and Guide to a New England Environment.* Hanover, N.H.: University Press of New England, 1998.

Chapters 1 to 4 take a thorough look at the evolution of the land and people through time for the environment found to the west of New Hampshire.

MacLeish, William. *The Day Before America: Changing the Nature of a Continent.* New York: Houghton Mifflin Co., 1994.

Sahlins, Marshall. *Stone Age Economics.* New York: Aldine Publishing Co., 1972.

Thaxter, Celia. *Among the Isles of Shoals.* Boston: James R. Osgood & Co., 1873; Portsmouth, N.H.: Peter E. Randall Publisher, 1994.

Thaxter's eloquent classic about New Hampshire's coast and culture is a delight.

Tudge, Colin. *The Variety of Life: A Survey and a Celebration of All the Creatures that Have Ever Lived.* Oxford, England: Oxford University Press, 2000.

Wessels, Tom. *Reading the Forested Landscape: A Natural History of New England.* Woodstock, Vt.: Countryman Press, 1997.

# INDEX

Page numbers in **bold italics** indicate illustrations and photographs.

Mourning, 205
*Msiwajok* (Massachusett), culture of, 134,
169
Museum of New Hampshire History (Concord), 124, 223
Music, 204
Musk ox, 47, 71, 77, 92
Muskrats, 99, 100, 127, 184

Nantucket Island, 49, 50, 52
Nash Bog Pond, 109
Nashua *(Nansawi)*, culture of, **219**
Nashua (New Hampshire), 53, 123, 165
Nashua River, 116, 117, 164; location of,
as *Nansawi*, **219**
Native peoples: earliest human presence in
Americas, 89; time living in New
Hampshire, 2. *See also* Alnôbak (Abenaki); Archaic people; Paleo-people;
Woodland period
Neolithic culture, 138–39
Nets, seine, 179, 181
New Boston (New Hampshire), 65
New England: beneath Iapetus Sea, 18; in
the Ice Age, 49–50; oldest-known rocks
of, 9. *See also* Maine; Massachusetts;
New Hampshire; Vermont
New England Room at Harvard Mineralogical Museum (Cambridge, Massachusetts), 223
Newfound Lake, 100, 161, 164, 165; location of, as *Basadômkik,* **160**
New Hampshire: Archaic people in, 94–
113; bedrock of, 12, 14, **25**; borders of,
xi; boundary with Vermont established,
23; coastline of, xi, 1, 11, 12, 40–41,
126; contact period in, 209–15; geological history of, 7–45; geological time
span of, xi, 1; inland wetlands of, 1;
Lakes Region, 54, 55, 106; in Laurentia,
17; oldest rocks in, 15, 23; paleo-people
in, 75–93; during Pleistocene epoch, 46–
72; terranes of, 16, *16;* the warming
time, 94–113; Woodland period in,
114–208. *See also* White Mountains;
*towns and physical features by name*
New Hampshire Historical Society (Concord), 223
New Hampshire magma, 24
Newichwannock River, 169

Newichwannock *(Nôwijoanek)*, culture of,
**219**
New London (New Hampshire), 164
Newport (New Hampshire), 224
*Niwaskw Zigwan* (Spirit of Spring), 153–54
Norridgewock *(Molôjoak),* culture of, 171
North Conway (New Hampshire), 53,
170–71
North corn *(bebonki skamon),* 144
Northern pike, 127, 171, 179
North Hampton (New Hampshire), 53
North Rochester (New Hampshire), 67
North Stratford (New Hampshire), 162
Northumberland (New Hampshire), 162
North Walpole (New Hampshire), 22
North Woodstock (New Hampshire), 42
Notches, 65
Nulhegan River (Vermont), 162
Nuthatches, 155
Nuts: acorns, 98, 101, 127, 146, 183, 186;
Alnôbak eating, 182; Archaic people eating, 98, 101; beechnuts, 101, 146, 183;
butternuts, 101, 119, 127, 146, 172,
183, 186; chestnuts, 125, 146, 183, 186;
cultivation of nut-bearing plants, 120;
hazelnuts, 127, 146, 183; hickory nuts,
127, 146, 186; walnuts, 127, 146, 154

Oak trees, 38, 91, 97, 98
*Odanak, 160,* 162
Odiornes Point, 42, *44,* 126, 142
Old Man of the Mountains, 33, 68, **69**
Oliverian Notch, 162
Oneida *(Onayatakono),* culture of, 210
Orford (New Hampshire), 164
Ospreys, 80
Ossipee (New Hampshire), 54, 63, 90
Ossipee Lake, 54, 124, 171; location of, as
*Awasibagok, 160*
Ossipee Mountains, 33, *35,* 61, *62,* 99,
101, 106
Ossipee River, 171
Ossipee *(Awasibagok),* culture of, **219**
Ostracods, 17
*Otozoum,* 33
Otters, 100, 127, 184
Outwash plains, 52–53, *59*
Oyster River, 169

Pack Monadnock, 26